DEVELOPING AIRPORT SYSTEMS IN ASIAN CITIES
SPATIAL CHARACTERISTICS, ECONOMIC EFFECTS, AND POLICY IMPLICATIONS
Hironori Kato and Jin Murakami

DECEMBER 2022

ASIAN DEVELOPMENT BANK

 Creative Commons Attribution 3.0 IGO license (CC BY 3.0 IGO)

© 2022 Asian Development Bank
6 ADB Avenue, Mandaluyong City, 1550 Metro Manila, Philippines
Tel +63 2 8632 4444; Fax +63 2 8636 2444
www.adb.org

Some rights reserved. Published in 2022.

ISBN 978-92-9269-912-3 (print); 978-92-9269-913-0 (electronic); 978-92-9269-914-7 (ebook)
Publication Stock No. TCS220548-2
DOI: http://dx.doi.org/10.22617/TCS220548-2

The views expressed in this publication are those of the authors and do not necessarily reflect the views and policies of the Asian Development Bank (ADB) or its Board of Governors or the governments they represent.

ADB does not guarantee the accuracy of the data included in this publication and accepts no responsibility for any consequence of their use. The mention of specific companies or products of manufacturers does not imply that they are endorsed or recommended by ADB in preference to others of a similar nature that are not mentioned.

By making any designation of or reference to a particular territory or geographic area, or by using the term "country" in this document, ADB does not intend to make any judgments as to the legal or other status of any territory or area.

This work is available under the Creative Commons Attribution 3.0 IGO license (CC BY 3.0 IGO) https://creativecommons.org/licenses/by/3.0/igo/. By using the content of this publication, you agree to be bound by the terms of this license. For attribution, translations, adaptations, and permissions, please read the provisions and terms of use at https://www.adb.org/terms-use#openaccess.

This CC license does not apply to non-ADB copyright materials in this publication. If the material is attributed to another source, please contact the copyright owner or publisher of that source for permission to reproduce it. ADB cannot be held liable for any claims that arise as a result of your use of the material.

Please contact pubsmarketing@adb.org if you have questions or comments with respect to content, or if you wish to obtain copyright permission for your intended use that does not fall within these terms, or for permission to use the ADB logo.

Corrigenda to ADB publications may be found at http://www.adb.org/publications/corrigenda.

Notes:
In this publication, "$" refers to United States dollars.
ADB recognizes "China" as the People's Republic of China; "Hong Kong" as Hong Kong, China; "Vietnam" as Viet Nam; "Bangalore" as Bengaluru; and "Hanoi" as Ha Noi.

All photos are owned by ADB unless otherwise stated.

Cover design by Joe Mark Ganaban.

Contents

Tables and Figures	v
About the Authors	vii
Acknowledgments	viii
Abbreviations	ix
Executive Summary	xi

1. **Motivation and Scope of Study** — 1

2. **Review of the Spatial Characteristics and Economic Effects of Airport System Development** — 4
   - 2.1 Overview — 4
   - 2.2 Macroeconomic Studies — 6
   - 2.3 Airport-Centric Development—From Normative Models to Practical Challenges — 8
   - 2.4 Urban Spatial Structure—Evidence for Airport-Centric Development — 10
   - 2.5 Hedonic Price Studies—Evidence for Externalities from Airports — 11
   - 2.6 Ground Transportation and Airport Access by Public Transportation — 12

3. **Airport System Development in Megacities: A Global Comparison and Classification** — 23
   - 3.1 Introduction — 23
   - 3.2 Megacities — 23
   - 3.3 New Airport Construction, Relocation, and Multi-Airport Formation — 28
   - 3.4 Airport Terminal Expansion — 32
   - 3.5 Airport Location and Access Rail Link — 33
   - 3.6 Air Traffic Flows, Classification, and Economic Production — 38
   - 3.7 Summary of Key Findings — 48

4. **Impacts from Improvement of Ground Rail Accessibility to/from City Airport to Local Economies: Case Study of Tokyo, Japan** — 51
   - 4.1 Introduction — 51
   - 4.2 Airport Rail Links in Tokyo Metropolitan Area — 52
   - 4.3 Method — 53
   - 4.4 Zone-Based Analysis — 56
   - 4.5 Point-Based Analysis — 65
   - 4.6. Discussion — 70
   - 4.7 Conclusion — 72

5. Economic Impacts of Airport Upgrading on the Regional Economy: Case Study of the People's Republic of China — 75

- 5.1 Introduction — 75
- 5.2 Models — 76
- 5.3 Data — 78
- 5.4 Results — 82
- 5.5 Discussion — 88
- 5.6 Conclusion — 89

6. Survival Analysis of Airport Upgrade Intervals: Evidence from the People's Republic of China — 94

- 6.1 Introduction — 94
- 6.2 Literature Review — 95
- 6.3 Model — 97
- 6.4 Data — 98
- 6.5 Results — 103
- 6.6 Discussion — 108
- 6.7 Conclusion — 108

7. Detailed Case Surveys: Airport System Development Practices in Ha Noi, Jakarta, and Manila — 111

- 7.1 Introduction — 111
- 7.2 Ha Noi — 112
- 7.3 Jakarta — 115
- 7.4 Manila — 120
- 7.5 Summary of Key Findings — 124

8. Conclusions — 127

- 8.1 Findings — 127
- 8.2 Discussion — 130
- 8.3 Policy Implications — 132

Tables and Figures

Tables

3.1	Descriptive Statistics of Air Transportation Movements, 2018	39
3.2	A Typology of 25 Single-Airport Megacities Based on the ACI Annual World Airport Traffic Data Set, 2011–2018	42
3.3	A Typology of 19 Multi-Airport Megacities Based on the ACI Annual World Airport Traffic Data Set, 2011–2018	44
4.1	Descriptive Statistics of Zone-Based Data Set	57
4.2	Estimation Results of Spatial DID Models	60
4.3	Estimation Results of Propensity Score Function	61
4.4	Estimation Results of ATE and ATT with PS Matching	62
4.5	Estimation Results of the Inverse Probability Weighting Model	62
4.6	Robustness Analysis – Estimation Results of OLS Model with Spatial Diffusion Effects	63
4.7	Descriptive Statistics in Point-Based Analysis	66
4.8	Estimation Results of OLS Models for Point-Based Land Prices	67
4.9	Estimation Results of OLS Models for Point-Based Land Prices by City Planning Zone	69
5.1	Descriptive Statistics of the Data Set	80
5.2	Treatment and Control Groups in Data Set	82
5.3	Estimation Results of DID Models	84
5.4	Continuous-Year Frame DID Models Estimated with Two Subgroups	86
5.5	Results of Counterfactual Tests with Pooled Data Set and Lower Subgroup Data	87
5.6	Estimation Results of Model C3 with Interaction Terms	88
A5-1	Cities and Their Regions in the Data Set	91
A5-2	Definitions of Aerodrome Reference Code for 4A to 4F	92
6.1	Airport Classification in the PRC	101
6.2	Descriptive Statistics of Data Set	102
6.3	Interval of Airport Upgrade and Urban Characteristics: The Gap Model	106
7.1	Comparison of Ha Noi, Jakarta, and Manila in Urbanized Area, Population, and Economic Production	112

Figures

2.1	Spatial Distribution of Commercial Land Use Rights in Shanghai	11
3.1	Five Urban Agglomerations in Guangzhou Urban Center	25
3.2	Distribution of 45 Megacities across Global Regions	25
3.3	The Emergence of Megacities by Region, 1950–2035	26
3.4	Scale and Pace of Megacity Growth by Region/Country, 1950–2035	27

3.5	Changes in Urbanized Area and Population Density across 45 Megacities, 1990–2015	27
3.6	Multi-Airport Formation in the Relationship between Urbanized Area and Population Density in 45 Megacities in 2015	29
3.7	Year Lead/Lag Distributions of Airport System Development to/from the Emergence of Megacities, 1950–2021	30
3.8	Cumulative Number of Megacities with Multi-Airport Formation by Region, 1950–2020	30
3.9	Comparison of Percentage Changes in Urbanized Area and Population Density in 45 Megacities with/without Airport System Development, 1990–2015	31
3.10	Comparison of Straight Distances from the Nearest City Centers to Airports without Terminal Expansion, with Terminal Expansion for One Period, and with Terminal Expansion in Sequence, 1990–2021	33
3.11	Comparison of the Built or Commercialized Years of Airports within and beyond Urbanized Areas	34
3.12	Locational Distribution of 82 Airports in 45 Megacities	34
3.13	Comparison of Straight-Line Distances from Nearest Centers to Airports by Type of Rail System	35
3.14	Distribution of 58 Airport Rail Link Systems by Region	36
3.15	Year Lead/Lag Distributions of Airport Rail Link Projects, 1950–2021	37
3.16	Comparison of Percentage Change in Urbanized Area across 45 Megacities with and without Airport Rail Link Investment, 1990–2015	37
3.17	Air Transportation Movements (Frequencies) to/from 45 Megacities, 2018	38
3.18	Comparison of Annual Movement Length in Kilometers per 1,000 Inhabitants across Megacities, 2015	40
3.19	Comparison of GDP 2015 and Change in GDP from 1990 to 2015 across the 11 Types of Airport System Development	47
4.1	Changes in Accessibility to Haneda Airport in the Tokyo Metropolitan Area from 2000 to 2010	58
4.2	Land Points Observed in Point-Based Analysis in Tokyo Metropolitan Area	65
5.1	GDP per Capita Versus Air Passengers in 2004 and 2015	81
6.1	Multiple Airport Upgrade Projects in the Data Set	99
6.2	Airport Upgrade in Different Decades	100
6.3	Time to First Upgrade of Airports versus Age of Airports as of 2019	103
6.4	Kaplan–Meier Empirical Hazard (Time from Entry)	104
6.5	Kaplan–Meier Empirical Hazard (Time from Previous Event-Gap Model)	104
6.6	Cumulative Hazard for Consecutive Events	105
7.1	Air Traffic Flow to and from Ha Noi in 2018	113
7.2	Air Traffic Flow to and from Jakarta in 2018	116
7.3	Location of Kemayoran Airport, Halim Perdanakusuma Airport, and Soekarno–Hatta International Airport in Jakarta	117
7.4	Soekarno–Hatta Airport Rail Link with Two New Stations and Three Renovated Stations	119
7.5	Air Traffic Flow to and from Manila in 2018	120

About the Authors

HIRONORI KATO

Hironori Kato has been a full professor at the Department of Civil Engineering, Graduate School of Engineering, University of Tokyo, since November 2013. After graduating from the Department of Civil Engineering of the University of Tokyo in 1993, he received his doctoral degree from the University of Tokyo in 1999. He has been studying transportation planning and policy since 1995, first as a research associate at the University of Tokyo, then as a project manager at the Institute of Transport Policy Studies in Tokyo, and for the past 22 years at the University of Tokyo. Since September 2016, he has also been co-director of the master's program in infrastructure engineering at Vietnam Japan University in Ha Noi. His research and teaching interests focus on transportation planning and policy, transportation economics, transportation finance, and travel behavior analysis.

JIN MURAKAMI

Jin Murakami is an assistant professor of urban planning and policy in the humanities, arts, and social sciences cluster; a master of urban science, policy and planning program; and the SGP Aviation sector at the Singapore University of Technology and Design. His research projects include an international case study on transit-oriented development and land value capture, a spatial analysis of airport system development, and an empirical analysis of real estate investment trusts as socially responsible investments in Asia. In addition, J. Murakami was appointed as a lead author for the Intergovernmental Panel on Climate Change's Fifth and Sixth Assessment Reports under Working Group III. He holds a PhD in city and regional planning from the University of California, Berkeley, and a master's degree in civil engineering from the University of Tokyo.

Acknowledgments

This study of developing airport systems in Asian cities: spatial characteristics, economic effects, and policy implications was prepared by the Asian Development Bank (ADB) under the technical assistance project, Asia Infrastructure Insights (TA-9441 REG). The Economic Research and Regional Cooperation Department (ERCD) led the study under the guidance and supervision of Edimon Ginting, Rana Hasan, and Lei Lei Song. Aimee Hampel-Milagrosa, economist, ERCD, and Kiyoshi Taniguchi, principal economist at the Pakistan Resident Mission, completed the study.

All chapters were written by Hironori Kato of the University of Tokyo and Jin Murakami of Singapore University of Technology and Design. The empirical analyses were prepared by Jian He (University of Tokyo), Hirokazu Mizuno (University of Tokyo), Takayoshi Tsuchiya (Creative Research and Planning, Co.), and Naoki Okunobo (Creative Research and Planning, Co.). Case study interviewees include Phan Le Binh (Japan International Cooperation Agency), Crispin E. Diaz (University of the Philippines), Sadayuki Yagi (Alemec Co.), and Hirohisa Kawaguchi (Oriental Consultants Global Co.).

Kuancheng Huang (National Yang Ming Chiao Tung University) provided an excellent technical review. We also thank Yidan Luo, Southeast Asia Department (SERD); Chaorin Shim, SERD; and Gloria Gerilla-Teknomo, East Asia Department, for their thorough review and insightful comments.

Lotis C. Quiao provided technical assistance. Amanda Isabel B. Mamon assisted in the management of the TA. Tuesday Soriano copyedited; and Kiyoshi Taniguchi, Aimee Hampel-Milagrosa, and Lotis C. Quiao proofread the entire document. Joe Mark Ganaban did graphic design, layout, and typesetting.

Abbreviations

ADB	Asian Development Bank
AIC	Akaike Information Criterion
ARC	Aerodrome Reference Code
ATE	average treatment effect
ATT	average treatment effect on treated
AUP	Airport Upgrade Project
BCR	building coverage ratio
BGC	Bonifacio Global City
BOT	build–operate–transfer
CAAC	Civil Aviation Administration of China
CBD	central business district
COVID-19	coronavirus disease
dB	decibel
DID	difference-in-differences
EU	European Union
FAR	floor area ratio
FDI	foreign direct investment
GDP	gross domestic product
GRP	gross regional production
ha	hectare
HSR	high-speed rail
ICAO	International Civil Aviation Organization
IPW	inverse probability weighting
JICA	Japan International Cooperation Agency
km	kilometer
km^2	square kilometer
LFAI	local fixed asset investment
LOS	level-of-service
LVC	land value capture
m^2	square meter
MAS	multi-airport system
ODA	official development assistance
OLS	ordinary least squares
PRC	People's Republic of China
PS	propensity score
SAC	spatial autoregressive model with a correlated error term

Abbreviations

SEM	spatial error model
SLM	spatial lag model
SP	stated preference
T1	Terminal 1
T2	Terminal 2
T3	Terminal 3
TMA	Tokyo Metropolitan Area
TOD	transit-oriented development
UCDB	Urban Centre Database
UK	United Kingdom
UN 2018WUP	2018 Revision of World Urbanization Prospects
US	United States
UURA	urgent urban renewal area
WTA	willingness to accept
WTP	willingness to pay

Executive Summary

Asia's emerging and growing megacities are expected to handle a large volume of air traffic flows for regional, national, and/or local economic development in wider production networks. Such a demand projection and economic policy will require a series of major capital investments to improve airport capacity and accessibility within megacities in some phases of development. Yet very little is known about the influences of the dynamic and complex development of airport systems, including the provision of ground transportation infrastructure and services, on the spatial transformation of megacities in Asia and other global regions.

This study attempts to provide answers or implications to three key questions: (i) what types of urban policies have been discussed and practiced with regard to airport system development in megacities?; (ii) how has airport system development influenced the spatial transformation of Asian cities?; and (iii) could policy options for airport system development affect the economic performance of Asian cities? (Chapter 1). The research consists of four major analyses and a conclusion section.

First, the literature review highlights five bodies of studies on airport system development: (i) macroeconomic studies, including empirical analyses of the linkage between air traffic, airport capacity and connectivity, and economic growth; (ii) airport-centric development, including normative and empirical studies; (iii) empirical studies of the relationship between the intra-metropolitan distribution of employment and transportation infrastructure and accessibility, including airports; (iv) hedonic pricing studies of airport externalities from airports; and (v) studies of ground transportation to/from airports and access to airports by public transportation (Chapter 2).

Second, descriptive statistics present the spatial characteristics of airport system development in megacities in Asia and the other global regions. The main findings from this illustrative analysis are six: (i) the construction of new airports was popular in emerging megacities in Asia, while the expansion of airport terminals occurs sequentially in both established and growing megacities in North America, Europe, and Asia; (ii) the formation of multi-airports is relatively new, but is gradually rising in the established and growing megacities of Asia; (iii) new airports are usually built outside urban areas and connected by various airport rail link systems, depending on the distance of access or egress to/from the city centers; (iv) the construction of airport–rail links has been intensive in recent decades and can be coordinated both proactively and reactively with the emergence and growth of megacities in Asia; (v) emerging megacities in South Asia and Africa have not yet played a nodal role with the development of single-airport systems for limited air traffic flows; and (vi) megacities with the development of single- and multi-airport systems have shown varying levels of economic production and growth in Asia and global regions (Chapter 3).

Third, three case studies were conducted in Tokyo and cities in the People's Republic of China (PRC) to understand the relationships between airport system development and socioeconomic factors in urban areas. Intracity empirical analysis of the Tokyo case study showed that improving the accessibility of an airport by investing in the urban rail network has a significant impact on employment density and land prices. Intercity empirical analysis of the PRC found that regional gross domestic product per capita could be increased by 11.0% to 12.2% by upgrading the airports. The economic impact was significant in regions with smaller airports, while it may not have been significant in regions with larger airports. Further empirical analysis using data from the airport development system in the PRC suggested that the proportion of tertiary industry production was negatively associated with the time interval of airport development, while airport status and the distance between the airport and the city center were positively associated with the time interval (Chapters 4, 5, and 6).

Fourth, the case surveys based on personal interviews, public reports, statistics, and other supplementary materials shed light on further details and local knowledge about airport system development practices in three Asian cities (Ha Noi, Manila, and Jakarta) with different population, urbanization, and economic production backgrounds. The main lessons learned from the detailed case surveys are as follows: (i) the complexity of airport system development (e.g., construction of a single new airport, expansion of airport capacity, and formation of multi-airports) depends on the degree of urbanization and the stage of economic development; (ii) international development agencies can play an important role in enhancing the economic impact of airport capacity expansion along with ground transportation investment through loan programs and/or technical assistance in emerging economies; (iii) the location of a (former) military air base in a metropolitan area is one of the critical factors in the formation of multi-airports, as the selection of sites for the construction or relocation of new airports is significant to the availability and accessibility of public land for airport capacity expansion; (iv) Asia's major corporations could take on the development and management of airport systems in an integrated way by internalizing the broader economic benefits of building new airports by developing land around new airport terminals and along ground transportation corridors if governments (or international development agencies) offer generous incentives to private partners, such as a range of tax breaks (Manila); (v) coordinating land use for airport-linked economic development often requires addressing the issue of land acquisition and resettlement of communities surrounding highway interchanges and/or rail stations with airport access. Military agencies may need to be involved in the land use coordination process for airport development as public landowners in the vicinity of airports or former airbases; (vi) relocation of an airport may lead to significant and transformative development opportunities in inner-city locations, while limiting the possibility of secondary or tertiary airport use (Jakarta); (vii) the development of new secondary and/or tertiary airports is proposed to mitigate the concentration of traffic around existing primary and/or secondary airports in dense inner-city locations. However, the formation of multi-airports is likely to necessitate additional investments in ground transportation infrastructure and services, especially airport rail links for reliable passenger travel services, between city-center and city-fringe locations (Ha Noi, Jakarta, and Manila); (viii) investment in airport rail connections requires coordination of development among jurisdictions and/or sectors to improve connectivity and last-mile accessibility, although the direct benefits of investments in airport rail connections for travelers are still debatable; and (ix) the broader economic benefits of developing the airport system may rely on municipal governments proactively adjusting land use zoning codes around airports and/or along ground transportation corridors with airport connections (Chapter 7).

Finally, this study draws important conclusions from the above findings for the three levels of urban policy and development practice: (i) national-level agencies are expected to play a critical role in developing a locational strategy for more dynamic and complex airport systems to ensure the competitiveness and sustainability of emerging and growing megacities in wider production networks with financial and/or technical support from international development agencies; (ii) metropolitan-level entities are encouraged to collaborate horizontally in the strategic provision of ground transportation infrastructure and services, including airport rail links and expressways, by overcoming the problem of jurisdictional and/or sectoral fragmentation to promote seamless travel experiences between cities and airports to improve accessibility and thus promote airport-linked economic development; (iii) municipal- and/or district-level agencies can take strong initiatives to enhance and capture the net economic impacts of dynamic and complex airport-system development through proactive land use coordination and unique business promotion/stewardship in collaboration with private developers, landowners, and other local stakeholders. The three levels of policy implications are interdependent, suggesting that multilevel governance is essential for the competitiveness and sustainability of emerging and growing megacities with the successful implementation of dynamic and complex airport system development on unique evolutionary pathways across metropolitan, national, regional, and global production networks (Chapter 8).

Chapter 1

Motivation and Scope of Study

Many countries in Asia are expected to face an unprecedented volume of air traffic flows arising from rapid urbanization and economic development, especially in their emerging and growing megacities (Boeing 2018; ICAO 2018). Certainly, the coronavirus disease (COVID-19) pandemic and following fuel price inflation have overshadowed the growth of air transportation markets globally for more than a few years. Nevertheless, in both optimistic and pessimistic scenarios, global air traffic is forecasted to reach pre-COVID-19 levels by around 2025 (ACI 2021; IATA 2022). Such demand forecasts will continue to require a series of major capital investments to improve airport capacity and accessibility within megacities across several different phases of system development.

Initially, the relevant authorities would promote general programs to increase the capacity of primary airports, including the construction of additional runways and the modernization of passenger terminals, as well as the improvement of ground transportation connections. However, because old primary airports operate in already built-up areas, they are usually physically limited for further capacity expansion. As a result, megacities are planning to build new secondary airports, usually in the suburbs and exurbs where there is plenty of land available for future growth, but where extensive ground transportation is critical for accessibility within the city. In this process, relevant authorities must consider two major development approaches—building a multi-airport system or replacing an old primary airport—depending on the spatial characteristics and economic progress stages of megacities on divergent development pathways.

The development pathways are the other way around, as the two approaches to airport system development are very likely to influence the spatial configuration and economic productivity of emerging and growing megacities to a significant degree in the coming decades. The former approach could benefit rapidly expanding megacities by separating larger catchment areas at different locations within the city, but would require more expensive infrastructure investments and more complex service arrangements for ground transportation systems (Murakami, Matsui, and Kato 2016). In contrast, the latter approach could benefit already congested megacities by eliminating airport-related negative externalities and height restrictions, and by creating large-scale developable sites for urban regeneration in already built-up areas (Murakami and Kato 2020). But this would drive up intracity travel costs to and from newly constructed suburban and extraurban airports. The economic efficiency of impending urbanization would depend progressively on the development of such an airport system along with supportive policy measures, as well as favorable market conditions.

Yet, there is little empirical research on the spatial transformation and economic performance of megacities associated with airport system development. We can foresee that this issue will be of particular importance to urban transportation, land use, and economic development policies in Asia's growing and emerging megacities, which currently operate very congested primary airports near old downtowns. There is a need to plan for the development and management of (multi-) airport systems with ground transportation and land use coordination for the coming decade, such as in Ha Noi, Ho Chi Minh City, Jakarta, and Manila.

From this perspective, our research questions can be summarized as follows:

(a) What types of urban policies have been discussed and/or introduced with regard to airport development and investment in airport infrastructure in megacities?
(b) How has airport system development influenced the spatial transformation of Asian cities?
(c) Could policy options for airport system development influence the economic performance of Asian cities?

These three main questions are outlined by the following four objectives:

(a) Objective 1: Review institutional coordination and policy implementation practices related to the development and management of existing airports and airport access infrastructure.
(b) Objective 2: Conduct geospatial data analysis on the relationship between airport system development (airport location and multimodal access) and economic performance in a selected Asian megacity.
(c) Objective 3: Carry out an international comparative analysis of airport system development policies, practices, and outcomes in major cities in Asia.
(d) Objective 4: Give policy recommendations for the economic competitiveness of growing and emerging megacities along medium- to long-term strategies for airport system development in Asia.

References

Airports Council International (ACI). 2021. The Impact of COVID-19 on the Airport Business and the Path to Recovery. https://aci.aero/2021/03/25/the-impact-of-covid-19-on-the-airport-business-and-the-path-to-recovery/.

Boeing. 2018. Boeing's World Air Cargo Forecast 2018–2037. https://www.boeing.com/commercial/market/cargo-forecast/.

International Air Transport Association (IATA). 2022. Air Passenger Numbers to Recover in 2024. Press Release No: 10. https://www.iata.org/en/pressroom/2022-releases/2022-03-01-01/.

International Civil Aviation Organization (ICAO). 2018. ICAO Long-Term Traffic Forecasts: Passenger and Cargo. https://www.icao.int/sustainability/documents/ltf_charts-results_2018edition.pdf.

Murakami, J. and H. Kato. 2020. The Intra-metropolitan Distribution of Airport Accessibility, Employment Density, and Labor Productivity: Spatial Strategy for Economic Development in Tokyo. *Applied Geography*. 125. pp.102309. https://doi.org/10.1016/j.apgeog.2020.102309.

Murakami, J., Y. Matsui, and H. Kato. 2016. Airport Rail Links and Economic Productivity: Evidence from 82 Cities with the World's 100 Busiest Airports. *Transport Policy*. 52. pp. 89–99. https://doi.org/10.1016/j.tranpol.2016.07.009.

Chapter 2

Review of the Spatial Characteristics and Economic Effects of Airport System Development

2.1 Overview

Air transportation has played an increasingly important role in the global economy—particularly in global trade, logistics, tourism, and producer services—since a worldwide political swing toward deregulation and privatization took place in the 1980s. Despite a series of global disease outbreaks, terrorist attacks, and economic setbacks in the early 21st century, demand for airport transportation continues to grow significantly. According to recent trends, air passenger traffic is expected to double to 8.2 billion by 2037, which could create 100 million jobs worldwide (IATA 2018). Similarly, air cargo, which represents less than 1% of global trade by tonnage but currently accounts for more than 35% of global trade by value, is expected to more than double over the next 2 decades, especially as e-commerce grows (Boeing 2018).

However, this growth appears to be geographically uneven and complex. Advances in aircraft technology, along with open-skies agreements and airline alliances, have helped economize the geography of air passenger and freight services toward explicit hub-and-spoke formations worldwide (Bowen 2012; O'Kelly 2014; Walcott and Fan 2017; Wang and Jin 2007). In addition, low-cost carriers are having a greater impact on regional connectivity and catchment area coverage by increasing their share of passenger and cargo markets. The Asia and Pacific region is leading this market expansion and territorial transformation as it manages growing traffic flows to and from multiple hub cities and/or megacities with multiple airports, accompanied by its newly emerging economies and middle-income population (O'Connor and Fuellhart 2016; O'Connor 1995). From this perspective, geographic studies typically examine how the development of air transportation networks affects the ranking of cities in terms of their competitiveness in regional and global hierarchies at a macro (inter-metropolitan) scale.

Rapid growth and overconcentration of air passenger and cargo traffic require billions of dollars of investment in airport capacity development, including expansion of existing airports, terminal upgrades, relocation of city airports, and/or construction of secondary airports, along with ground transportation improvement programs (ITF 2014). Over the next 4 decades, $1.1 trillion in public–private investment in airport infrastructure projects is currently planned or underway—$255 billion in new greenfield airport projects and $845 billion in existing airport projects (CAPA 2015). In particular, Asia and the Pacific and the Middle East are spending higher amounts on new airport construction projects than the other global regions. However, the decision between building new and/or expanding existing airports depends on many idiosyncratic factors, including environmental risks and community opposition (Graham and Morell 2016). Policy makers and other stakeholders around the world are currently faced with a series of critical decisions about the adequacy of developing airport systems for future competitive and sustainable cities. Indeed, competitive cities (or "entrepreneurial" city agencies under neoliberalism) tend to encourage such large-scale capital investments not only to improve the operational efficiency of air transportation systems for the direct benefit of users, but rather to generate wider economic impacts around major airports as "engines of growth" in micro (intra-metropolitan) contexts (Banister and Berechman 2001; Berechman and Paaswell 2005; Goetz 2015; Mosbah and Ryerson 2016).

In traditional location theory, transportation investments are expected to reduce travel costs and improve accessibility for users, cities, and even regions. By improving accessibility, cities are expected to increase economic output, labor productivity, and local employment. Consistent with studies on new economic geography (or urban spatial structure), access to airports can be assumed to be one of the key factors for competitive firms in choosing locations and forming industrial clusters for agglomeration economies (Fujita and Thisse 1996; Krugman 1991; Porter 1996). In recent years, several aviation studies have summarized the economic effects of airport system development into four large categories (Bowen and Rodrigue 2020; CAPA 2015; Goetz 2015; IHLG 2019; ITF 2014):

- **Direct Effects:** Activities at the airport itself, services to passengers (e.g., check-in, security, boarding), cargo (e.g., loading and unloading), and aircraft (e.g., fueling, cleaning). This category also includes concessionaires operating in airport terminals.
- **Indirect Effects:** Activities powered by backward linkages from the airport—production (e.g., jet fuel suppliers, electricity producers and other utilities, and fresh food sold in restaurants at the airport). An airport requires many different inputs, and the flow of these inputs into the airport generates a counterflow of money into the economy of the local area and beyond.
- **Induced Effects:** Activities driven by forward linkages—consumption, especially spending by people who work at the airport and passengers who pass through the airport. Notably, airport workers at a major hub spend their income on basic goods and services, including retail, local transportation, and housing. The restaurants and hotels that surround many airports also fall into this category.
- **Catalytic Effects:** Activities that attract and retain airports through reduced transportation costs, improved network connectivity and accessibility, and enhanced agglomeration economies. This category can include a range of speed-sensitive, airport-using businesses, such as global trade, logistics, high-tech manufacturing, tourism, and producer services, which tend to co-locate near airports and/or airport-linked industrial zones.

The "catalytic" category may offer greater benefits, but also more complex impacts to be measured by transportation planners and economic analysts than the other three categories. While the link between airport investment and economic growth is generally very likely, the magnitude and patterns of airport-related economic development are still debatable, as there is little knowledge synthesis on such wide-ranging economic impacts, including both positive spillover effects and negative externalities of airport system development from different disciplinary perspectives, in different industry sectors, and at different geographic scales (Goetz 2015; Mosbah and Ryerson 2016). Thus, prior to examining the spatial characteristics and economic effects of airport system development in Asian cities, we attempt to provide a systemic framework of interdisciplinary, cross-sectoral, and multi-scale analyses based on the above-mentioned (spatial and economic) rationales by reviewing relevant (i) macroeconomic studies; (ii) airport-centric development; (iii) urban spatial structure; (iv) hedonic price studies; and (v) ground transportation and airport access by public transportation.

2.2 Macroeconomic Studies

There is a relatively large body of macroeconomic studies that empirically examine the relationship between air traffic, airport capacity and/or connectivity, and economic growth. The first papers to discuss the economic benefits of hub airports are Button and Lall (1999) and Button et al. (1999), who analyzed the bidirectional relationships between high-tech employment, hub-and-spoke services, and air passenger flows in four selected metropolitan areas in the United States (US) (Pittsburgh, Cincinnati, Nashville, and Milwaukee) between 1980 and 1990. Likewise, Button and Taylor (2000) point to the importance of international air services in the new economy by demonstrating the relationship between local employment and air passenger flows to and from Europe in 41 US metropolitan areas. Debbage and Delk (2001) also statistically confirm that a significant relationship exists between administrative employment and air passenger volumes for the top 50 urban–airport complexes in the US from 1973 to 1996. Brueckner (2003) finds that the level of airline service with airport expansion matters to contemporary firms because it affects the cost of managing face-to-face interactions with business partners in other cities. His empirical results from 91 US metropolitan areas for 1996 show that a 10% increase in airport passenger traffic (enplanements) leads to a 1% increase in service-related employment.

In later years, macroeconomic studies have paid increasing attention to the direction of causality between airport traffic and economic development. Using panel data and instrumental variable regression methods for 83 US metropolitan areas between 1990 and 2000, Green (2007) tested whether the various measures of airport activity (e.g., passenger volumes, originations, hub status, and cargo volumes) are a cause of urban employment and population growth. This econometric analysis showed that air passenger traffic is a strong predictor of economic growth, but air cargo traffic is not. Bel and Fageda (2008) also identified the causal relationship between the location of large firms' headquarters and the supply of direct intercontinental flights in 52 European urban areas from 1992 to 2000 using the two-step efficient generalized method of moments (GMM) estimator. Bilotkach (2015) applied the dynamic panel data GMM estimator to estimate the impact of air passenger service volume and the number of destinations served by nonstop flights on the growth of total employment and average wages in all US metropolitan areas with major airports from 1993 to 2009.

The following studies examine the direction of causality between air traffic and economic growth by applying Granger causality analysis to relatively long-term panel data sets from different global regions. Mukkala and Tervo (2013) found that there is causality between air passenger volumes and regional economic growth (employment and gross domestic product [GDP]) in peripheral regions of Europe, while the causality is less clear in core regions. Marazzo, Scherre, and Fernandes (2010) showed that air passenger-kilometers are sensitive to economic growth (GDP), but GDP tended to have a slower and weaker response to a change in air passenger kilometers in Brazil from 1966 to 2006. Baker, Merkert, and Kamruzzaman (2015) provided evidence that there are both short- and long-term causal links between air passenger traffic and economic growth (aggregate real taxable income) by analyzing 88 regional airports in Australia from 1985/1986 to 2010/2011. Mehmood, Aleem, and Shahzad (2015) proved that there is a bidirectional relationship between air traffic (career departures) and economic growth (gross national income) in Asian countries from 1970 to 2014. On the other hand, using panel data from South Asia (i.e., Afghanistan,[1] Bangladesh, Bhutan, Maldives, Nepal, Pakistan, and Sri Lanka), Hakim and Merkert (2016) demonstrated more of a long-run unidirectional causality from economic growth and air travel from 1973 to 2014, suggesting that the lack of bidirectional and short-run causality is likely due to spatial idiosyncrasy and contextual heterogeneity of the case countries.

Another trend in macroeconomic research is to measure the "sector-specific" economic impacts of airport system development. Neal (2012) examined the causal relationship between airline passengers and "creative" employment (workers in the arts, design, entertainment, sports, and media) using panel data sets from 128 US metropolitan areas with 145 major commercial airports from 2000 to 2008. This analysis infers that attracting tourist and business travel flows can only lead to creative job growth if the national economy is growing. Similarly, Florida, Mellander, and Holgersson (2015) statistically tested the relationships between creative employment (e.g., human capital and Bohemian index), airport development, and economic productivity (gross regional product per capita) based on cross-sectional data from 120 US metropolitan areas for 2010. According to this research, a city with creative bohemians is very likely to have an airport, and cities with human capital development tend to have high economic productivity associated with the airport system development. Sheard (2014) claimed that the effect of airport size on total employment is insignificant, but expansion of airport capacity leads to industrial specialization and significant growth in tradable services employment, based on the results of a series of two-stage least square regressions for sectoral employment in 290 metropolitan areas for 2007.

Some empirical work in recent years has examined in more detail the impact of air freight transportation on regional economic development. For example, Chang and Chang (2009) used Granger causality analysis to examine the causal relationship between air cargo and economic growth in Taipei,China from 1974 to 2006, demonstrating a long-term equilibrium and bidirectional relationship. Button and Yuan (2013) also tested causality between air cargo volumes and a number of economic growth measures (total employment, personal income, and per capita income) using panel data from 32 US metropolitan areas with 35 airports from 1990 to 2009. Uniquely, Chi and Baek (2013) found that the 11 September 2001 terrorist attacks and the severe acute respiratory syndrome (SARS) epidemic had a negative impact on air passenger traffic in both the short and long term, but the same shocks had little impact on air cargo traffic, which tended to increase with economic growth (real income). A few macroeconomic studies have looked at airport location planning and investment policy attributes. For example, Percoco (2010) measured the "territorial spillover effects" of air passenger traffic on economic growth among neighboring airports using province-level data sets from Italy for 2002. Tittle, McCarthy, and Xiao (2013) examined the effects of "airport runway capacity" (e.g., the number of runways and maximum runway length) on various economic measures using panel data sets for 35 US metropolitan areas from 2000 to 2007.

---

[1] ADB placed on hold its assistance in Afghanistan effective 15 August 2021. See ADB (2021).

2.3 Airport-Centric Development—From Normative Models to Practical Challenges

A growing body of applied research in airport operations, economic geography, urban planning, public policy, and real estate business is examining not only the overall extent, but also the detailed patterns of airport system development and its contribution to local economic growth and restructuring within districts, cities, and metropolitan areas as "normative" land use models for the 21st century. Indeed, urban planning studies and practices in the last century had tended to overlook airports, despite their potential role in shaping urban form (De Barros 2013; Mosbah and Ryerson 2016; Freestone and Baker 2011). Most notably, Kasarda (2001, 2019, 2020) saw the changing importance of major airports as drivers of development, as they attract a variety of speed-sensitive commercial activities and relevant value-added services both in the immediate business zones—called "airport city"—and along radiating ground transportation corridors up to 30 kilometers (km) outward—called "aerotropolis." In recent years, the airport city and/or aerotropolis concept has been gradually adopted by policy makers and urban planners in cities with hub airports for competitiveness reasons not only in North America (e.g., Memphis and Denver) but also in other regions of the world, including Asia (e.g., Hong Kong, China; Incheon; and Singapore) (Cox 2010; Goetz 2015; Kasarda 2006; Kasarda and Lindsay 2011).

Importantly, the wider economic impacts of airport system development can occur in different locations and at different territorial scales. Therefore, several studies have coined different terms to illustrate the evolutional stages of airport-centric development driven by specific owners and/or stakeholders as normative models. Freestone and Baker (2011) summarized the six development models as follows:

(1) **Airfront:** Airport-related commercial zone at the airport fringe, managed by a local community and/or through public–private partnerships
(2) **Decoplex:** New airport community in the regional setting led by a master developer
(3) **Airport City:** Planned mixed-use development on airport site led by the airport owner-lessee
(4) **Airport Corridor:** Coordinated provision of infrastructure and commercial development along the airport–central business district (CBD) axis led by private developers and/or public infrastructure authorities
(5) **Aerotropolis:** Time-sensitive scatter of aviation-oriented land uses across the airport-centered metropolitan area driven by the private market
(6) **Airea:** Discrete spatial clusters of airport-related development in the metropolitan subregion driven by the private market

While these normative models for urban competitiveness in globalization have gained political popularity, the sustainability and/or complexity of airport-centric development in practice has been increasingly debated in several studies. Charles et al. (2007) criticized the industry-focused aerotropolis model in three unsustainable aspects—energy, security, and export-oriented economy—for years to come. Similarly, Freestone (2009) and Boquet (2018) pointed out that traditional community opposition (or so-called "NIMBY" reactions) to airport capacity expansion projects is evolving into more fundamental problems for the aviation industry as a whole, such as nonrenewable energy consumption and global climate change.

A number of studies address land use policies and planning practices related to privatized airports in Australia. Freestone (2011) argued that neoliberal land policies around federally leased major airports lead to new commercial real estate developments (e.g., factory outlets and big-box retailing) for the non-aeronautical revenue streams of major airports; but such "light-handed" land regulation inevitably leads to conflicts with local planning systems and practices. In the same context, Freestone, Baker, and Stevens (2011) examined the pragmatic attitudes of airport planners and property managers toward the regulatory risks and uncertainties associated with non-aeronautical commercial development. Baker and Freestone (2012) showed that while private airport owners embrace the airport city concept, local planning agencies and key stakeholders struggle with inadequate coordination of infrastructure in and around airports due to differing values and interests. Freestone and Wiesel (2014) further claimed that local planning conflicts with the airport city concept occur not only in cities with capital status and large airports, but also around smaller secondary airports that are slated for privatization and revenue diversification. Analogous land use patterns, local planning challenges, and potential development risks have been increasingly reported from cities with capital status and hub airports in Europe and Africa, such as Paris-Charles de Gaulle (Kasioumi 2015), Amsterdam-Schiphol (Van Wijk, Brattinga, and Bontje 2011), Accra Airport (Arthur 2018), and Cape Town and OR Tambo International Airports (Mokhele 2017, 2018).

On the other hand, an emerging body of research is attempting to evaluate the performance of land use planning around airports and/or identify the key factors for competitive airport-centric development. Wang and Hong (2011) and Wang et al. (2011) demonstrated a systematic analysis to support the development of airport-based economic zones into an airport city with 30 key (planning) factors and seven (development) trends using the case of the Taoyuan International Airport in Taipei,China. Yeo, Wang and Chou (2013) and Wang, Chou, and Yeo (2013) identified "hub status," "geographic location," "airport access mode," "land use planning and cost" as the main criteria for the competitiveness (or service quality) of an aerotropolis by applying a fuzzy multiple criteria decision-making method for five city cases in East Asia—Beijing; Hong Kong, China; Incheon; Shanghai; and Taoyuan. In the US, GAO (2013) identified "development at the airport," "air and surface connectivity," "funding sources," "development in the region," and "stakeholder collaboration" as five factors that facilitate airport-centric development based on reviews, interviews, and 14 in-depth case studies. Drawing from this government report, Boloukian and Siegmann (2016) emphasized the role of "urban logistics" in extensive airport-centric planning and development. However, Janic (2016) indicated how "compatible" land use criteria for the airside area (aeronautical activities for operational efficiency, public safety, and environmental consideration) are different from those for the landside area (non-aeronautical revenues and real estate values). Wang, Gong, and Yang (2018) used the case of Dalian New International Airport in the People's Republic of China (PRC) as an example to illustrate the optimal location patterns for basic industries, employees' housing locations, and service industries to locate in an airport-linked economic zone based on cargo, passenger, information, and monetary flows.

2.4 Urban Spatial Structure—Evidence for Airport-Centric Development

Studies of "urban spatial structure" in urban economics and/or regional science provide empirical evidence of the intra-metropolitan distribution of employment, with particular interest in transportation infrastructure and accessibility, including airports, as key determinants of economic growth during rapid suburbanization. Indeed, the evidence on the degree and patterns of airport-centric development in different phases and/or different contexts appears to be mixed. Giuliano and Small (1991) initially identified mixed industry and specialized manufacturing employment centers around five suburban airports in the Los Angeles region using the 1980 Census data. Giuliano and Small (1999) further suggested that the growth of suburban employment centers in the Los Angeles region between 1970 and 1980 is statistically explained by access to the primary airport and the other three regional airports. However, Giuliano et al. (2012) found that access to the primary airport and the other regional airports appears to be statistically insignificant in explaining the growth of suburban employment centers in the Los Angeles region under the relatively weak economic conditions between 1990 and 2000. Similarly, McMillen and McDonald (1998) showed that access to O'Hare International Airport is a significant determinant of employment density in the Chicago region between 1980 and 1990. On the other hand, Greene (2008) noted the decline of an airport-related employment center around O'Hare in Chicago between 1990 and 2000. Lang et al. (2009) argued that suburban employment centers tend to lose their competitive advantages and become "edgeless" as congestion increases, by presenting the spatial distribution of office development around major transportation interchanges, including airports, in 13 US metropolitan areas.

In recent years, there has been a growing body of empirical work examining the impact of airports on the distribution of employment in US metropolitan areas. Appold and Kasarda (2013) identified the spatial concentration of employment within 2.5 miles (or about 4 km) of 25 major airports in 22 US metropolitan areas in nine industry sectors for 2010. However, Cidell (2014) claimed that the airport city/aerotropolis concept in the US context ignores the spatial complexity of individual metropolitan areas and overstates the influence of an airport on regional economic development by showing the spatial variations in the distribution of employment in professional and administrative service sectors at 25 US major airports for 2007. Based on the results of spatial regressions for 51 US metropolitan areas for 2000, Appold (2015a, 2015b) further suggested that (i) access to airports determines the location of "aviation-providing" employment (e.g., airline services, aircraft maintenance, and airport operations); (ii) urban land costs and agglomeration benefits influence the presence of "aviation-supporting" employment (e.g., accommodations and retail) and "aviation-using" employment (e.g., producer services and manufacturing); and (iii) airport cities develop primarily as cities expand rather than as a direct consequence of aviation services.

Evidence on airport-centric development is not limited to US metropolitan areas. Verburg et al. (2004), for example, estimated access to hub airports and noise levels as key drivers of long-term land use change in the Netherlands. Zheng et al. (2017) concluded that access to airports can be interpreted as one of the key characteristics for the emergence of industrial jobs around city-fringe locations in the PRC. On the other hand, Huang and Wei (2014) reported that airport access explains the location patterns of foreign direct investment (FDI) in Wuhan only marginally. Murakami and Chang (2018) showed that both the supply of and demand for commercial land use (office, retail, and hotel properties) tend to be high near an inner-city domestic airport with high-speed rail and metro lines (such as the Shanghai Hongqiao Integrated Transport Hub), but not near an extraurban international airport (such as Shanghai Pudong International Airport) in the context of Shanghai's rapid suburbanization from 2004 to 2016 (Figure 2.1).

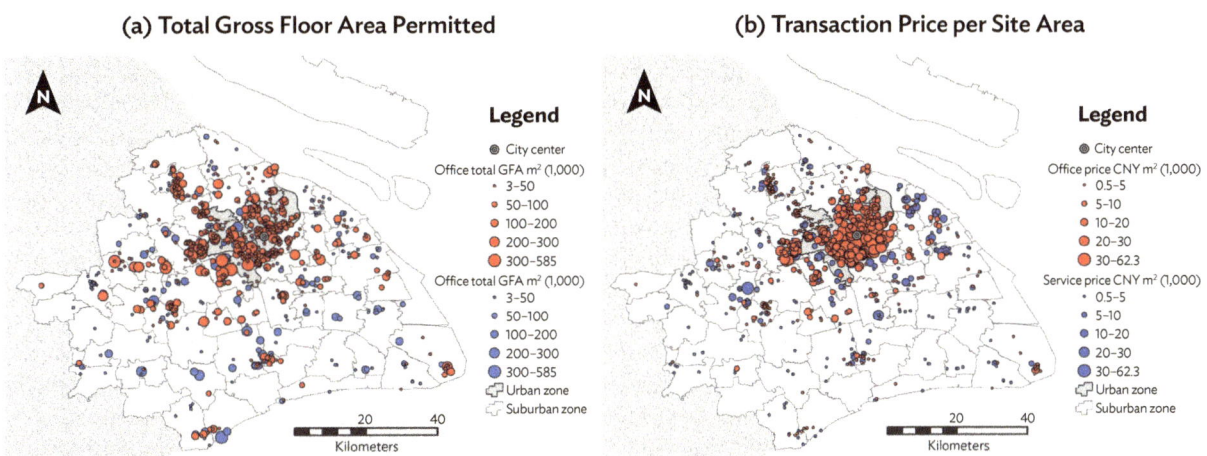

Figure 2.1: Spatial Distribution of Commercial Land Use Rights in Shanghai

GFA = gross floor area, m² = square meter.
Note: This map was produced by Murakami and Zhang (2018). The boundaries, colors, denominations, and any other information shown on this map do not imply, on the part of the Asian Development Bank, any judgment on the legal status of any territory, or any other endorsement or acceptance of such boundaries, colors, denominations, or information.
Source: Murakami and Chang (2018).

2.5 Hedonic Price Studies—Evidence for Externalities from Airports

Since the 1970s, numerous hedonic pricing studies have been conducted to examine the spatial impact of airport noise on residential communities. For example, Nelson (1979) reported on the negative effects of aircraft noise on housing prices near six major US airports—San Francisco, St. Louis, Cleveland, New Orleans, San Diego, and Buffalo. This early work addressed the potential problem of controlling for the appreciation effect of access when measuring the net depreciation impact of noise. Tomkins et al. (1998) suggested that the positive impacts of improved accessibility and employment opportunities around Manchester Airport may be valued more highly by local communities than the negative externalities of proximity to the airport, such as noise pollution and traffic congestion. Nelson (2004) conducted a meta-analysis to test the negative impact of airport noise pollution on residential property values by considering 33 hedonic price estimates of noise discount for 23 airports in the US and Canada over the past few decades. The results of this meta-analysis indicated that a given residential property with a noise exposure of 55 decibels (dB) would sell for about 10% to 12% less if located near a 75 dB airport. In addition, the same meta-analysis indicated that the discount for noise appears to be higher in Canada than in the US, likely due to differences in regulatory requirements and other socioeconomic conditions.

Some unique case studies assess the spatial impact of the airport system development on surrounding properties. McMillen (2004) estimated that residential property prices in the densely populated area around Chicago's O'Hare International Airport could increase by nearly $300 million if a new runway is built. This estimate suggests that some advances in aircraft technology and airport design are likely to lead to greater opportunities for land rezoning and real estate development. Thanos, Wardman, and Bristow. (2011) examined how the relocation of Athens Airport from Hellenikon (population 150,000) to Eleftherios Venizelos (population 53,000) affects two residential values—willingness to pay (WTP) and willingness to accept (WTA)—for significant changes in aircraft noise exposure using stated preference (SP) data sets. Ahlfeldt and Maennig (2013) measured the impact of two city airports (Tegel and Tempelhof) and one suburban airport (Schönefeld) on commercial property values in Berlin. The results of this spatial analysis suggest that the operation of city airports is undesirable for densely developed commercial areas due to the significant noise costs and insignificant accessibility benefits.

2.6 Ground Transportation and Airport Access by Public Transportation

Ground transportation is considered one of the critical elements for competitiveness and sustainability of airport-related developments or, more specifically, "airport-linked" commercial real estate developments. Kasarda and Appold (2014) reiterated the importance of reducing first- and last-mile travel costs and improving the efficiency of the logistics industry by integrating the airport city/aerotropolis model into ground transportation planning. In fact, several studies are being conducted to understand the integration of ground transportation infrastructure and services with airport system development from different perspectives.

A group of studies in Europe addresses the intermodal integration of air and ground transportation systems at the national or regional level. Stubbs and Jegede (1998) discuss the need for nationwide coordination to reap the benefits of air and rail integration, given the increasing congestion on roads around airports due to very piecemeal planning in the context of mainland Britain. Givoni and Banister (2006) argue that high-speed rail (HSR) and other intercity rail systems should be projected as part of airport system development to achieve both passenger and environmental benefits by examining the case of Heathrow International Airport in the context of United Kingdom (UK) transportation policy. Givoni and Banister (2007) also suggest that the development of HSR networks in conjunction with the airline industry could provide better passenger service for medium distance (800 km) as a positive alternative and make better use of available airport capacity by examining intermodal substitution in detail in the context of European transportation markets. Thomson (1995) suggests that HSR-airport interchanges, in combination with motorway networks and state-of-the-art telecommunication facilities, can create new employment clusters and generate economic gains by facilitating commercial trade and exchange by presenting the example of the Lyon Satolas International Airport/High-Speed Rail Hub in France. On the other hand, Givoni and Chen (2017) claim that the institutional division between air and ground transportation systems limits the potential development benefits of intermodal integration imported to the PRC from the US and Europe by describing the "disintegrated" status of the Shanghai Hongqiao Integrated Transport Hub.

A larger body of studies address intra-metropolitan arrangements for ground access infrastructure and services to airports. In practice, first- and last-mile of ground transportation between airport terminals and cities are sometimes more burdensome for travelers in terms of out-of-pocket expenses, travel time, and baggage handling than air transportation between airports, especially "short-haul" and "medium-haul" services. In particular, the spatiotemporal coordination of ground access to airports by public transportation (rail, bus, shuttle, and taxi services) for both airline passengers and airport employees can be discussed from various policy perspectives in different market conditions and development contexts around the world (Coogan 2008; Gosling 1997; Murakami, Matsui, and Kato 2016; Vespermann and Wald 2011).

A series of case studies from the UK and Australia discuss the role of ground access to airports by public transportation from an environmental perspective. Humphreys et al. (2005) illustrated how UK airports have developed policy goals for ground transportation in response to growing public concern about traffic congestion and environmental degradation. Humphreys and Ison (2005) also reported that the UK government has initiated airport ground access programs, including public transportation, to address the heavy reliance of airport employees on private cars for commuting to work. Budd et al. (2011a, 2011b) note the importance of reducing "kiss-and-fly" travel by airline passengers in private cars to achieve environmental benefits, while commercial pressures to maximize the non-aeronautical revenues from airport parking are increasing in the context of airport privatization in the UK. In contrast to UK airports, Ison, Merkert, and Mulley (2014) noted that while major (federally privatized) airports in Australia have experienced growth in both aeronautical and non-aeronautical activities, their ground access strategies do not include environmental policy goals or educational activities that should aim to reduce traffic congestion and shrink their carbon footprint. Drawing on the experience of London's six business traveler airports, Budd et al. (2016) listed a number of policy initiatives that could promote the supply and use of public transportation to meet environmental targets.

Of the public transportation options, the construction of airport rail links has gained political popularity worldwide. However, such megaprojects are controversial from a financial perspective, especially in metropolitan areas in the US. It is unlikely that the environmental benefits will guarantee a sufficient return on the billions of dollars invested in airport rail links. Notably, urban rail projects worldwide tend to raise the issue of cost overruns and demand shortfalls in favor of global competitiveness and environmental sustainability (Dimitriou 2006; Dimitriou and Trueb 2005; Flyvbjerg 2007). This evaluation bias may be worse for airport rail link projects, which typically require higher costs but reach fewer intercity passengers than general urban rail systems planned for daily intracity commuters (de Neufville 2006; Guerra and Cervero 2011). However, in Asian hub cities with sufficient urban density, such as Singapore and Hong Kong, China, airport rail link projects may be justified for economic efficiency and competitiveness (Phang 2003; Cervero and Murakami 2009). Murakami et al. (2016) noted that greater investment in airport rail link infrastructure and dedicated express services may be justified by the broader economic benefits derived from airport-connected accessibility premiums and agglomeration economies in city centers by examining the relationship between airport rail links and economic productivity in 82 cities with the world's 100 busiest airports in 10 regions. Despite the potential economic importance of airport rail links, knowledge and evidence on the intra-metropolitan influences of ground transportation infrastructure and services (as part of airport system development) on employment location and business productivity are still limited globally. Rothfeld et al. (2019) recently used Google Maps to visualize the spatial configuration of airport arrival and departure times in six major European metropolitan areas. Similarly, Liu (2019) geospatially measures the distribution of airport access times by public transportation and private car in selected cities in the PRC. Furthermore, Murakami and Kato (2020) describe the intra-metropolitan distribution patterns of airport accessibility, employment density, and labor productivity using municipality-level data sets from the Tokyo metropolitan region. The cross-sectional analyses suggest that labor productivity tends to be high in municipalities with high accessibility to the inner-city airport and a high degree of firm co-location for urbanization economies, although their causal relationships are still debatable.

References

Ahlfeldt, G. M. and W. Maennig. 2013. External Productivity and Utility Effects of City Airports. *Regional Studies*. 47 (4). pp. 508–529. https://doi.org/10.1080/00343404.2011.581652.

Appold, S. J. 2015a. Airport Cities and Metropolitan Labor Markets: An Extension and Response to Cidell. *Journal of Economic Geography*. 15 (6). pp. 1145–1168. https://doi.org/10.1093/jeg/lbv021.

Appold, S. J. 2015b. The Impact of Airports on US Urban Employment Distribution. *Environment and Planning A*. 47 (2). pp. 412–429. https://doi.org/10.1068/a130114p.

Appold, S. J. and J. D. Kasarda. 2013. The Airport City Phenomenon: Evidence from Large US Airports. *Urban Studies*. 50 (6). pp. 1239–1259. https://doi.org/10.1177/0042098012464401.

Arthur, I. K. 2018. Exploring the Development Prospects of Accra Airport City, Ghana. *Area Development and Policy*. 3 (2). pp. 258–273. https://doi.org/10.1080/23792949.2018.1428112.

Asian Development Bank (ADB). 2021. ADB Statement on Afghanistan. 10 November. Manila.

Baker, D. and R. Freestone. 2012. Land Use Planning for Privatized Airports: The Australia Experience. *Journal of the American Planning Association*. 78 (3). pp. 328–341. https://doi.org/10.1080/01944363.2012.716315.

Baker, D., R. Merkert, and M. Kamruzzaman. 2015. Regional Aviation and Economic Growth: Cointegration and Causality Analysis in Australia. *Journal of Transport Geography*. 43. pp. 140–150. https://doi.org/10.1016/j.jtrangeo.2016.09.006.

Banister, D. and Y. Berechman. 2001. Transport Investment and the Promotion of Economic Growth. *Journal of Transport Geography*. 9 (3). pp. 209–218. https://doi.org/10.1016/S0966-6923(01)00013-8.

Bel, G. and X. Fageda. 2008. Getting There Fast: Globalization, Intercontinental Flights and Location of Headquarters. *Journal of Economic Geography*. 8 (4). pp. 471–495. https://doi.org/10.1093/jeg/lbn017.

Berechman, J. and R. E. Paaswell. 2005. Evaluation, Prioritization and Selection of Transportation Investment Projects in New York City. *Transportation*. 32 (3). pp. 223–249. https://doi.org/10.1007/s11116-004-7271-x.

Bilotkach, V. 2015. Are Airports Engines of Economic Development? A Dynamic Panel Data Approach. *Urban Studies.* 52 (9). pp. 1577–1593. https://doi.org/10.1177/0042098015576869.

Boeing. 2018. Boeing's World Air Cargo Forecast 2018–2037. https://www.boeing.com/commercial/market/cargo-forecast/.

Boloukian, R. and J. Siegmann. 2016. Urban logistics; A Key for the Airport-Centric Development—A Review on Development Approaches and the Role of Urban Logistics in Comprehensive Airport-Centric Planning. *Transportation Research Procedia.* 12. pp. 800–811. https://doi.org/10.1016/j.trpro.2016.02.033.

Boquet, Y. 2018. From Airports to Airport Territories: Expansions, Potentials, Conflicts. *Human Geographies: Journal of Studies and Research in Human Geography.* 12 (2). http://dx.doi.org/10.5719/hgeo.2018.122.1.

Bowen, J. and J. P. Rodrigue. 2020. Airport Terminals. In J. P. Rodrigue. *The Geography of Transport Systems.* New York: Routledge. https://transportgeography.org/?page_id=3717.

Bowen Jr, J. T. 2012. A Spatial Analysis of FedEx and UPS: Hubs, Spokes, and Network Structure. *Journal of Transport Geography.* 24. pp. 419–431. https://doi.org/10.1016/j.jtrangeo.2012.04.017.

Brueckner, J. K. 2003. Airline Traffic and Urban Economic Development. *Urban Studies.* 40 (8). pp. 1455–1469. https://doi.org/10.1080/0042098032000094388.

Budd, L., S. Ison, and T. Budd. 2016. Improving the Environmental Performance of Airport Surface Access in the UK: The Role of Public Transport. *Research in Transportation Economics.* 59. pp. 185–195. https://doi.org/10.1016/j.retrec.2016.04.013.

Budd, T., S. Ison, and T. Ryley. 2011a. Airport Surface Access Management: Issues and Policies. *Journal of Airport Management.* 6 (1). pp. 80–97. https://doi.org/10.1016/j.rtbm.2011.05.003.

Budd, T., S. Ison, and T. Ryley. 2011b. Airport Surface Access in the UK: A Management Perspective. *Research in Transportation Business & Management.* 1 (1). pp. 109–117. https://doi.org/10.1016/j.rtbm.2011.05.003.

Button, K. and S. Lall. 1999. The Economics of Being an Airport Hub City. *Research in Transportation Economics.* 5. pp. 75–105. https://doi.org/10.1016/S0739-8859(99)80005-5.

Button, K., S. Lall, R. Stough, and M. Trice. 1999. High-Technology Employment and Hub Airports. *Journal of Air Transport Management.* 5 (1). pp. 53–59. https://doi.org/10.1016/S0969-6997(98)00038-6.

Button, K. and S. Taylor. 2000. International Air Transportation and Economic Development. *Journal of Air Transport Management.* 6 (4). pp. 209–222. https://www.sciencedirect.com/science/article/pii/S0969699700000156.

Button, K. and J. Yuan. 2013. Airfreight Transport and Economic Development: An Examination of Causality. *Urban Studies.* 50 (2). pp. 329–340. https://doi.org/10.1177/0042098012446999.

Centre for Aviation (CAPA). 2015. Europe's Airports. Economic Impact – The Theory and the Practice. ACI Europe Report. Part 1. https://centreforaviation.com/analysis/reports/europes-airports-economic-impact--the-theory-and-the-practice-aci-europe-report-part-1-207594.

Cervero, R. and J. Murakami. 2009. Rail and Property Development in Hong Kong: Experiences and Extensions. *Urban Studies.* 46 (10). pp. 2019–2043. https://doi.org/10.1177/0042098009339431.

Chang, Y. H. and Y. W. Chang. 2009. Air Cargo Expansion and Economic Growth: Finding the Empirical Link. *Journal of Air Transport Management.* 15 (5). pp. 264–265. https://doi.org/10.1016/j.jairtraman.2008.09.016.

Charles, M. B., P. Barnes, N. Ryan, and J. Clayton. 2007. Airport Futures: Towards A Critique of The Aerotropolis Model. *Futures.* 39 (9). pp. 1009–1028. https://doi.org/10.1016/j.futures.2007.03.017.

Chi, J. and J. Baek. 2013. Dynamic Relationship between Air Transport Demand and Economic Growth in the United States: A New Look. *Transport Policy.* 29. pp. 257–260. https://doi.org/10.1016/j.tranpol.2013.03.005.

Cidell, J. 2014. The Role of Major Infrastructure in Subregional Economic Development: An Empirical Study of Airports and Cities. *Journal of Economic Geography*. 15 (6). pp. 1125–1144. https://doi.org/10.1093/jeg/lbu029.

Coogan, M. A. and Transportation Research Board. 2008. *Ground Access to Major Airports by Public Transportation*. Vol. 4. Airport Cooperative Research Program Report 4.

Cox, L. 2010. Evolving the Memphis Aerotropolis. *Journal of Airport Management.* 4 (2). pp. 149–155.

De Barros, A. G. 2013. Sustainable Integration of Airports into Urban Planning – A Review. *International Journal of Urban Sciences.* 17 (2). pp. 226–238. https://doi.org/10.1080/12265934.2013.776286.

De Neufville, R. D. 2006. Planning Airport Access in an Era of Low-Cost Airlines. *Journal of the American Planning Association.* 72 (3). pp. 347–356. https://doi.org/10.1080/01944360608976756.

Debbage, K. G. and D. Delk. 2001. The Geography of Air Passenger Volume and Local Employment Patterns by US Metropolitan Core Area: 1973–1996. *Journal of Air Transport Management.* 7 (3). pp. 159–167. https://doi.org/10.1016/S0969-6997(00)00045-4.

Dimitriou, H. T. 2006. Urban Mobility and Sustainability in Asia and the Power of Context. *Transportation Research Record.* 1983 (1), pp.140–150. https://doi.org/10.1177/0361198106198300119.

Dimitriou, H. T. and O. Trueb. 2005. Transportation Research Record. 1924 (1). pp. 59–68. https://doi.org/10.1177/0361198105192400108.

Florida, R., C. Mellander, and T. Holgersson. 2015. Up in the Air: The Role of Airports for Regional Economic Development. *The Annals of Regional Science*. 54 (1). pp. 197–214. https://doi.org/10.1007/s00168-014-0651-z.

Flyvbjerg, B. 2007. Cost Overruns and Demand Shortfalls in Urban Rail and Other Infrastructure. *Transportation Planning and Technology*. 30 (1). pp. 9–30. https://doi.org/10.1080/03081060701207938.

Freestone, R. 2009. Planning, Sustainability and Airport-Led Urban Development. *International Planning Studies*. 14 (2). pp. 161–176. https://doi.org/10.1080/13563470903021217.

Freestone, R. 2011. Managing Neoliberal Urban Spaces: Commercial Property Development at Australian Airports. *Geographical Research*. 49 (2). pp. 115–131. https://doi.org/10.1111/j.1745-5871.2010.00679.x.

Freestone, R. and D. Baker. 2011. Spatial Planning Models of Airport-Driven Urban Development. *Journal of Planning Literature*. 26 (3). pp. 263–279. https://doi.org/10.1177/0885412211401341.

Freestone, R., D. Baker, and N. Stevens. 2011. Managing Airport Land Development Under Regulatory Uncertainty. *Research in Transportation Business & Management*. 1 (1). pp. 101–108. https://doi.org/10.1016/j.rtbm.2011.05.006.

Freestone, R. and I. Wiesel. 2014. The Making of an Australian 'Airport City'. *Geographical Research*. 52 (3). pp. 280–295. https://doi.org/10.1111/1745-5871.12069.

Fujita, M. and J. F. Thisse. 1996. Economics of Agglomeration. *Journal of the Japanese and International Economies*. 10 (4). pp. 339–378. https://doi.org/10.1006/jjie.1996.0021.

Giuliano, G., C. Redfearn, A. Agarwal, and S. He. 2012. Network Accessibility and Employment Centres. *Urban Studies*. 49 (1). pp. 77–95. https://doi.org/10.1177/0042098011411948.

Giuliano, G. and K. A. Small. 1991. Subcenters in the Los Angeles Region. *Regional Science and Urban Economics*. 21. pp. 163–182. https://doi.org/10.1016/0166-0462(91)90032-I.

Giuliano, G. and K. A. Small. 1999. The Determinants of Growth of Employment Subcenters. *Journal of Transport Geography*. 7 (3). pp. 189–201. https://doi.org/10.1016/S0966-6923(98)00043-X.

Givoni, M. and D. Banister. 2006. Airline and Railway Integration. *Transport Policy*. 13 (5). pp. 386–397. https://doi.org/10.1016/j.tranpol.2006.02.001.

Givoni, M. and D. Banister. 2007. Role of the Railways in the Future of Air Transport. *Transportation Planning and Technology*. 30 (1). pp. 95–112. https://doi.org/10.1080/03081060701208100.

Givoni, M. and X. Chen. 2017. Airline and Railway Disintegration in China: The Case of Shanghai Hongqiao Integrated Transport Hub. *Transportation Letters*. 9 (4). pp. 202–214. https://doi.org/10.1080/19427867.2016.1252877.

Goetz, A. R. 2015. The Expansion of Large International Hub Airports. In R. Hickman, M. Givoni, D. Bonilla, and D. Banister, eds. *Handbook on Transport and Development*. Edward Elgar Publishing. https://www.elgaronline.com/view/edcoll/9780857937254/9780857937254.00031.xml.

Gosling, G. D. 1997. Airport Ground Access and Intermodal Interface. *Transportation Research Record*. 1600 (1). pp. 10–17. https://doi.org/10.3141/1600-02.

Graham, A. and P. Morrell. 2016. *Airport Finance and Investment in the Global Economy*. Routledge.

Green, R. K. 2007. Airports and Economic Development. *Real Estate Economics*. 35 (1). pp. 91–112. https://doi.org/10.1111/j.1540-6229.2007.00183.x.

Greene, R. P. 2008. Urban Peripheries as Organizers of What Remains of the Center: Examining the Evidence from Los Angeles and Chicago. *Urban Geography*. 29 (2). pp. 138–153. https://doi.org/10.2747/0272-3638.29.2.138.

Guerra, E. and R. Cervero. 2011. Cost of a Ride: The Effects of Densities on Fixed-Guideway Transit Ridership and Costs. *Journal of the American Planning Association*. 77 (3). pp. 267–290. https://doi.org/10.1080/01944363.2011.589767.

Hakim, M. M. and R. Merkert. 2016. The Causal Relationship between Air Transport and Economic Growth: Empirical Evidence from South Asia. *Journal of Transport Geography*. 56. pp. 120–127. https://doi.org/10.1016/j.jtrangeo.2016.09.006.

Huang, H. and Y. D. Wei. 2014. Intra-Metropolitan Location of Foreign Direct Investment in Wuhan, China: Institution, Urban Structure, and Accessibility. *Applied Geography*. 47. pp. 78–88. https://doi.org/10.1016/j.apgeog.2013.11.012.

Humphreys, I. and S. Ison. 2005. Changing Airport Employee Travel Behaviour: The Role of Airport Surface Access Strategies. *Transport Policy*. 12 (1). pp. 1–9. https://doi.org/10.1016/j.tranpol.2004.07.002.

Humphreys, I., S. Ison, G. Francis, and K. Aldridge. 2005. UK Airport Surface Access Targets. *Journal of Air Transport Management*. 11 (2). pp. 117–124. https://doi.org/10.1016/j.jairtraman.2004.10.001.

Industry High Level Group (IHLG). 2019. Aviation Benefits Report 2019. https://www.icao.int/sustainability/Documents/AVIATION-BENEFITS-2019-web.pdf.

International Air Transport Association (IATA). 2018. IATA Forecast Predicts 8.2 Billion Air Travelers in 2037. https://www.iata.org/pressroom/pr/Pages/2018-10-24-02.aspx.

International Transport Forum (ITF). 2014. Expanding Airport Capacity in Large Urban Areas. ITF Round Tables. No. 153. Paris: OECD Publishing. https://doi.org/10.1787/9789282107393-en.

Ison, S., R. Merkert, and C. Mulley. 2014. Policy Approaches to Public Transport at Airports – Some Diverging Evidence from the UK and Australia. *Transport Policy*. 35. pp. 265–274. https://doi.org/10.1016/j.tranpol.2014.06.005.

Janic, M. 2016. Analyzing, Modeling, and Assessing the Performances of Land Use by Airports. *International Journal of Sustainable Transportation.* 10 (8). pp. 683–702. https://doi.org/10.1080/15568318.2015.1104566.

Kasarda, J. 2001. From Airport City to Aerotropolis. *Airport World.* 6 (4). pp. 42–45. http://aerotropolis.com/airportcity/wp-content/uploads/2018/10/2001_09AirportWorld_FromAirportCityToAerotropolis-1.pdf.

Kasarda, J. D. 2006. Asia's Emerging Airport Cities. *International Airport Review.* 10 (2). https://www.internationalairportreview.com/article/1704/asias-emerging-airport-cities/.

Kasarda, J. D. 2019. Aerotropolis. *The Wiley Blackwell Encyclopedia of Urban and Regional Studies.* pp. 1–7. https://doi.org/10.1002/9781118568446.eurs0436.

Kasarda, J. D. 2020. About the Aerotropolis. http://aerotropolis.com/airportcity/index.php/about/.

Kasarda, J. D. and S. J. Appold. 2014. Planning a Competitive Aerotropolis. *The Economics of International Airline Transport.* pp. 281–308.

Kasarda, J. and G. Lindsay. 2011. *Aerotropolis: the Way We'll Live Next.* New York: Farrar.

Kasioumi, E. 2015. Emerging Planning Approaches in Airport Areas: The case of Paris-Charles de Gaulle (CDG). *Regional Studies, Regional Science.* 2 (1). pp. 408–414. https://doi.org/10.1080/21681376.2015.1064012.

Krugman, P. 1991. Increasing Returns and Economic Geography. *Journal of Political Economy.* 99 (3). pp. 483–499. https://doi.org/10.1086/261763.

Lang, R. E., T. W. Sanchez, and A. C. Oner. 2009. Beyond Edge City: Office Geography in the New Metropolis. *Urban Geography.* 30 (7). pp. 726–755. https://doi.org/10.2747/0272-3638.30.7.726.

Liu, X. 2019. Assessing Airport Ground Access by Public Transport in Chinese Cities. *Urban Studies.* 57 (2). pp. 267–285. https://doi.org/10.1177/0042098019828178.

Marazzo, M., R. Scherre, and E. Fernandes. 2010. Air Transport Demand and Economic Growth in Brazil: A Time Series Analysis. *Transportation Research Part E: Logistics and Transportation Review.* 46 (2). pp. 261–269. https://doi.org/10.1016/j.tre.2009.08.008.

McMillen, D. P. 2004. Airport Expansions and Property Values: The Case of Chicago O'Hare Airport. *Journal of Urban Economics.* 55 (3). pp. 627–640. https://doi.org/10.1016/j.jue.2004.01.001.

McMillen, D. P. and J. F. McDonald. 1998. Suburban Subcenters and Employment Density in Metropolitan Chicago. *Journal of Urban Economics.* 43 (2). pp. 157–180. https://doi.org/10.1006/juec.1997.2038.

Mehmood, B., M. Aleem, and N. Shahzad. 2015. Air-Transport and Macroeconomic Performance: An Analysis. *Pakistan Journal of Applied Economics.* 25 (2). pp. 179-192. http://aerc.edu.pk/wp-content/uploads/2016/08/Article_59Paper-642-III-Bilal-Mehmood-2.pdf.

Mokhele, M. 2017. Spatial Economic Evolution of the Airport-Centric Developments of Cape Town and OR Tambo International Airports in South Africa. *Town and Regional Planning*. 70 (1). pp. 26–36. http://dx.doi.org/10.18820/2415-0495/trp70i1.3.

Mokhele, M. 2018. Spatial Economic Attributes of OR Tambo and Cape Town Airport-Centric Developments in South Africa. *Journal of Transport and Supply Chain Management*. 12 (1). pp. 1–12. https://doi.org/10.4102/jtscm.v12i0.344.

Mosbah, S. and M. S. Ryerson. 2016. Can US Metropolitan Areas Use Large Commercial Airports as Tools to Bolster Regional Economic Growth?. *Journal of Planning Literature*. 31 (3). pp. 317–333. https://doi.org/10.1177/0885412216653100.

Mukkala, K. and H. Tervo. 2013. Air Transportation and Regional Growth: Which Way Does the Causality Run?. *Environment and Planning A*. 45 (6). pp. 1508–1520. https://journals.sagepub.com/doi/abs/10.1068/a45298.

Murakami, J. and Z. Chang. 2018. Polycentric Development under Public Leasehold: A Spatial Analysis of Commercial Land Use Rights. *Regional Science and Urban Economics*. 71. pp. 25–36. https://doi.org/10.1016/j.regsciurbeco.2018.05.001.

Murakami, J. and H. Kato. 2020. The Intra-metropolitan Distribution of Airport Accessibility, Employment Density, and Labor Productivity: Spatial Strategy for Economic Development in Tokyo. *Applied Geography*. 125. pp.102309. https://doi.org/10.1016/j.apgeog.2020.102309.

Murakami, J., Y. Matsui, and H. Kato. 2016. Airport Rail Links and Economic Productivity: Evidence from 82 Cities with the World's 100 Busiest Airports. *Transport Policy*. 52. pp. 89–99. https://doi.org/10.1016/j.tranpol.2016.07.009.

Neal, Z. 2012. Creative Employment and Jet Set Cities: Disentangling Causal Effects. *Urban Studies*. 49 (12). pp. 2693–2709. https://doi.org/10.1177/0042098011431282.

Nelson, J. P. 1979. Airport Noise, Location Rent, and the Market for Residential Amenities. *Journal of Environmental Economics and Management*. 6 (4). pp. 320–331. https://doi.org/10.1016/0095-0696(79)90011-1.

Nelson, J. P. 2004. Meta-Analysis of Airport Noise and Hedonic Property Values. *Journal of Transport Economics and Policy (JTEP)*. 38 (1). pp. 1–27. https://doi.org/10.1097/01.inf.0000129687.12470.af.

O'Connor, K. 1995. Airport Development in Southeast Asia. *Journal of Transport Geography*. 3 (4). pp. 269–279. https://doi.org/10.1016/0966-6923(95)00032-1.

O'Connor, K. and K. Fuellhart. 2016. Airports and Regional Air Transport Markets: A New Perspective. *Journal of Transport Geography*. 53l. pp. 78–82. https://doi.org/10.1016/j.jtrangeo.2015.10.010.

O'Kelly, M. E. 2014. Air Freight Hubs in the FedEx System: Analysis of Fuel Use. *Journal of Air Transport Management*. 36. pp. 1–12. https://doi.org/10.1016/j.jairtraman.2013.12.002.

Percoco, M. 2010. Airport Activity and Local Development: Evidence from Italy. *Urban Studies.* 47 (11). pp. 2427–2443. https://doi.org/10.1177/0042098009357966.

Phang, S. Y. 2003. Strategic Development of Airport and Rail Infrastructure: The Case of Singapore. *Transport Policy.* 10 (1). pp. 27–33. https://doi.org/10.1016/S0967-070X(02)00027-6.

Porter, M. E. 1996. Competitive Advantage, Agglomeration Economies, and Regional Policy. *International Regional Science Review.* 19 (1–2). pp. 85–90. https://doi.org/10.1177/016001769601900208.

Rothfeld, R., A. Straubinger, A. Paul, and C. Antoniou. 2019. Analysis of European Airports' Access and Egress Travel Times Using Google Maps. *Transport Policy.* 81. pp. 148–162. https://doi.org/10.1016/j.tranpol.2019.05.021.

Sheard, N. 2014. Airports and Urban Sectoral Employment. *Journal of Urban Economics.* 80. pp. 133–152. https://doi.org/10.1016/j.jue.2014.01.002.

Stubbs, J. and F. Jegede. 1998. The Integration of Rail and Air Transport in Britain. *Journal of Transport Geography.* 6 (1). pp. 53–67. https://doi.org/10.1016/S0966-6923(97)00039-2.

Thanos, S., M. Wardman, and A. L. Bristow. 2011. Valuing Aircraft Noise: Stated Choice Experiments Reflecting Inter-Temporal Noise Changes from Airport Relocation. *Environmental and Resource Economics.* 50 (4). pp. 559–583. https://doi.org/10.1007/s10640-011-9482-x.

Thompson, I. B. 1995. High-Speed Transport Hubs and Eurocity Status: The Case of Lyon. *Journal of Transport Geography.* 3 (1). pp. 29–37. https://doi.org/10.1016/0966-6923(94)00004-9.

Tittle, D., P. McCarthy, and Y. Xiao. (2012). Airport Runway Capacity and Economic Development: A Panel Data Analysis of Metropolitan Statistical Areas. *Economic Development Quarterly.* 27 (3). pp. 230–239. https://doi.org/10.1177/0891242412467228.

Tomkins, J., N. Topham, J. Twomey, and R. Ward. 1998. Noise Versus Access: The Impact of an Airport in an Urban Property Market. *Urban Studies.* 35 (2). pp. 243–258. https://doi.org/10.1080/0042098984961.

US Government Accountability Office (GAO). 2013. *Airport Centric Development.* National Airspace System – Report to Congressional Requesters. GAO-13-261. Washington, DC. https://www.gao.gov/products/GAO-13-261.

Van Wijk, M., K. Brattinga, and M. A. Bontje. 2011. Exploit or Protect Airport Regions from Urbanization? Assessment of Land-Use Restrictions in Amsterdam-Schiphol. *European Planning Studies.* 19 (2). pp. 261–277. https://doi.org/10.1080/09654313.2011.532671.

Verburg, P. H., J. R. R. van Eck, T. C. de Nijs, M. J. Dijst, and P. Schot. 2004. Determinants of Land-Use Change Patterns in the Netherlands. *Environment and Planning B: Planning and Design.* 31 (1). pp. 125–150. https://doi.org/10.1068/b307.

Vespermann, J. and A. Wald. 2011. Intermodal Integration in Air Transportation: Status Quo, Motives and Future Developments. *Journal of Transport Geography*. 19 (6). pp. 1187–1197. https://doi.org/10.1016/j.jtrangeo.2011.05.003.

Walcott, S. M. and Z. Fan. 2017. Comparison of Major Air Freight Network Hubs in the US and China. *Journal of Air Transport Management*. 61. pp. 64–72. https://doi.org/10.1016/j.jairtraman.2016.06.006.

Wang, D., Z. Gong, and Z. Yang. 2018. Design of Industrial Clusters and Optimization of Land Use in an Airport Economic Zone. *Land Use Policy*. 77. pp. 288–297. https://doi.org/10.1016/j.landusepol.2018.05.048.

Wang, J. and J. Jin. 2007. China's Air Passenger Transport: An Analysis of Recent Trends. *Eurasian Geography and Economics*. 48 (4). pp. 469–480. https://doi.org/10.2747/1538-7216.48.4.469.

Wang, K. J. and W. C. Hong. 2011. Competitive Advantage Analysis and Strategy Formulation of Airport City Development. *Transport Policy*. 18 (1). pp. 276–288. https://doi.org/10.1016/j.tranpol.2010.08.011.

Wang, K. J., W. C. Hong, S. H. Chen, and J. T. Jiang. 2011. Strategic Development Trend and Key Factors Analysis of Airport City in Taipei,China. *Journal of Transport Geography*. 19 (4). pp. 807–820. https://doi.org/10.1016/j.jtrangeo.2010.10.003.

Wang, Y., C. C. Chou, and G. T. Yeo. 2013. Criteria for Evaluating Aerotropolis Service Quality. *The Asian Journal of Shipping and Logistics*. 29 (3). pp. 395–414. https://doi.org/10.1016/j.ajsl.2013.12.006.

Yeo, G. T., Y. Wang, and C. C. Chou. 2013. Evaluating the Competitiveness of the Aerotropolises in East Asia. *Journal of Air Transport Management*. 32. pp. 24–31. https://doi.org/10.1016/j.jairtraman.2013.06.004.

Zheng, S., W. Sun, J. Wu, M. E. Kahn. 2017. The Birth of Edge Cities in China: Measuring the Effects of Industrial Parks Policy. *Journal of Urban Economics*. 100. pp. 80–103. https://doi.org/10.1016/j.jue.2017.05.002.

Chapter 3

Airport System Development in Megacities: A Global Comparison and Classification

3.1 Introduction

Both policy makers and academic researchers worldwide have paid much attention to the emergence and growth of megacities in terms of sustainable development over the decades (ADB 1997; Gottmann 1957; Gurjar et al. 2008; Hall 1999; Lang and Knox 2009; Li et al. 2018; Mage et al. 1996; WHO 1992). Traditionally, successive expansions of cities have been explained by changes in the accessibility around extraurban locations. Billion-dollar investments in urban transportation systems (e.g., railways and roads) have been viewed as critical drivers of greater metropolitan formation, or "centrifugal force," pushing out human settlements along an inward–outward development pathway (Cervero 1998; Duranton and Turner 2012; Hanson and Giuliano 2004; Lang and LeFurgy 2003; Pojani and Stead 2015; Reilly, O'Mara, and Seto 2009).

On the other hand, both city leaders and urban theorists have increasingly addressed the economic importance of intercity transportation (e.g., high-speed rail and airport) and telecommunication networking as a "centripetal force" of urban agglomeration in the era of globalization (Bulu 2011; Hall and Pain 2006; OECD 2006; Rondinelli, Johnson Jr, and Kasarda 1998; Sassen 2018; Taylor and Derudder 2015; Yeo, Wang, and Chou 2013). General households continue to manage daily social activities within larger metropolitan areas in the traditional sense of "the space of places." Competitive firms appear to form clusters of economic activity in cities with world-class infrastructure (including airports and rail transit links) as global nodes of supply chain networks and information flows. Thus, to promote competitiveness and sustainability, it is increasingly necessary to study the geospatial progress of megacities (as economic entities) with nodal functions in the dynamics of global, regional, and national production systems based on the logic of the "space of flows" (Castells 1996; 2015; Doel and Hubbard 2002). Nevertheless, little attention has been paid to the geospatial associations of airport system development and the emergence and growth of megacities worldwide.

3.2 Megacities

A megacity is generally defined as an urbanized area with a total population of more than 10 million. This study first sought to identify both existing and emerging megacities worldwide based on the 2018 Revision of World Urbanization Prospects (UN 2018WUP) published by the United Nations (UN) Department of Economic and Social Affairs (UN DESA 2018). According to the estimates of UN 2018WUP, 34 "urban agglomerations" with more than 10 million inhabitants are observed by 2020, and 12 more urban agglomerations are expected to become megacities by 2035. However, the territorial definition of an urban agglomeration varies from country to country, making global comparison difficult. In particular, several of the large urban agglomerations (e.g., Greater Los Angeles and Pearl River Delta) have gradually evolved into larger metropolitan areas by combining multiple cities and towns in a polycentric pathway across the territorial boundaries of urban agglomerations indicated in the UN 2018WUP statistics.

To overcome the problem of international differences in the territorial definition of an urban agglomeration, this study geospatially associates the UN 2018WUP estimates with the figures reported by the European Commission in the Urban Centre Database UCDB R2019A (EU2015UrbanCentres) (European Commission 2018). The territorial coverage of an "urban center" reported by EU2015UrbanCentres is broader based on the degree and pattern of urbanization (e.g., urban density and contiguity) than that of an urban agglomeration, which is based on the size of the urban population estimated for statistical units (or administrative areas). Indeed, the EU2015UrbanCentres database is beneficial in capturing the polycentric formation of megacities and the emergence and growth of multiple urban agglomerations, while the UN 2018WUP estimate is suitable for capturing the dynamics of urban population over the last 7 decades (1950–2020) and the next 15 years (2020–2035).

This study finally identifies 45 megacities ("urban centers"), of which 14 megacities contain more than one urban agglomeration, based on geospatial data association. In particular, the Guangzhou Urban Center combines two large urban agglomerations (Guangzhou and Shenzhen) and three other neighboring urban agglomerations (Dongguan, Foshan, and Jiangmen) into one megacity with a total population of 42 million in 2020 (Figure 3.1). Note that very large urban centers without any large urban agglomeration (less than 10 million population in 2035) are not considered megacities in this study to highlight the ambiguity of the emerging megacity formation accompanied by the spatial influences of the airport system development.

The distribution of the 45 megacities appears to be uneven across global regions (Figure 3.2). Importantly, 30 of the 45 megacities are concentrated in Asia (66.6%), followed by six in Central and South America (13.3%) and four in Africa (8.8%). Only three megacities are located in Europe (6.6%) and two in North America (4.4%). Of the 30 megacities in Asia, nine are growing in the PRC (30.0%), five in Southeast Asia (16.7%), four in (other) South Asia (13.3%), three in East Asia (10.0%), and one in West Asia (3.3%). The emergence of megacities has gradually increased over the past 7 decades (Figure 3.3). By 1950, there were only three megacities—i.e., New York, Osaka, and Tokyo. However, new megacities (i.e., Los Angeles, Mexico City, Sao Paulo, and Seoul) appeared from 1970 to 1980, followed by Buenos Aires and Jakarta from 1980 to 1990. The number of megacities has increased dramatically since the 1990–2000 period. In fact, 25 of the 45 megacities (55.5%) emerged during the 1990–2020 period, largely due to the rapid urbanization of 17 fast-growing cities (national or provincial capitals) in Asia, including Bangkok, Beijing, Bengaluru, Guangzhou (Pearl River Delta), Ho Chi Minh City, Istanbul, Manila, and Shanghai. Only 21 of the 45 megacities (46.6%) have capital status in their nations, so megacities do not necessarily grow out of cities with capital status. Nine more megacities are predicted to emerge during the 2020–2035 period, which will continue to be driven by emerging and growing Asian cities such as Chengdu, Kuala Lumpur, Nanjing, Wuhan, and Xi'an.

Figure 3.1: Five Urban Agglomerations in Guangzhou Urban Center

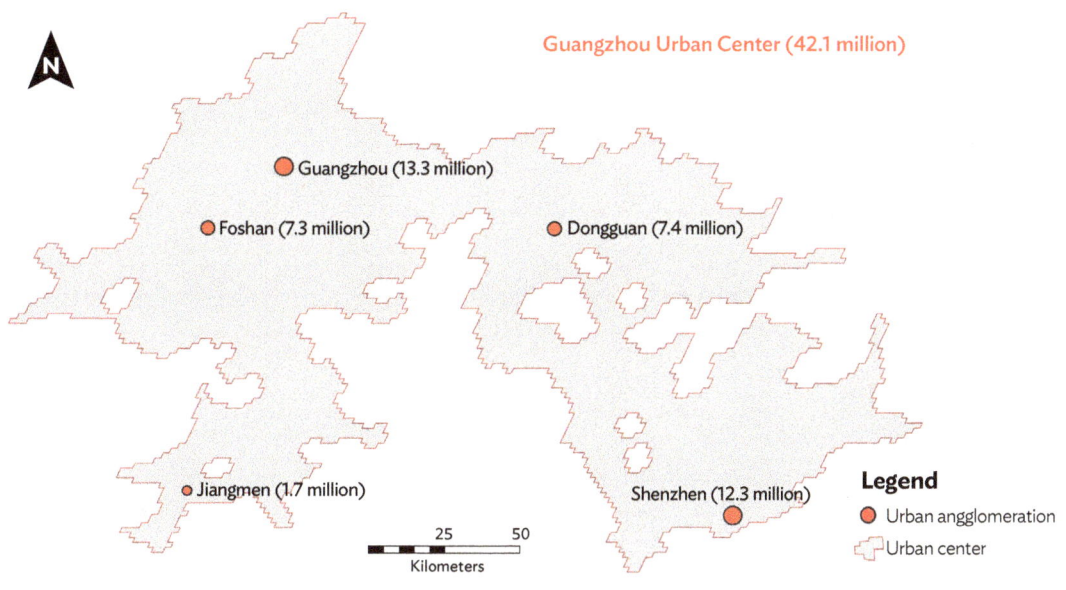

Note: This map was produced by the Authors, with data from European Commission (2018) and UN Department of Economic and Social Affairs (2018). The boundaries, colors, denominations, and any other information shown on this map do not imply, on the part of ADB, any judgment on the legal status of any territory, or any other endorsement or acceptance of such boundaries, colors, denominations, or information.
Sources: Authors, with data from European Commission (2018) and UN Department of Economic and Social Affairs (2018).

Figure 3.2: Distribution of 45 Megacities across Global Regions

Note: This map was produced by the Authors, with data from European Commission (2018). The boundaries, colors, denominations, and any other information shown on this map do not imply, on the part of ADB, any judgment on the legal status of any territory, or any other endorsement or acceptance of such boundaries, colors, denominations, or information.
Source: Authors, with data from European Commission (2018).

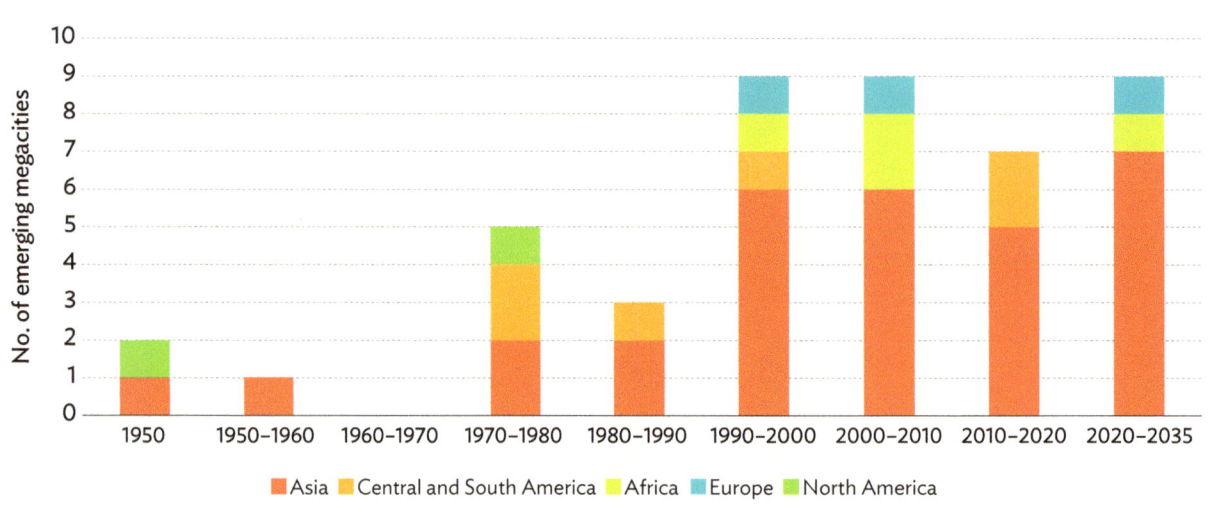

Figure 3.3: The Emergence of Megacities by Region, 1950–2035

Sources: Authors, with data from European Commission (2018) and UN Department of Economic and Social Affairs (2018).

The extent and pace of megacity growth also appear to vary by region or country (Figure 3.4). The population size of three megacities in East Asia is particularly large, ranging from 19.2 million to 37.4 million residents in 2020, but two megacities in Japan—Tokyo and Osaka—are projected to experience gradual population declines (–3.7% and –4.3%, respectively) between 2020 and 2035. In contrast, the size of four megacities in Africa is still rather modest in 2020, but is projected to grow rapidly from 2020 to 2035 (+36.4% to +99.7%). In the PRC, there are some megacities with exceptionally large populations of about 20 million to 40 million (e.g., Guangzhou and Shanghai) that are expected to grow by +21.9% to +27.1% by 2035. Certainly, the scale and pace of growth of megacities in South Asia and Southeast Asia are relatively large and/or rapid compared with traditional capital megacities in Europe (e.g., Paris, London, and Moscow). However, megacities such as Istanbul in West Asia show mixed trends (large scale but moderate growth) between Asia and Europe. The population size of eight megacities in North America, Central America, and South America is as large as that of some megacities in Asia. Nevertheless, the growth of the eight megacities in America is likely to be moderate from 2020 to 2035 (+10.0% to +21.0%).

The emergence and growth of megacities are likely to distribute increasing numbers of inhabitants not only along a horizontal expansion but also along a vertical development (Figure 3.5). Indeed, both urbanized area and population density increased significantly in many megacities between 1990 and 2015, as shown by the trend line drawn for 45 megacities in Figure 3.5(a) shifting upward to the right over the period. However, the percentage increase in population density over the same period was generally much greater than the percentage increase in urbanized area, regardless of the population size of the megacities, as shown in Figure 3.5(b). The ratio of the percentage change in population density to the percentage change in urbanized area averages 3.98 across the 45 megacities and is high in many megacities in the PRC, as well as in some megacities with geographic constraints on horizontal expansion (e.g., Bogota and Chongqing). It is important to note that the percentage increases in both urbanized area (horizontal expansion) and population density (vertical development) were remarkably high in Guangzhou on the Pearl River Delta, where the total population grew to about 38.9 million in 2015 (+64.9% horizontally and +301.8% vertically).

Figure 3.4: Scale and Pace of Megacity Growth by Region/Country, 1950–2035

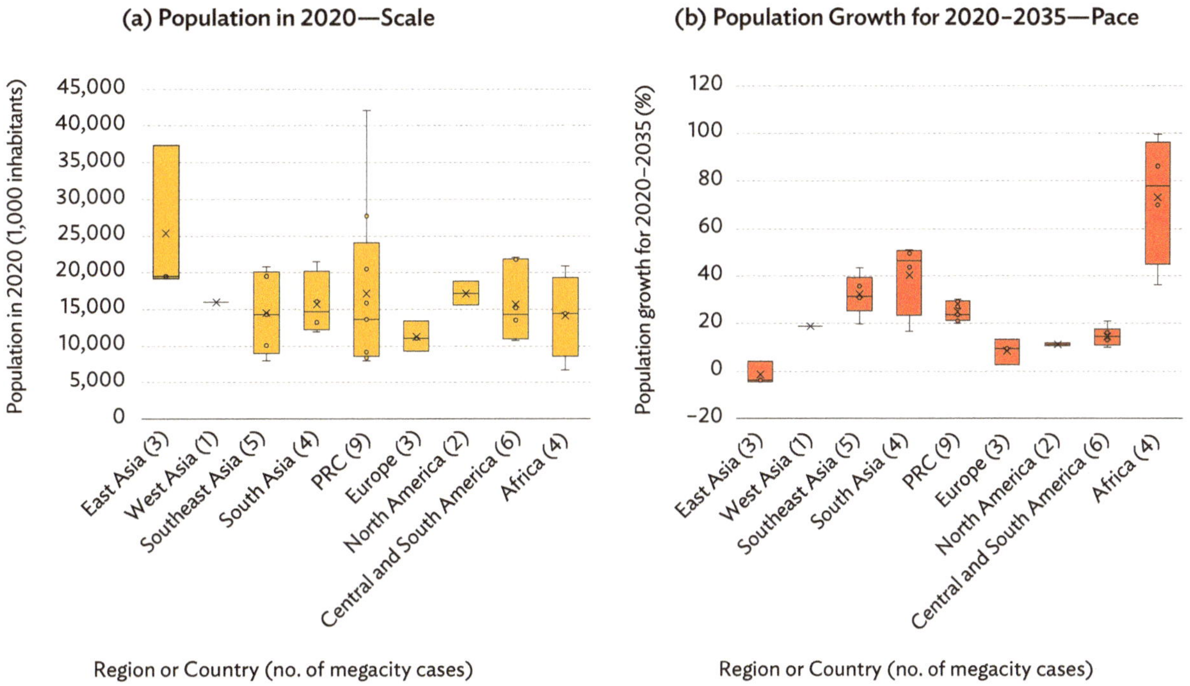

(a) Population in 2020—Scale

(b) Population Growth for 2020–2035—Pace

PRC = People's Republic of China.
Sources: Authors, with data from European Commission (2018) and UN Department of Economic and Social Affairs (2018).

Figure 3.5: Changes in Urbanized Area and Population Density across 45 Megacities, 1990–2015

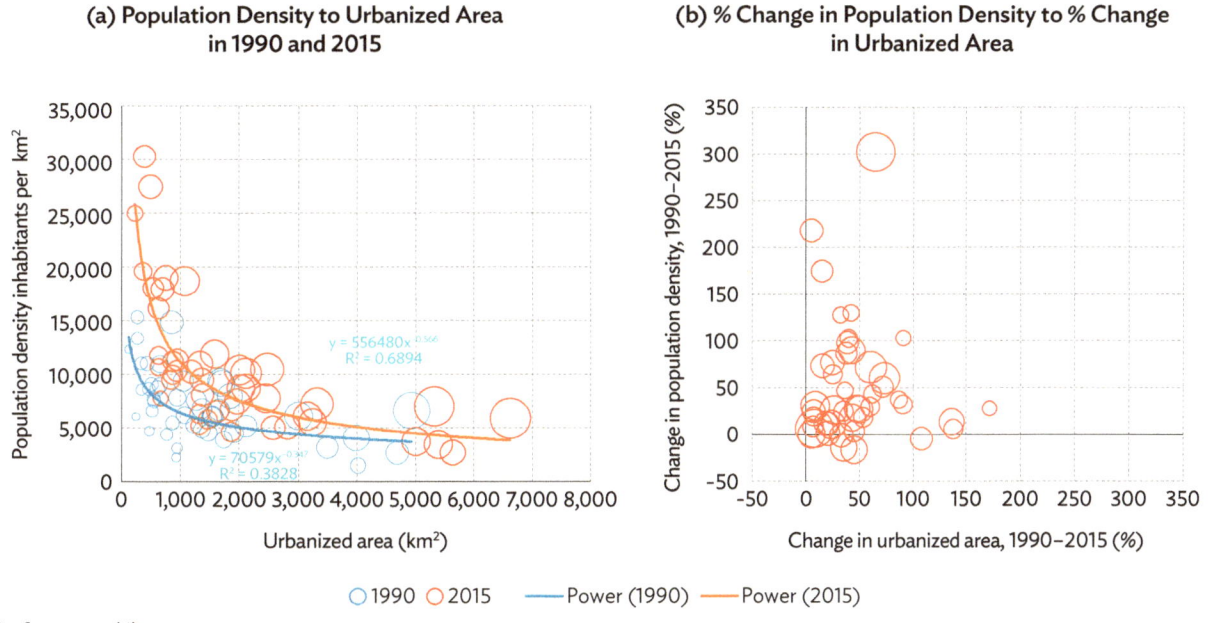

(a) Population Density to Urbanized Area in 1990 and 2015

(b) % Change in Population Density to % Change in Urbanized Area

○ 1990 ○ 2015 —— Power (1990) —— Power (2015)

km^2 = square kilometer.
Note: The size of a bubble indicates the population of each megacity in 1990 (blue) and 2015 (red).
Sources: Authors, with data from European Commission (2018) and UN Department of Economic and Social Affairs (2018).

On the other hand, the ratio was less than 1 in New York (0.45), Seoul (0.45), Bangkok (0.90), and Osaka (0.98), and less than 1 in Los Angeles (1.05), Tehran (1.10), Dhaka (1.23), and Dar es Salaam (1.44), which may indicate rapid suburbanization or metropolitan sprawl during the 1990–2015 period. This study assumes that different development strategies for airport systems are spatiotemporally associated with the vertical and horizontal distribution patterns of urban residents in megacities.

3.3 New Airport Construction, Relocation, and Multi-Airport Formation

In this study, information on the locations and year of completion of the airport system for each of the 45 megacities was collected from various sources (e.g., ACI Annual World Airport Traffic Dataset, official websites of individual airport agencies, airport-technology.com, CAPA Centre for Aviation, and iFly.com, supplemented by Wikipedia). There is neither an internationally integrated nor a formally established global database on airport investment attributes (e.g., new airport construction, relocation, and multi-airport formation) with particular interest in the spatial influences of airport system development on megacities. The information collected on airport system development was geocoded using an online satellite imagery technique and spatiotemporally associated with data on 45 megacities identified in the previous section. This data work looks only at commercial airports (those operating regular scheduled flight services), excluding general airports, heliports, and military airports (air bases).

This study identifies 82 airports serving the 45 existing and emerging megacities worldwide from 1990 to 2021. Of the 82 airports, 22 opened or became operational in the last 3 decades (26.8%), including 7 between 1990 and 1999 (8.5%), 10 between 2000 and 2010 (12.2%), and 5 between 2011 to 2021 (6.1%). In the 3 decades, only two major inner-city airports (Wuhan Nanhu Airport in 1995 and Beijing Nanyuan Airport in 2019) were permanently closed and relocated to newly constructed outer-city airports (Wuhan Tianhe International Airport in 1995 and Beijing Daxing International Airport in 2019). Notably, 21 of the 22 new or newly operating airports were developed for megacities in Asia, including Istanbul in West Asia, and 8 of them appear to work for those in the PRC (36.4%). Surprisingly, only one new airport was built to serve Moscow in Europe (4.5%).

Of the 45 megacities, 20 deployed multi-airport formations with more than one airport in 2021 (44.4%). London and Los Angeles have six and five airports, respectively, followed by one megacity with four airports (Moscow) and six megacities with three airports (Guangzhou, Istanbul, New York, Osaka, Paris, and Rio de Janeiro). Of the 30 megacities in Asia, 12 operate multi-airport formations with more than one airport (40%). However, none of Africa's four existing and emerging megacities will develop more than one airport by 2021. Moreover, 12 of the 20 megacities with multiple airports have a national capital status (60.0%). These figures imply that the probability of developing multi-airport systems in megacities may depend on the funding power of nations or regions and the degree and pattern of urbanization in megacities. Indeed, "population size" alone does not numerically explain the likelihood of multi-airport formation in the 45 megacities, while both "urbanized area" and "population density" do (Figure 3.6). Territorially large and dense megacities (with an urbanized area of more than 1,000 square kilometers [km^2] and population density of less than 12,000 inhabitants per km^2) are most likely to have more than one airport, and all five megacities with an urbanized area of more than 5,000 km^2 have multi-airports.

Figure 3.6: Multi-Airport Formation in the Relationship between Urbanized Area and Population Density in 45 Megacities in 2015

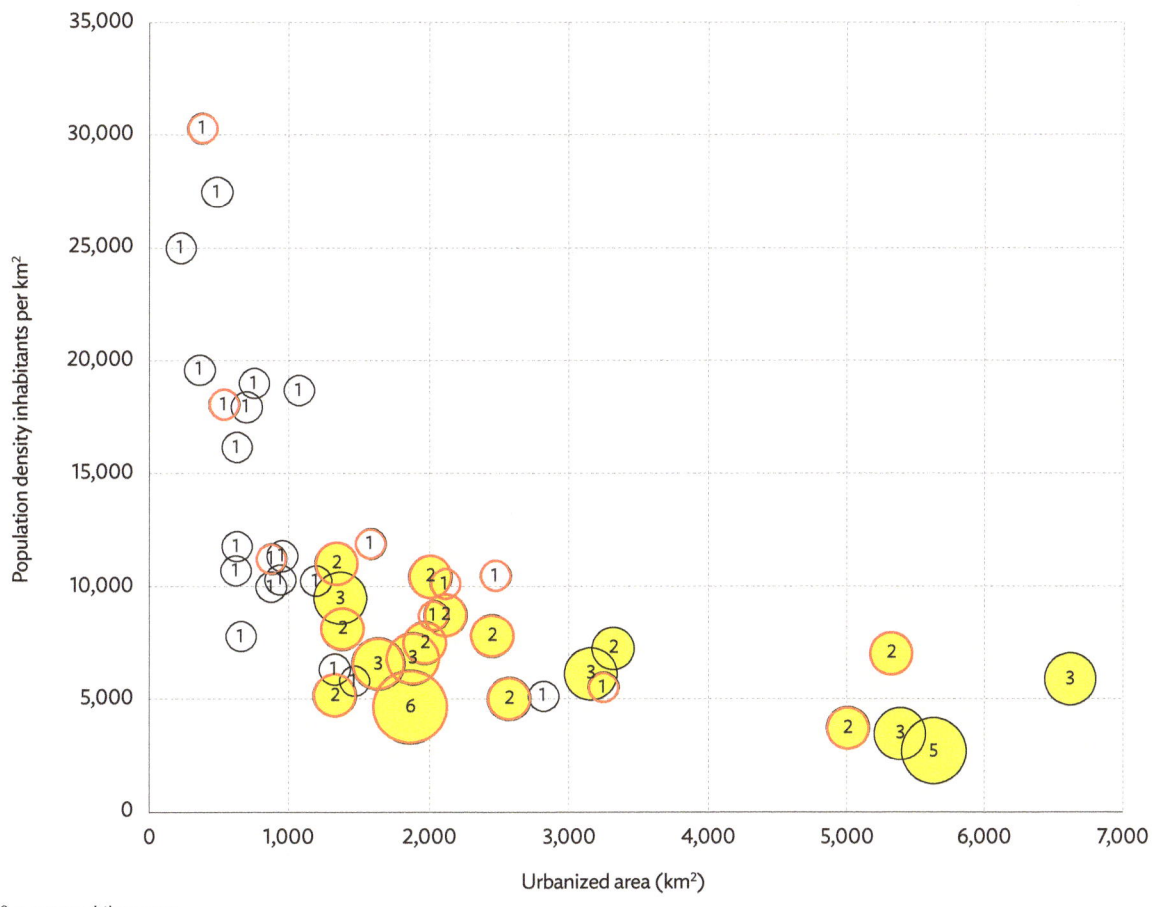

km² = square kilometer.
Notes: The size of a bubble indicates the number of airports developed in each megacity by 2015; yellow bubbles indicate megacities with more than one airport and red outlines indicate megacities with a national capital status.
Sources: Authors, with data from European Commission (2018) and UN Department of Economic and Social Affairs (2018).

This study further examines the sequential association of airport system development with the emergence and growth of megacities over the 1950–2021 period by illustrating the distributions of the leading and/or lagging years for the construction of new airports and the formation of multi-airports with mean, standard deviation, skewness, and kurtosis (Figure 3.7). Apparently, the distribution patterns in both Figure 3.7(a) and Figure 3.7(b) are largely skewed toward the leading side. Of the 82 airports, 71 opened before the emerging megacities reached a total population of over 10 million inhabitants (86.6%). Nine of the 11 airports that were newly built after the emergence and growth of megacities (81.8%) are located near seven megacities in Asia—Tokyo (Haneda in 1953 and Narita in 1978), Osaka (Kansai in 1994 and Kobe in 2006), Seoul (Incheon in 2001), Beijing (Daxing in 2019), Shanghai (Pudong in 1999), Guangzhou (Bai Yun in 2004), and Istanbul (New Istanbul in 2019). These nine airports were developed to build a multi-airport formation for the seven Asian megacities. Nonetheless, 14 of the 20 megacities with more than one airport are leading this year, which means that the development and management of multiple airports will be applied before they reach a total population of more than 10 million. In fact, the number of megacities with more than one airport has gradually increased since the 1970s. However, the rapid increase in multi-airport formation over the 1990–2020 period was led primarily by 11 emerging and growing megacities in Asia (Figure 3.8).

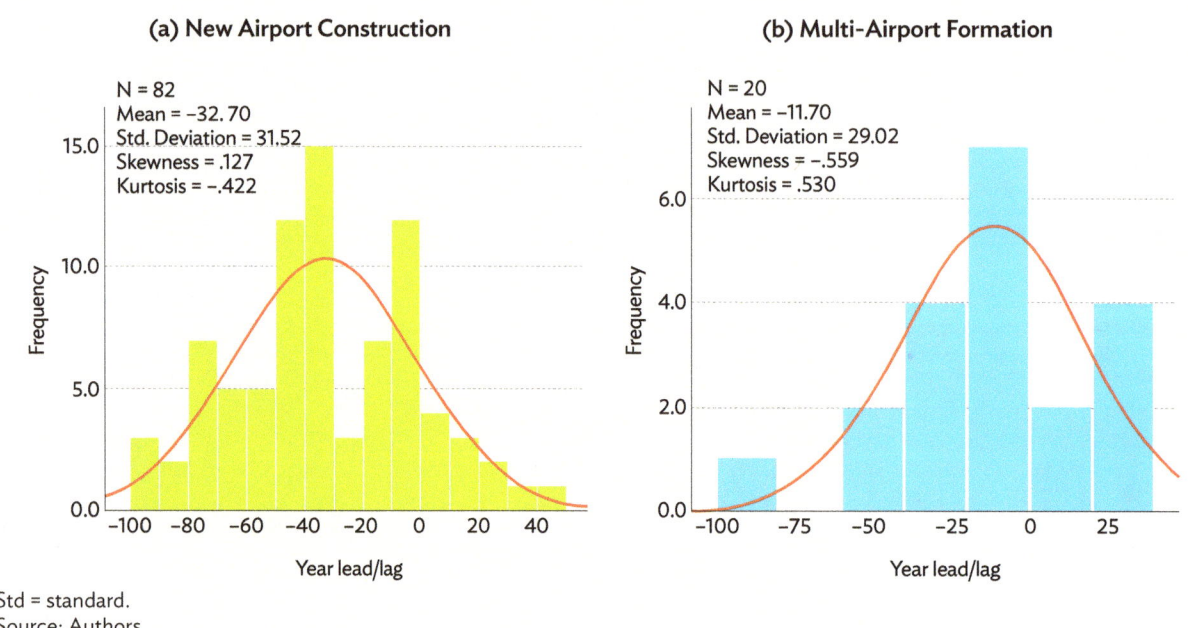

Figure 3.7: Year Lead/Lag Distributions of Airport System Development to/from the Emergence of Megacities, 1950–2021

Std = standard.
Source: Authors.

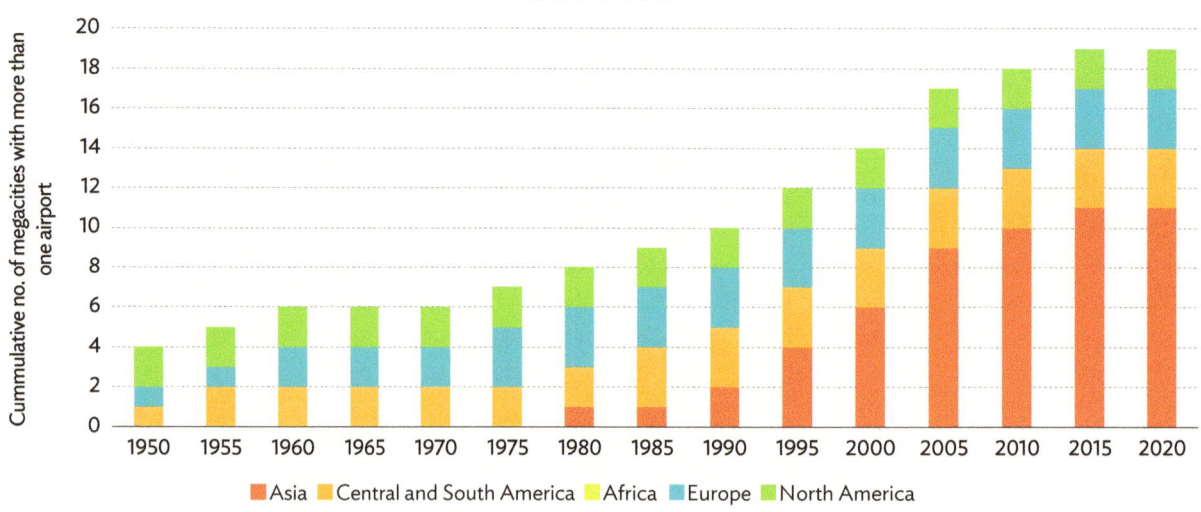

Figure 3.8: Cumulative Number of Megacities with Multi-Airport Formation by Region, 1950–2020

Source: Authors.

The spatial influences of airport system development can be assessed by comparing the percentage changes in urbanized area and population density in the 45 megacities: (i) without the construction of any new airport, (ii) with a new airport, and (iii) with multi-airport formation from 1990 to 2015 (Figure 3.9). On average, megacities with a new airport (+63.9%) experienced a 21.6% increase in urbanized areas compared with cities without new airport construction (+42.3%). Megacities with multi-airports (+50.0%) experienced a 7.7% increase in urbanized area compared with cities without new airport construction. Similarly, megacities with a new airport (+163.1%) recorded a 60.3% increase in population density compared with cities without any new airport construction (+102.8%). On the other hand, population density in megacities with multi-airports (+147.5%) increased by 44.7% compared with cities without new airport construction.

To see these changes in detail, multivariate regression analysis must be applied by controlling for the spatial effects of many other factors in explaining urbanized area and population density to measure the net impact of airport system development. Nonetheless, these simple comparisons with and without suggest that airport system development is likely to have both suburbanization and densification effects on megacities. The descriptive statistics also suggest that both the suburbanization and densification effects of building new airports may be more significant for megacities than those of forming multi-airports.

Figure 3.9: Comparison of Percentage Changes in Urbanized Area and Population Density in 45 Megacities with/without Airport System Development, 1990–2015

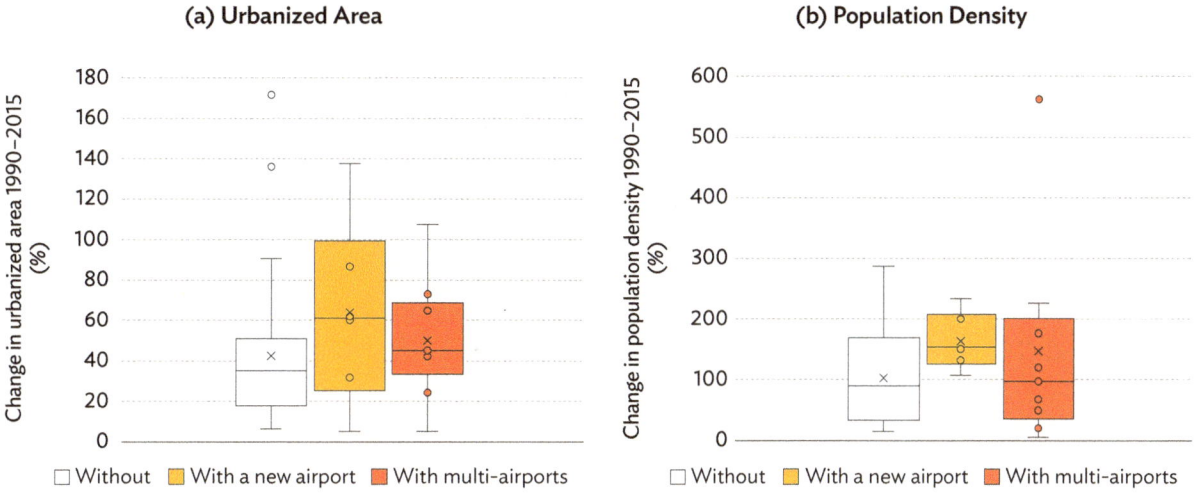

Sources: Authors, with data from European Commission (2018) and UN Department of Economic and Social Affairs (2018).

3.4 Airport Terminal Expansion

In this study, information on the years of completion of airport terminal expansion, such as new terminal construction projects and modernization programs, for the 82 airports around the 45 megacities was compiled from various sources (e.g., ACI Annual World Airport Traffic Dataset, official websites of individual airport agencies, airport-technology.com, CAPA Centre for Aviation, and iFly.com, supplemented by Wikipedia). This study focuses on airport "terminal" expansion instead of "capacity" expansion for two reasons. First, it is difficult to collect globally consistent, comprehensive, and accurate information on airport capacity expansion projects, including runway extensions and taxiway improvements. Second, terminal expansion projects are in many cases delivered along with other capacity expansion projects.

According to the data collected, 67 of the 82 airports in the 45 megacities had some type of terminal expansion from 1990 to 2021 (81.7%). Of the 67 airports, 37 have sequentially delivered multiple terminal expansion projects over the past 3 decades (55.2%). The sequential distribution of the 67 airports with terminal expansion projects over the period is 18 during the 1990s (26.9%), 45 from 2000 to 2010 (67.2%), and 53 from 2011 to 2021 (79.1%). The distribution of terminal expansion projects appears to be not only more sequential but also more ubiquitous than that of new airport construction projects in global regions. All 12 and 4 airports in Europe and Africa, respectively (100%), 7 of the 8 airports in North America (87.5%), and 9 of the 10 airports in Central and South America (90.0%) completed at least one terminal expansion project from 1990 to 2021, while there had been no new airport construction in these regions during this period. In contrast, only 17 of the 44 airports in Asia completed more than one terminal expansion project in sequence during the 1990–2021 period (36.9%), as 21 of the 22 newly built or commercialized megacity airports began operations in Asia during the same period.

It is assumed that airport terminal expansion is highly dependent on the availability of land for expansion in inner-city and outer-city locations, which can be measured by the straight-line distance from the nearest city center to an airport with/without terminal expansion. In fact, the average distance from the nearest city center to an airport without terminal expansion (26.1 km) appears to be 0.9 km longer than to an airport with expansion for one period (24.2 km), but 4.9 km shorter than to an airport with expansion in sequence (31.0 km), respectively, although the distance range is wide, especially within a group of airports with terminal expansion in sequence (Figure 3.10).

Figure 3.10: Comparison of Straight Distances from the Nearest City Centers to Airports without Terminal Expansion, with Terminal Expansion for One Period, and with Terminal Expansion in Sequence, 1990–2021

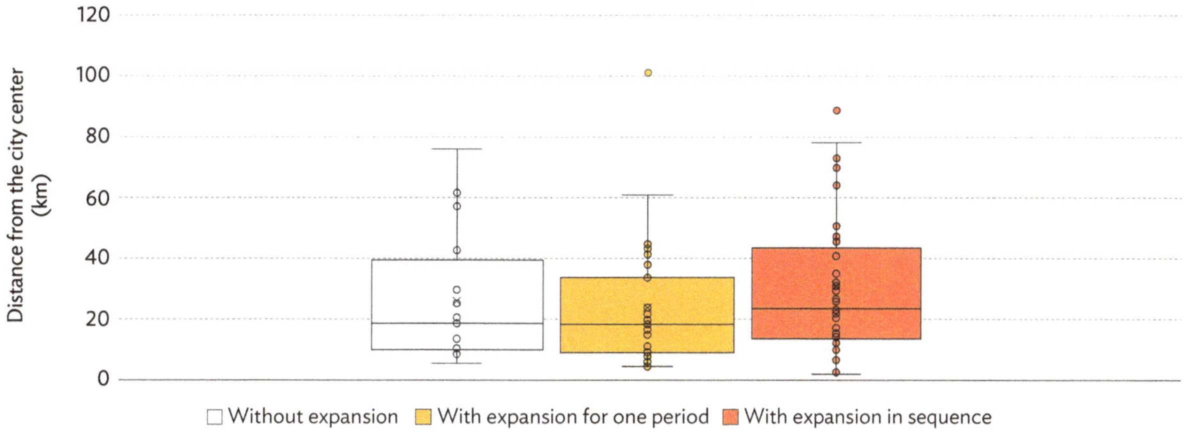

☐ Without expansion ☐ With expansion for one period ☐ With expansion in sequence

km = kilometer.
Sources: Authors, with data from European Commission (2018) and UN Department of Economic and Social Affairs (2018).

3.5 Airport Location and Access Rail Link

The locational distribution of airports within and around megacities is a critical determinant of airport accessibility and, in turn, the spatial influences of airport system development and ground transportation investment in theory. Twenty-eight of the 82 airports are located outside the urbanized areas of 22 megacities (34.1%), and 21 of the 28 outer-city airports operate as part of the multi-airport formation. Noticeably, London, Paris, Moscow, and Beijing have more than one outer-city airport beyond urban boundaries, and Osaka places two offshore airports on artificial islands. On average, the year of construction (or age) of 28 airports outside urbanized areas (1985) is about 25 years younger than that of 54 airports within urbanized areas (1960) (Figure 3.11). The average network distance from the nearest city center for the 82 airports in and around the 45 megacities is about 27.5 km and ranges from 1.9 km to 101.4 km (Figure 3.12).

This study also collected information on ground transportation attributes (e.g., airport rail link availability, type of rail system, and year of completion) for each of the airports in and around the 45 megacities from various sources (e.g., official websites of each airport and public transit agencies, Google Map and Earth Pro, and UrbanRail.Net, supplemented by Wikipedia). Note that the typical travel times for two major modes (private car and public transit) were originally compiled but not used for this data analysis for two reasons: (i) travel time information is inconsistent across countries, and (ii) travel restrictions during the COVID-19 pandemic most likely influence travel times across the 45 megacities.

Figure 3.11: Comparison of the Built or Commercialized Years of Airports within and beyond Urbanized Areas

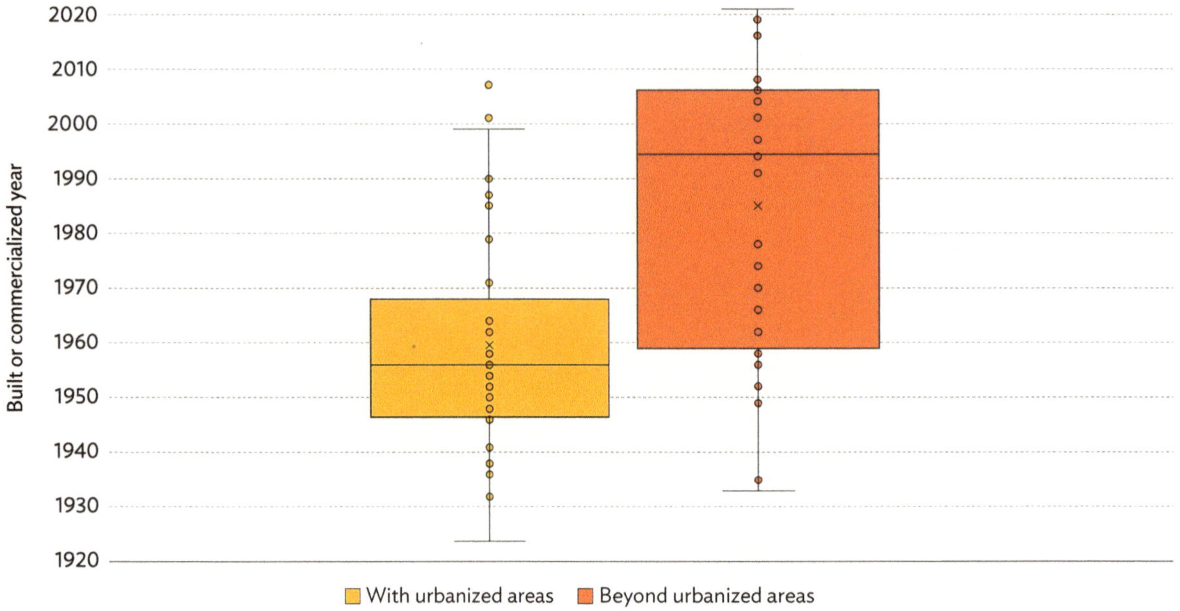

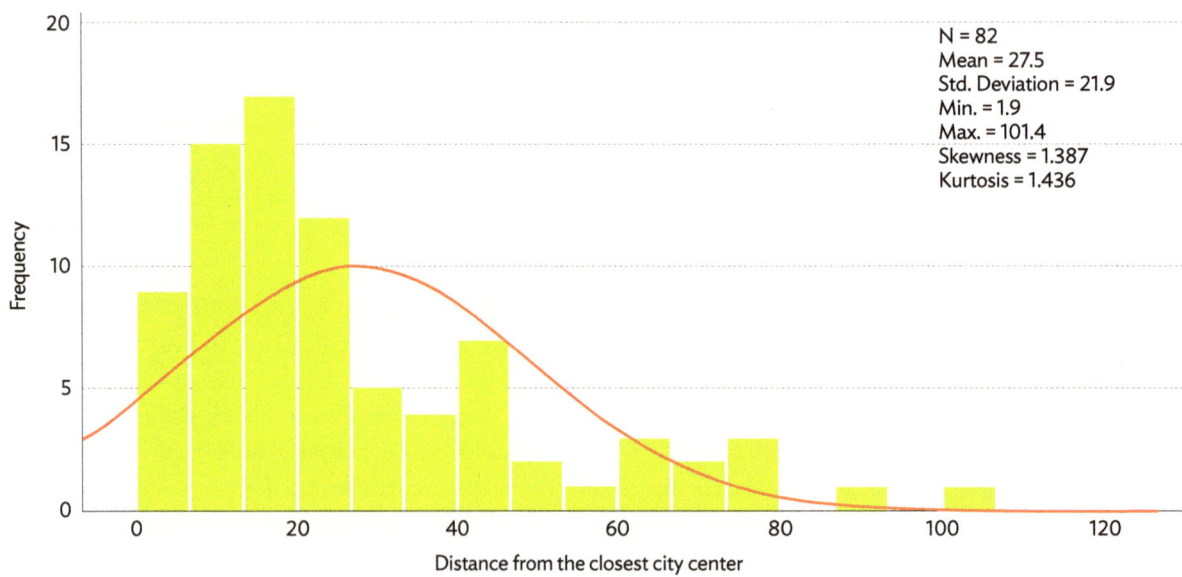

Sources: Authors, with data from European Commission (2018) and UN Department of Economic and Social Affairs (2018).

Figure 3.12: Locational Distribution of 82 Airports in 45 Megacities

N = 82
Mean = 27.5
Std. Deviation = 21.9
Min. = 1.9
Max. = 101.4
Skewness = 1.387
Kurtosis = 1.436

Std = standard.
Source: Authors.

Forty-six of the 82 airports have at least one airport rail link by 2021 (56.1%), and 19 of the 46 airports provide airport express rail service (or dedicated rail access) to/from the nearest city centers (41.3%). There are 58 airport rail link systems (developed through 62 projects) serving the 46 airports, consisting of 27 metro and heavy rail (46.6%), 17 commuter rail (29.3%), 5 light rail and monorail (8.6%), 5 bus rapid transit guideways (8.6%), 2 high-speed rail (3.4%), and 2 maglev (3.4%). The average distance from one airport to the closest city center appears to vary by type of rail system: 33.3 km without airport rail link; 48.3 km with airport express; 29.4 km with metro; 40.9 km with heavy rail; 36.1 km with commuter rail; 15.9 km with light rail and monorail; 28.8 km with bus rapid transit; 22.3 km with high-speed rail; and 47.9 km with maglev (Figure 3.13). The distribution of several airport rail link systems also appears to be uneven across the global regions (Figure 3.14). In particular, 37 of the 58 airport rail link systems are concentrated in Asia (63.8%), where metros, heavy rail, and commuter rail systems (83.8%) predominate. Similarly, 10 of the 12 airports in three megacities (London, Paris, and Moscow) in Europe have airport rail links (83.3%), which are served mainly by metros, heavy rail, and commuter rail systems (83.8%). In contrast, two of the three airports in New York employ a mix of rail systems, and none of the five airports in Los Angeles in North America have airport rail links. Four of the 10 airports use bus rapid transit systems for six megacities in Central and South America (40.0%), while all four airports have not yet developed airport rail link systems for four megacities in Africa (0.0%).

Figure 3.13: Comparison of Straight-Line Distances from Nearest Centers to Airports by Type of Rail System

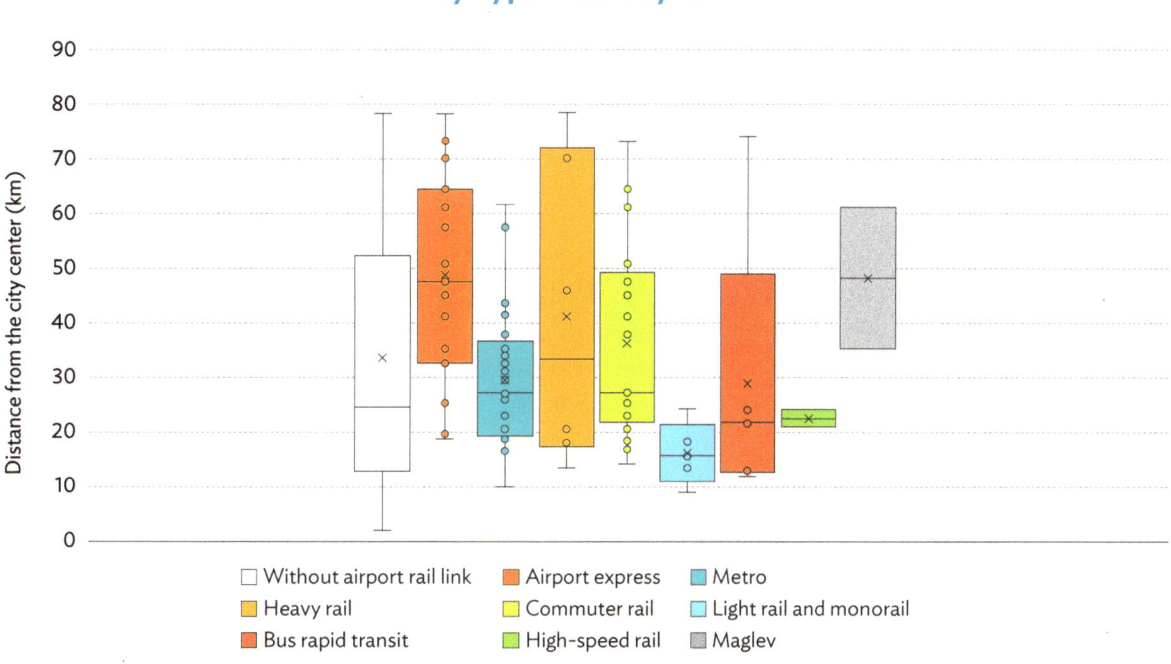

km = kilometer.
Source: Authors.

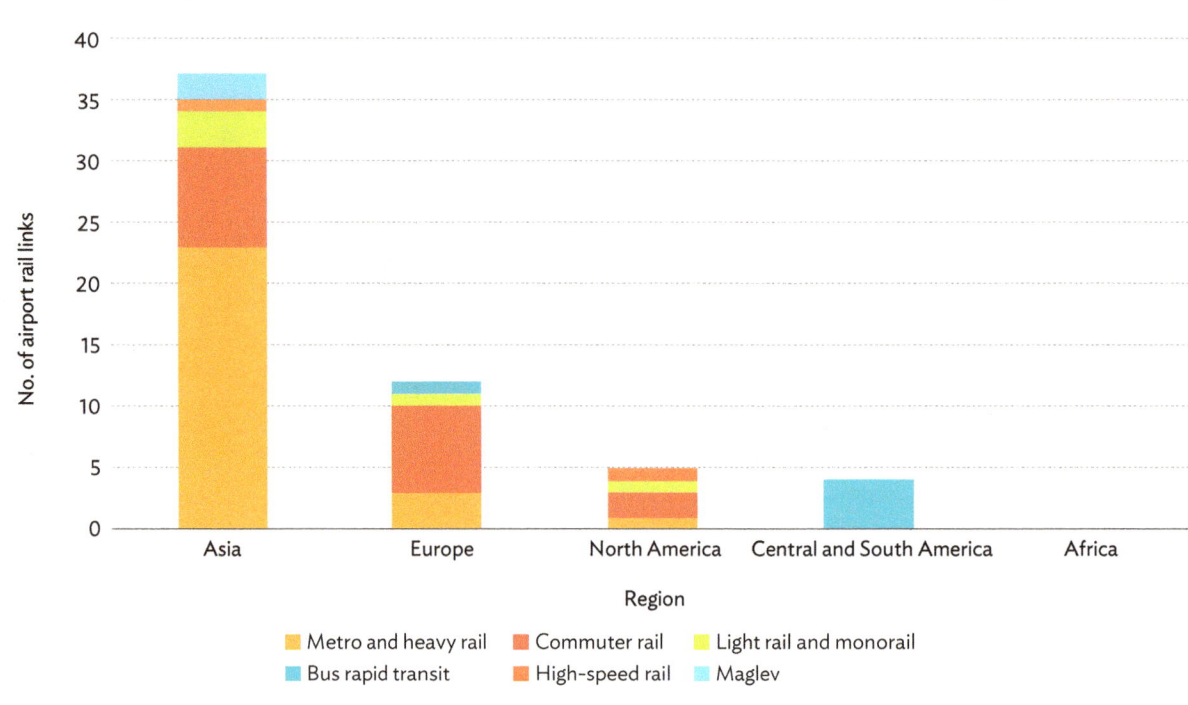

Figure 3.14: Distribution of 58 Airport Rail Link Systems by Region

Source: Authors.

The construction of airport rail links is a relatively new development practice in megacities worldwide, with 57 of the 62 airport rail link projects completed between 1990 and 2021 (91.9%), including 10 between 1990 and 1999 (16.1%), 20 between 2000 and 2010 (32.3%), and 27 between 2011 and 2021 (43.5%). The five airport rail links built before the 1990s are in two megacities: three projects for Gatwick Airport (1958) and Heathrow International Airport (1977 and 1986) in London; and two projects for Haneda Airport (1964) and Narita International Airport (1972) in Tokyo. Only four of the 62 airport rail links were opened along with new airports: Kansai International Airport (1994) and Kobe Airport (2006) in Osaka; Daxing International Airport (2019) in Beijing; and Tianfu International Airport (2021) in Chengdu. All other airport rail links were built after the completion of their new airports, as shown in Figure 3.15(a). However, the temporal distribution of airport rail link projects turns out to be a normal pattern with two tails (both lead years and lag years) before and after the emergence of the megacities, as shown in Figure 3.15(b). This may suggest that the construction of airport rail links, which was intensively delivered during the 1990–2021 period, may be spatiotemporally associated with the birth and growth of megacities during the 1950–2035 period.

Nonetheless, the influences of airport rail link investment on population density during the 1990–2015 period were more elusive than the influences of new airport construction and multi-airport formation. Instead, airport rail link projects were likely to mitigate the degree and pace of suburbanization or metropolitan sprawl, while the construction of new airports and the formation of multi-airports tended to expand the urbanized areas of megacities over the same period (Figure 3.16). It can also be presumed that municipalities within and around megacities with airport rail link projects newly adopted anti-sprawl land use measures around their airports and/or along their airport access corridors. Yet, the net spatial effects of new airport construction, the formation of multi-airports, and airport rail link investment (along with supportive land use measures) on suburbanization or metropolitan sprawl cannot be concluded from this simple data description.

Figure 3.15: Year Lead/Lag Distributions of Airport Rail Link Projects, 1950–2021

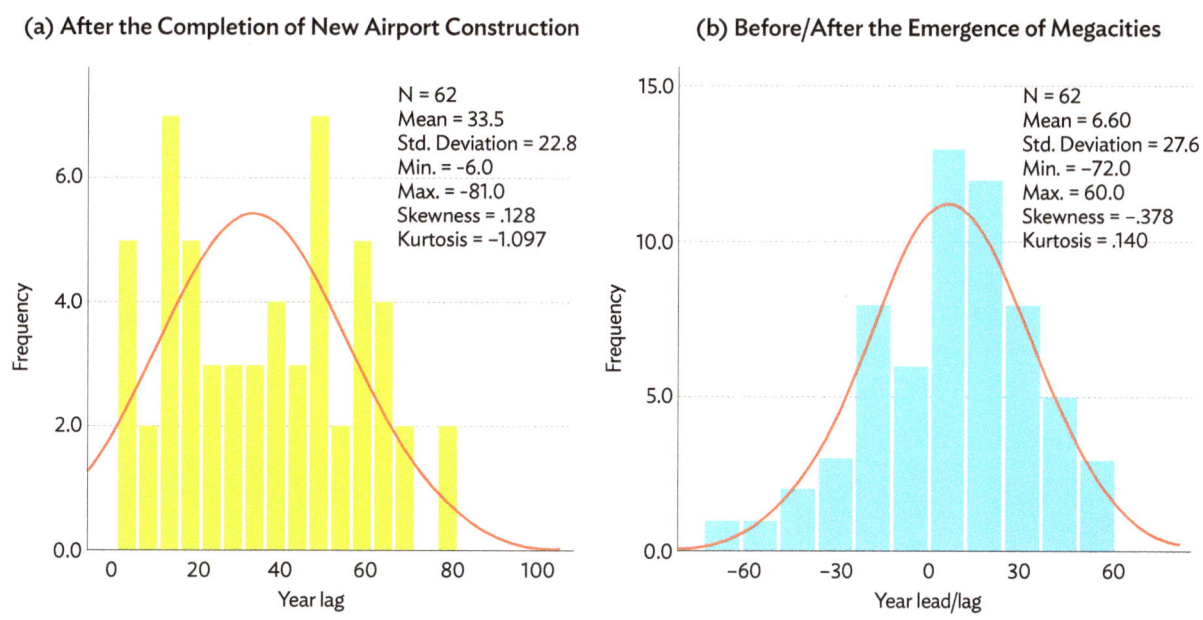

Max = maximum, Min = minimum, Std = standard.
Source: Authors.

Figure 3.16: Comparison of Percentage Change in Urbanized Area across 45 Megacities with and without Airport Rail Link Investment, 1990–2015

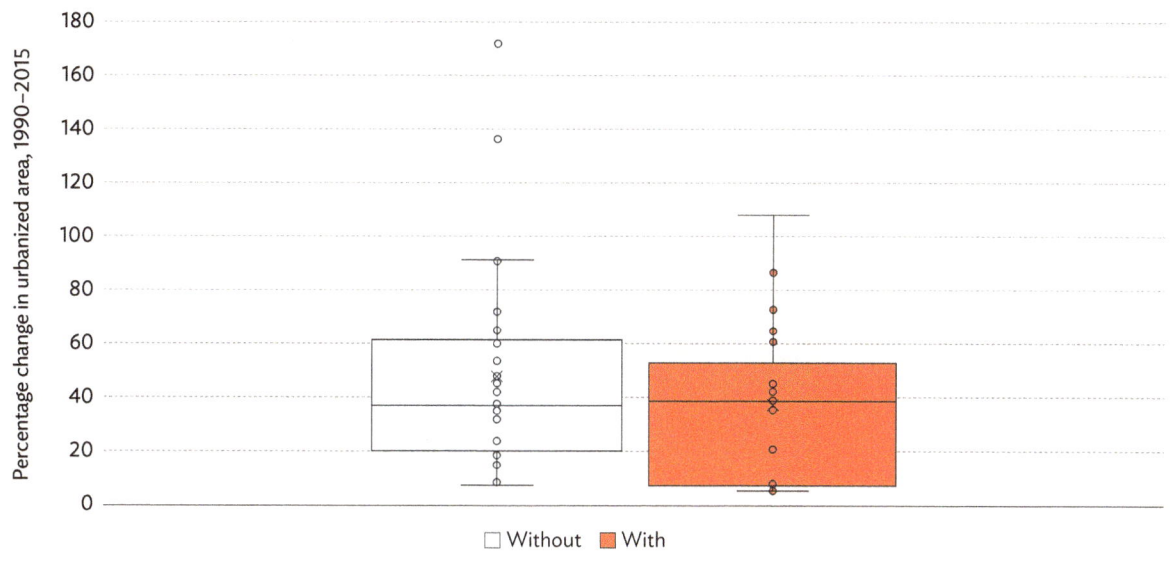

Sources: Authors, with data from European Commission (2018) and UN Department of Economic and Social Affairs (2018).

3.6 Air Traffic Flows, Classification, and Economic Production

This study illustrates the geospatial distribution pattern of air traffic flows to and from 45 megacities using International Civil Aviation Organization (ICAO) Traffic Flow Global Data, including the number of aircraft movements (frequency) for both departures and arrivals in each city and between cities, as well as the typical flight routes (distances) between cities, which appear to vary by location or country (Figure 3.17). On average, one megacity managed 369,418 aircraft movements (for both departures and arrivals) by connecting about 72 cities internationally and domestically in 2018, with a total flight length of 422,807 km (Table 3.1).

Among the 45 megacities, New York can be considered the busiest air transportation node, handling about 1.24 million movements to and from 140 cities in 2018, followed by London (1.13 million; 212 cities), Los Angeles (0.88 million; 158 cities), Guangzhou (0.79 million; 179 cities), and Shanghai (0.73 million; 120 cities). On the other hand, Kinshasa is the least busy node with only 9,602 aircraft movements to and from 17 cities in 2018, followed by Lagos (10,472; 6 cities), Karachi (30,215; 20 cities), and Lahore (48,046; 22 cities). These figures show that some of the

Figure 3.17: Air Transportation Movements (Frequencies) to/from 45 Megacities, 2018

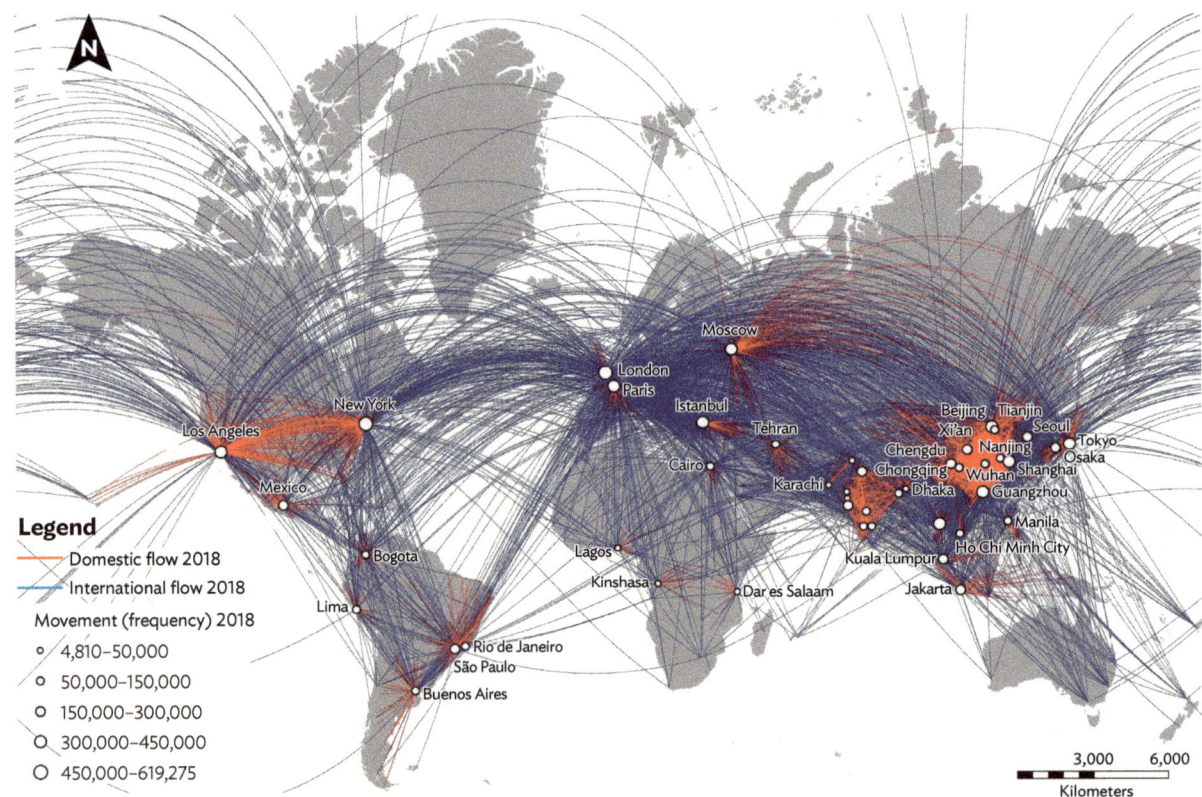

Note: This map was produced by the Authors, with data from ICAO, European Commission (2018), and UN Department of Economic and Social Affairs (2018). The boundaries, colors, denominations, and any other information shown on this map do not imply, on the part of ADB, any judgment on the legal status of any territory, or any other endorsement or acceptance of such boundaries, colors, denominations, or information.
Sources: Authors, with data from ICAO (2018), European Commission (2018), and UN Department of Economic and Social Affairs (2018).

Table 3.1: Descriptive Statistics of Air Transportation Movements, 2018
(N = 45 Megacities)

	Mean	S.D.	Minimum	Maximum
Year 2018				
Frequency – annual movements	369,418	295,743	9,602	1,238,521
Total length km	422,807	377,247	8,885	1,481,438
Annual movement length in km million	655.1	666.4	8.8	2,799.7
No. of cities connected	71.8	52.7	6.0	211.5
International Ratio				
Frequency – annual movements (%)	33.4	24.3	0.0	100.0
Total length km (%)	79.5	19.0	0.0	100.0
Annual movement length in km million (%)	56.6	26.6	0.0	100.0
No. of cities connected (%)	55.1	23.0	0.0	100.0
Change 2011–2018				
Frequency – annual movements	+91,693	+77,884	-45,802	+310,634
Total length km	+124,358	+124,356	-13,880	+468,855
Annual movement length in km million	+187.7	+163.1	-23.0	+549.8
No. of cities connected	+18.1	+16.9	-2.5	+68.5

km = kilometer, S.D. = standard deviation.
Note: "No. of cities connected" is the average of no. of cities connected for departures and arrivals.
Sources: Authors, with data from ICAO (2018), European Commission (2018), and UN Department of Economic and Social Affairs (2018).

megacities with more than 10 million inhabitants in developing countries do not always play (or have not yet played) a nodal role in global production networks. The share of international traffic flows (or international ratios in Table 3.1) also proved to vary widely across the 45 megacities in terms of frequency—annual movements, total length in km, annual movement length in million km, and number of cities connected, depending on geographic or regional configuration. Noticeably, the share of international traffic flows (frequency) in 2018 tended to be very high for megacities with capital status in and around Europe, such as London (90.8%), Cairo (82.4%), and Paris (81.9%), while they were relatively low for emerging and growing megacities in the PRC, such as Tianjin (4.8%), Chengdu (7.2%), Nanjing (9.2%), Wuhan (9.3%), Chongqing (9.4%), and Xi'an (10.0%). On average, from 2011 to 2018, one megacity experienced significant growth in frequency—annual movements (+91,693; +24.8%), total length in km (+124,358; +29.4%), annual movement length in million km (+187.7; +28.7%), and number of cities connected (+18.1; +25.2%), although there were four megacities with some reduction in volume and/or coverage of air traffic flows (Rio de Janeiro, Paris, Lagos, and Karachi).

This study comparatively describes the annual movement length of domestic and international air traffic flows normalized by population size (per 1,000 inhabitants) in 45 megacities in 2015, which is supposed to indicate the total amount of air transportation services per capita for each megacity (Figure 3.18). Of the 45 megacities, London had the largest annual movement length in km per 1,000 inhabitants with a high proportion of international flows (260,591 at 97.5%), well ahead of Paris (131,683 at 94.6%) and Istanbul (69,686 at 84.5%) as comparable megacities with hub status in and around Europe. New York, Los Angeles, and Moscow had high

Figure 3.18: Comparison of Annual Movement Length in Kilometers per 1,000 Inhabitants across Megacities, 2015

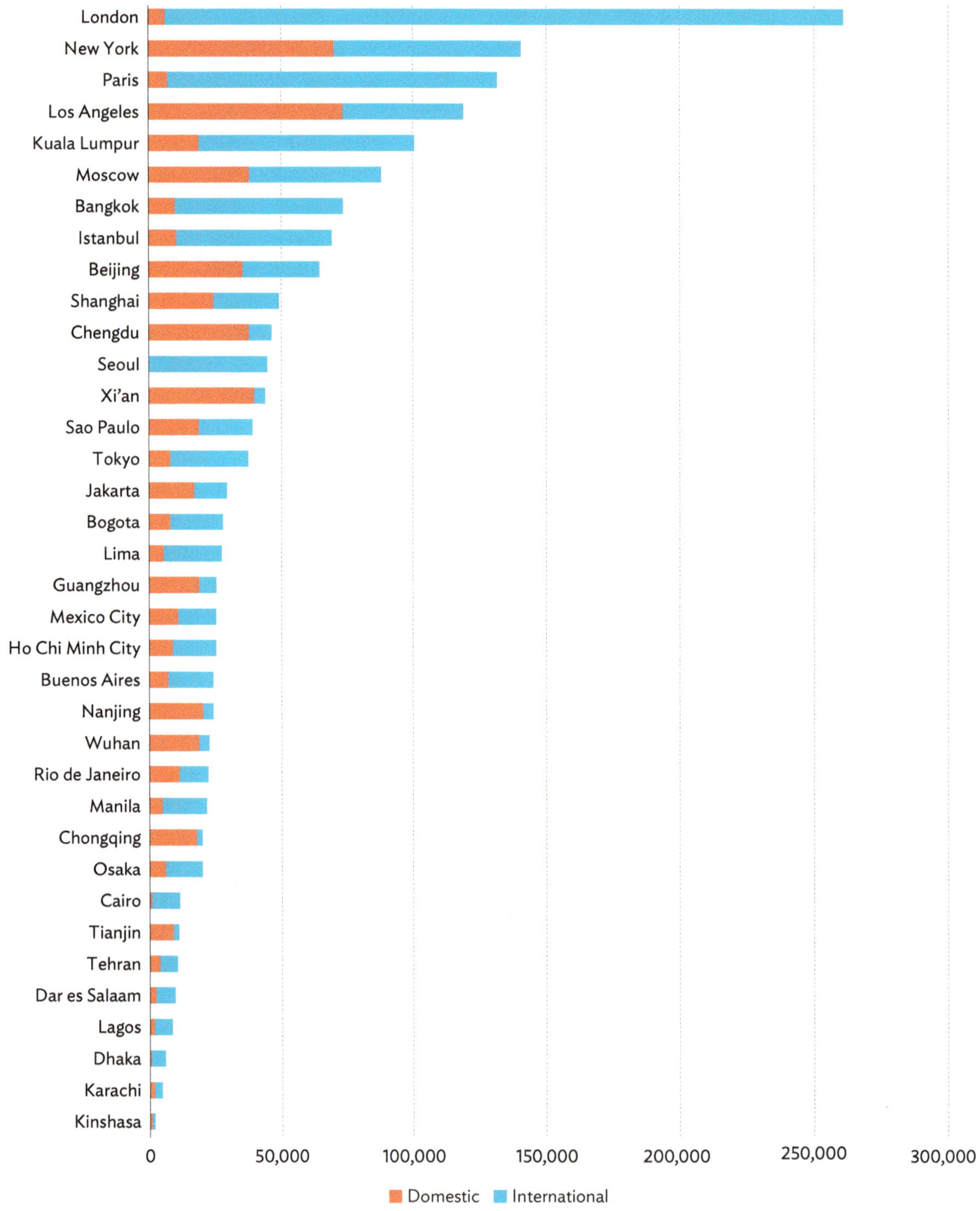

Sources: Authors, with data from ICAO (2015), European Commission (2018), and UN Department of Economic and Social Affairs (2018).

annual movement length in km per 1,000 inhabitants with a modest share of international flows (140,549 with 49.9%; 118,971 with 38.8%; and 88,022 with 56.7%, respectively) due to their large domestic territories and long-distance city pairs to be connected by air transportation networks. Similarly, Kuala Lumpur and Bangkok, as regional hubs, exhibited a large annual movement length in km per 1,000 inhabitants with a high proportion of international flows (100,784 with 80.9% and 73,822 with 86.4%, respectively), mainly due to their limited domestic territories/short-distance city pairs and cross-border tourism/trade economy in and around Southeast Asia. In contrast, due to their large domestic area and various large city pairs within the PRC, Beijing and Shanghai had a large annual movement length in km per 1,000 inhabitants with a modest share of international flows (64,719 with 45.5% and 49,382 with 50.7%, respectively). Notably, all emerging and growing megacities in South Asia still have relatively small annual movement length in km per 1,000 inhabitants with a moderate share of international flows compared with those in Southeast Asia and the PRC.

Furthermore, this study attempts to classify the geospatial assignment patterns of air traffic flows within 44 megacities. For this purpose, the ACI Annual World Airport Traffic Dataset is used, which records aircraft movements (frequency) and passenger and cargo volumes at each airport for the 2011–2018 period. Dhaka is excluded from this classification due to the incompleteness and inconsistency of air traffic data in the above and other comparable sources. First, a typology is created for 25 megacities with single-airport system development based on two criteria: (i) air traffic volumes, and (ii) the composition of international and domestic traffic flows. This illustrative analysis identifies four types of single-airport megacities, which are summarized in Table 3.2 along with information on megacity configuration and airport system development.

- **Type S1:** Five megacities with single-airport system development that handle a small volume of international and domestic air traffic (4.4 million passengers on average) within a relatively short distance from the city center (about 15.3 km) within a limited urban boundary (789 km²). This type of development is found in Africa and Pakistan without airport rail links, partly due to the relatively slow growth of air traffic (+17.0% for the 2011–2018 period).

- **Type S2:** Seven megacities controlling a medium volume of international and domestic air flows (average 39.1 million passengers) near the city center (about 11.8 km) in a relatively large urbanized area (1,583 km²). It is noticeable that most of these megacities (except Ho Chi Minh City) have the status of national capital in emerging economies. Yet, only two megacities offer airport express rail or bus rapid transit services (e.g., Bogota). Growth in air traffic to/from these megacities has been moderate until recent years (+36.6% for the 2011–2018 period).

- **Type S3:** Seven megacities with single-airport system development that accommodate a small to medium volume of predominantly domestic air flows (22.7 million passengers on average). Despite very rapid growth in air traffic flows (+279.4%), only one megacity has an airport rail link. This is probably because many of the airports are not far from the city center (about 15.5 km) and are located in an urbanized area averaging 989 km² and/or the development of urban rail networks to/from the airports is still in progress.

Table 3.2: A Typology of 25 Single-Airport Megacities Based on the ACI Annual World Airport Traffic Data Set, 2011–2018
(Selected)

Legend
- Urbanized area
- ○ City center
- ● International
- ● Domestic
- ◎ Both
- ◎ Air cargo
- xxx IATA airport code

	Type S1 Single Small Volume International and Domestic	Type S2 Single Medium Volume International and Domestic	Type S4 Single Medium Volume Domestic
Pax volume	4.4 M	39.1 M	36.2 M
International pax (%)	56.5	44.8	8.8
2011–2018 growth (%)	+17.0	+36.6	+81.0
Distance (km)	15.3	11.8	28.8
Urbanized area (km²)	789	1,583	767
Population	10.8 million	16.0 million	9.4 million
Airport rail links (no.)	0	2	7
Megacities (no.)	5	7	6
Megacity names (selected)	Dar es Salaam Kinshasa* Lagos* Karachi Lahore	Bogota* Lima* Mexico City* Cairo* Ho Chi Minh City Manila*	Chengdu Chongqing Nanjing Tianjin Wuhan Xi'an

ACI = Airports Council International, km = kilometer, km² = square kilometer.

Notes:
(i) The numbers presented in each column are the average of megacities by type; * = national capital; gray = megacity in Asia.
(ii) These maps were produced by Authors, with data from ACI (2019) and European Commission (2018). The boundaries, colors, denominations, and any other information shown on this map do not imply, on the part of the Asian Development Bank, any judgment on the legal status of any territory, or any other endorsement or acceptance of such boundaries, colors, denominations, or information.

Sources: Authors, with data from ICAO (2015), European Commission (2018), and UN Department of Economic and Social Affairs (2018).

- **Type S4:** Six megacities that manage a medium volume of predominantly domestic air flows (36.7 million passengers on average). Remarkably, all six emerging megacities (with nearly 10 million inhabitants) in the PRC belong to this single-airport system type with at least one metro line connection for an access or egress travel distance of about 28.8 km between the city center and the airport location. The location of the airport beyond an urbanized area of about 767 km^2 is probably advantageous to accommodate the rapid growth of air traffic flows (+81.0%) to and from the PRC's major cities and towns. Note that one of these megacities (Chengdu) opened a large secondary airport well outside the urban boundary in 2021.

Similarly, another typology is created for 19 megacities with the development of a multi-airport system based on seven criteria: (i) air traffic volume, (ii) composition of international and domestic traffic flows, (iii) assignment of air traffic volume among two or more airports, (iv) distribution of international and domestic flows among multiple airports, (v) assignment of air cargo flows among multiple airports, (vi) geospatial configuration of multiple airports, and (vii) monocentric or polycentric formation of megacities. In this work, six types of multi-airport megacities are found, as shown in Table 3.3.

- **Type M1:** Three megacities with a few airports handling a medium volume of international and domestic air traffic flows (37.5 million passengers with slow air traffic growth at +5.5% from 2011 to 2018) in an urbanized area of about 1,789 km^2. All three megacities are located in South America, where bus rapid transit or general bus services are widely used to provide an access or egress travel distance of about 16.8 km between the city center and a few airport locations. Of the two or three airports, the primary airport manages not only international and domestic passengers, but also all air cargo flows. The secondary and tertiary airports largely share domestic passengers, which account for about 28.4% of total passenger volume.

- **Type M2:** Six megacities with some airports that manage the large volume of international and domestic air flows (92.6 million passengers on average). All six entries are growing megacities with populations of about 16 million from Asia, and five of the six megacities (except Shanghai) have a national capital status. Thus, a large primary airport serves as a hub of international and national transportation networks for passenger and cargo traffic flows around the outer-city location of a highly urbanized area (2,593 km^2 on average). The secondary airport is dedicated to sharing domestic passengers around the inner-city location, which accounts for about 24.9% of total passenger volume. Remarkably, all six megacities have at least one airport rail link for an average access or egress travel distance of 28.6 km, and two of them (Shanghai and Seoul) use a maglev system to travel to or from the airport outside the city. Indeed, air traffic growth is sizable: +49.2% for the 2011–2018 period.

- **Type M3:** Two unique megacities (i.e., Bangkok and Tehran) with national capital status, where the primary airport is responsible for handling medium to large passenger volumes of about 63.5 million passengers in either international or domestic service, while the secondary airport is located elsewhere for lower volumes of opposite or mixed service (accounting for 16.7% of total passenger traffic volume). In both megacities, the outlying airports cater to international passenger and air cargo services to varying degrees.

Table 3.3: A Typology of 19 Multi-Airport Megacities Based on the ACI Annual World Airport Traffic Data Set, 2011–2018

	Type M1 Primary+ Medium Volume International and Domestic	Type M2 Primary+ Large Volume International and Domestic	Type M3 Primary+ Medium to Large Volume International or Domestic
Pax volume	37.5 million	92.6 million	63.5 million
International pax (%)	30.2	46.3	48.7
2011–2018 growth (%)	+5.5	+49.2	+71.5
Airports (no.)	2 to 3	2	2
Primary (%)	61.4	75.1	83.3
Distance (km)	16.8	28.6	28.1
Urbanized area (km²)	1,780	2,593	1,975
Population	16.2 million	17.0 million	12.0 million
Airport rail links (no.)	3	9	4
Megacities (no.)	3	6	2
Megacity names (selected)	Buenos Aires Rio de Janeiro São Paulo	Beijing* Istanbul* Jakarta*	Kuala Lumpur* Seoul* Shanghai	Bangkok* Tehran*

Legend: Urbanized area; City center; International; Domestic; Both; Air cargo; XXX IATA airport code

* = national capital, ACI = Airports Council International, km = kilometer, km² = square kilometer.

Notes:
(i) The numbers presented in each column are the average of megacities by type; gray = megacity in Asia.
(ii) These maps were produced by Authors, with data from ACI (2019) and European Commission (2018). The boundaries, colors, denominations, and any other information shown on this map do not imply, on the part of the Asian Development Bank, any judgment on the legal status of any territory, or any other endorsement or acceptance of such boundaries, colors, denominations, or information.

Sources: Authors, with data from ICAO (2015), European Commission (2018), and UN Department of Economic and Social Affairs (2018).

continued on next page

Table 3.3 continued

Airport System Development in Megacities 45

Legend

- Urbanized area
- ○ City center
- ● International
- ● Domestic
- ◉ Both
- ◎ Air cargo
- xxx IATA airport code

	Type M4 Primary and Secondary+ Large Volume International and Domestic	Type M5 Multiple for Monocentric Large Volume International	Type M6 Multiple for Polycentric Large Volume Domestic
	New York: EWR, LGA, JFK	London: LTN, STN, LHR, LCY, SEN, LGW	Los Angeles: BUR, LAX, CPM, ONT, SNA, LGB
	Tokyo: NRT, HND	Moscow: SVO, VKO, ZIA, DME	Guangzhou: CAN, FUO, SZX
Pax volume	133.5 million	127.8 million	93.3 million
International pax (%)	38.8	75.0	29.1
2011–2018 growth (%)	14.3	17.9	36.9
Airports (no.)	2 to 3	3 to 6	3 to 6
Primary (%)	56.0	52.7	65.4
Distance (km)	32.6	59.0	18.4
Urbanized area (km²)	5,351	1,795	5,138
Population	28.0 million	10.7 million	24.5 million
Airport rail links (no.)	6	10	5
Megacities (no.)	2	3	3
Megacity names (selected)	New York Tokyo*	London* Moscow* Paris*	Los Angeles Guangzhou Osaka

* = national capital, ACI = Airports Council International, km = kilometer, km² = square kilometer.

Notes:
(i) The numbers presented in each column are the average of megacities by type; gray = megacity in Asia.
(ii) These maps were produced by Authors, with data from ACI (2019) and European Commission (2018). The boundaries, colors, denominations, and any other information shown on this map do not imply, on the part of the Asian Development Bank, any judgment on the legal status of any territory, or any other endorsement or acceptance of such boundaries, colors, denominations, or information.

Sources: Authors, with data from ICAO (2015), European Commission (2018), and UN Department of Economic and Social Affairs (2018).

On the other hand, the inner-city airports are used for either "international and domestic passengers" or "domestic passengers and cargo flow" to varying degrees. With an average distance of about 28.1 km to/from the city center, each airport in these two megacities has an airport rail link station. The growth of air traffic to/from these two megacities is very fast (+71.5%) compared with that of megacities with other types of multi-airport development and management (+5.5% to +49.2%).

- **Type M4:** Two established megacities (New York and Tokyo), with an average population of 28 million, distribute the huge volume of international and domestic air traffic (about 133.5 million passengers) between two or three major airports in their own ways. Tokyo increasingly assigns both international and domestic passengers to its inner-city waterfront airport (56.0%), while its suburban airport (44.0%) continues to manage predominantly international passengers and air cargo flows. New York evenly splits the huge volume of international and domestic passengers and air cargo flows between the primary and secondary airports (accounting for 44.8% and 33.3% of the total passenger volume, respectively, while a portion of domestic passenger flows are allocated to the tertiary airport near the inner-city location (21.9% of total passengers). Almost all airports in these two established megacities are well connected by some types of rail systems, including airport express services and monorail links, so that the average access and egress travel distance is about 32.6 km on average. Air traffic growth from 2011 to 2018 was relatively moderate (+14.3%).

- **Type M5:** Three national capital megacities in Europe (London, Moscow, and Paris) with an average population of about 10 million cope with the enormous volume of primarily international air traffic (accounting for about 75.0% of the 127.8 million passengers) by establishing three or more airports on the outskirts of the cities or well outside a relatively limited urbanized area of 1,795 km². In London and Paris, international and domestic passenger and air cargo flows are largely concentrated in primary airports (accounting for 45.1% and 66.2% of total passenger volumes, respectively), while in Moscow, international and domestic passenger and air cargo flows are more evenly distributed among primary, secondary, and tertiary airports (accounting for 46.8%, 30.0%, and 21.9%, respectively). Many of these outlying airports are connected by airport express services and/or some types of urban rail systems, so that the travel distance to/from the main city center of the monocentric metropolitan formation is about 52.7 km. The growth of air traffic in the 2011–2018 period was relatively moderate (+17.9%).

- **Type M6:** Three megacities (Los Angeles, Guangzhou, and Osaka) with an average population of about 24.5 million handle a large volume of primarily domestic air traffic (accounting for about 70.9% of the 93.3 million passengers) with three or more airports in an area of 5,138 km² (which includes some or more major municipalities). Essentially, none of the three megacities has a national capital status, but they constitute the second- or third-largest urban agglomeration in each country. In the three megacities, both international and domestic passenger and air cargo flows are generally handled at the primary airports in outer-city or bayfront locations (which account for about 65.4% of total passenger traffic on average). On the other hand, some or several major municipalities in the same urbanized areas divide domestic passenger flows among secondary, tertiary, or wider airports. Los Angeles in North America does not yet have airport rail connections, while Guangzhou and Osaka in Asia offer some types of airport rail connections for relatively short arrival or departure distances of 18.4 km to/from the nearest city centers of polycentric metropolitan areas. The growth of air traffic in the 2011–2018 period tended to be substantial (+36.9%).

The geospatial associations of airport system development with megacities appear to vary not only by urban development attributes but also by economic development phases. Therefore, it is assumed that megacities, together with 10 types of single-airport system and multi-airport system development, show the different extents of economic production and growth. Based on this assumption, the "gross domestic product (GDP) in 2015" and "change in GDP for the 1990–2015 period" are calculated by type and compared with the 10 types, as shown in Figures 3.19(a) and 3.19(b). Noticeably, megacities with a multi-airport system tend to have larger GDP in 2015 and faster GDP growth for the 1990–2015 period than those with a single-airport system. Among megacities with a single-airport system, S2-type megacities had greater GDP and faster GDP growth than S1-type megacities (in Africa and Pakistan). Similarly, S4-type megacities (in the PRC) tended to have higher amounts of both economic production and growth than S3-type megacities.

Figure 3.19: Comparison of GDP 2015 and Change in GDP from 1990 to 2015 across the 11 Types of Airport System Development

(a) GDP 2015 $ Billion by Type

(b) Change in GDP 1990 to 2015 $ Billion by Type

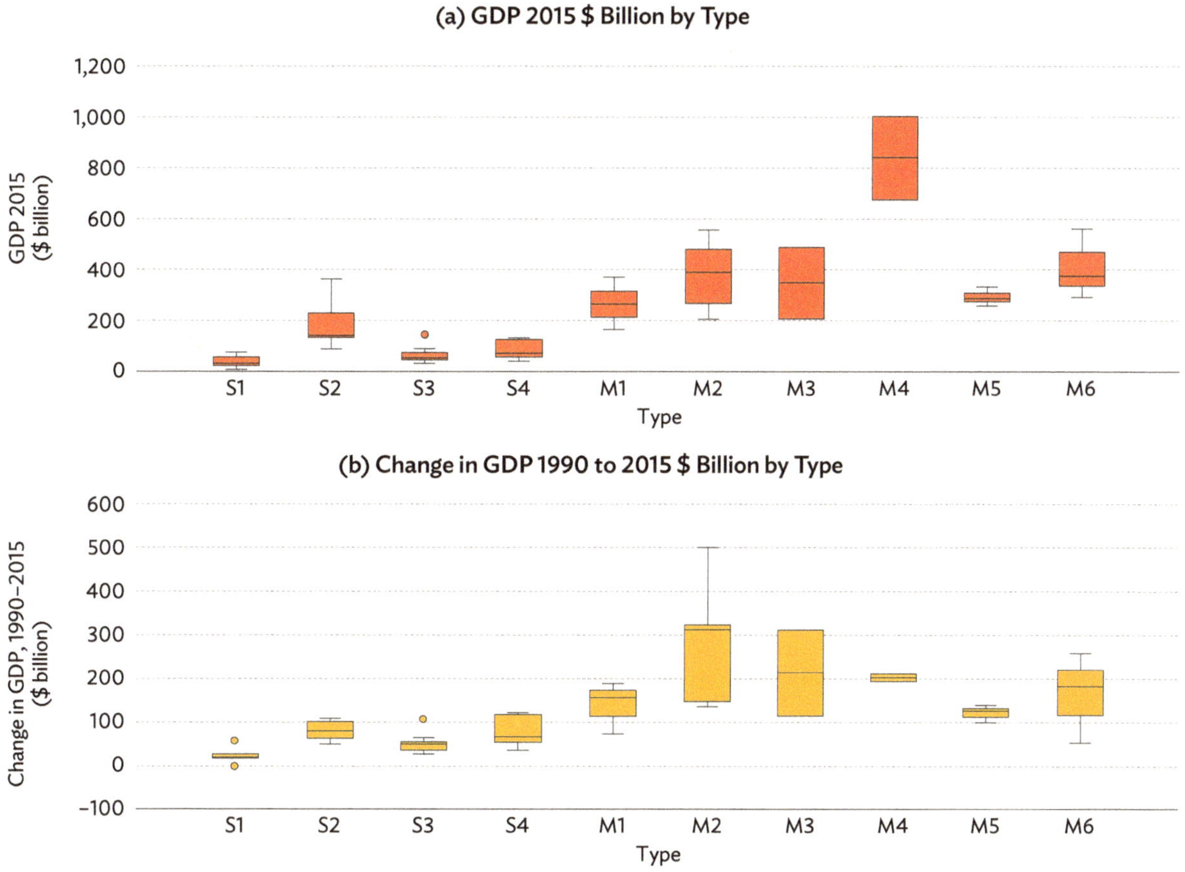

GDP = gross domestic product.
Source: Authors, with data from European Commission (2018).

Among megacities with a multi-airport system development, M4-type megacities (New York and Tokyo) had the largest GDP in 2015, but also relatively high GDP growth for the 1990–2015 period, while M1- and M5-type megacities (in South America and Europe) had comparatively lower economic production and growth. The M2-, M3-, and M6-type megacities exhibited a range of values in both GDP in 2015 and GDP change from 1990 to 2015, suggesting that there are other crucial, diverse, and unobservable determinants of economic production and growth in each global region, country, and/or megacity.

3.7 Summary of Key Findings

Finally, this chapter summarizes six key findings extracted from a series of descriptive statistics on megacities with airport systems in Asia and the other global regions:

(1) The geospatial characteristics of megacities are of particular importance to emerging and developing economies in Asia, as they involve increasing numbers of urban residents and not only horizontal expansion but also vertical development in the coming decade or more.
(2) The construction of new airports is popular in emerging megacities in Asia, while the expansion of airport terminals has been ongoing in both established and growing megacities in North America, Europe, and Asia. On the other hand, airport relocation is limited to a few megacities in the PRC.
(3) The formation of multi-airports is relatively new, but is gradually emerging in established and growing megacities in Asia. The emergence of multi-airports in megacities may depend on the financial capabilities (or political power) of nations or regions, as well as the degree and pattern of urbanization in megacities. However, the decentralization and densification effects of the formation of multi-airports still remain debatable.
(4) New airports are usually built outside the urbanized areas and connected by different airport rail systems, depending on the distance of access or egress to/from the city centers. The construction of airport rail links has been intensive in recent decades and can be coordinated both proactively and reactively with the emergence and growth of megacities in Asia.
(5) Established megacities in North America, Europe, and East Asia have managed large volumes of air traffic flows with the development of multi-airport systems in global, regional, and national production networks, while emerging megacities in South Asia and Africa have not yet played a nodal role with the development of single-airport systems for limited air traffic flows. Population size (or megacity size) alone is not a determinant of airport system development.
(6) Megacities can be classified on an evolutionary path from single-airport systems to multi-airport system development. Nevertheless, the geospatial assignment patterns of air traffic flows within megacities with multiple airports have been shown to follow divergent development pathways. Megacities with single- and multi-airport system development have shown different levels of economic production and growth in Asia and global regions.

It is important to note that these holistic data descriptions are not conclusive, but rather support the individual case studies and detailed case surveys that follow.

References

Airports Council International (ACI). 2019. *Annual World Airport Traffic Dataset 2011–2018*. https://store.aci.aero/product-category/economics-statistics/annual-world-airport-traffic-reports-watr/.

Asian Development Bank (ADB). 1997. The Asian Development Bank on Asia's Megacities. *Population and Development Review*. 23 (2). pp. 451–459. https://doi.org/10.2307/2137566.

Bulu, M. 2011. *City Competitiveness and Improving Urban Subsystems: Technologies and Applications: Technologies and Applications*. IGI Global.

Castells, M. 1996. The Space of Flows. *The Rise of the Network Society*. 1. pp. 376–482.

Castells, M. 2015. Space of Flows, Space of Places: Materials for A Theory of Urbanism in the Information Age. In *The City Reader*. pp. 263–274. Routledge.

Cervero, R. 1998. *The Transit Metropolis: A Global Inquiry*. Island Press.

Doel, M. and P. Hubbard. 2002. Taking World Cities Literally: Marketing the City in A Global Space of Flows. *City*. 6 (3). pp.351–368. https://doi.org/10.1080/1360481022000037779.

Duranton, G. and M. A. Turner. 2012. Urban Growth and Transportation. *Review of Economic Studies*. 79 (4). pp.1407–1440. https://doi.org/10.1093/restud/rds010.

European Commission (2018). *Urban Centre Database UCDB R2019A: Interactive Visualisation*, based on the First Release of the UCDB. https://ghsl.jrc.ec.europa.eu/ucdb2018visual.php.

Gottmann, J. 1957. Megalopolis or the Urbanization of the Northeastern Seaboard. *Economic Geography*. 33 (3). pp. 189–200.

Gurjar, B. R., T. M. Butler, M. G. Lawrence, and J. Lelieveld. 2008. Evaluation of Emissions and Air Quality in Megacities. *Atmospheric Environment*. 42 (7). pp.1593–1606. https://doi.org/10.1016/1352-2310(95)00219-7.

Hall, P. 1999. Planning for the Mega-City: A New Eastern Asian Urban Form?. In *East West Perspectives on 21st Century Urban Development*. pp. 3–36. Routledge.

Hall, P. G. and K. Pain. 2006. *The Polycentric Metropolis: Learning from Mega-City Regions in Europe*. Routledge.

Hanson, S. and G. Giuliano, G. 2004. *The Geography of Urban Transportation*. Guilford Press.

International Civil Aviation Organization (ICAO). 2021. Traffic Flow Global Data (Shape File). https://store.icao.int/en/traffic-flow-global-data-shape-file.

Lang, R. and P. K. Knox. 2009. The New Metropolis: Rethinking Megalopolis. *Regional Studies*. 43 (6). pp. 789–802. https://doi.org/10.1080/00343400701654251.

Lang, R. E. and J. LeFurgy. 2003. Edgeless Cities: Examining the Noncentered Metropolis. *Housing Policy Debate*. 14 (3). pp. 427–460. https://doi.org/10.1080/10511482.2003.9521482.

Li, D., J. Ma, T. Cheng, J. L. Van Genderen, and Z. Shao. 2018. Challenges and Opportunities for the Development of Megacities. *International Journal of Digital Earth*. 12 (12). pp. 1382–1395. https://doi.org/10.1080/17538947.2018.1512662.

Mage, D., G. Ozolins, P. Peterson, A. Webster, R. Orthofer, V. Vandeweerd, and M. Gwynne. 1996. Urban Air Pollution in Megacities of the World. *Atmospheric Environment*. 30 (5). pp. 681–686. https://doi.org/10.1016/1352-2310(95)00219-7.

Organisation for Economic Co-operation and Development (OECD). 2006. *Competitive Cities in the Global Economy*. Paris: OECD.

Pojani, D. and D. Stead. 2015. Sustainable Urban Transport in the Developing World: Beyond Megacities. *Sustainability*. 7 (6). pp. 7784–7805. https://doi.org/10.3390/su7067784.

Reilly, M. K., M. P. O'Mara, and K. C. Seto. 2009. From Bangalore to the Bay Area: Comparing Transportation and Activity Accessibility as Drivers of Urban Growth. *Landscape and Urban Planning*. 92 (1). pp. 24–33. https://doi.org/10.1016/j.landurbplan.2009.02.001.

Rondinelli, D. A., J. H. Johnson Jr, and J. D. Kasarda. 1998. The Changing Forces of Urban Economic Development: Globalization and City Competitiveness in the 21st Century. *Cityscape*. pp. 71–105. https://www.jstor.org/stable/20868460.

Sassen, S. 2018. *Cities in A World Economy*. Sage Publications.

Taylor, P. and B. Derudder. 2015. *World City Network: A Global Urban Analysis*. Routledge.

United Nations (UN) Department of Economic and Social Affairs. 2018. *2018 Revision of World Urbanization Prospects*. https://population.un.org/wup/Download/.

World Health Organization (WHO). 1992. *Urban Air Pollution in Megacities of the World*. Oxford: Blackwell.

Yeo, G. T., Y. Wang, and C. C. Chou. 2013. Evaluating the Competitiveness of the Aerotropolises in East Asia. *Journal of Air Transport Management*. 32. pp. 24–31. https://doi.org/10.1016/j.jairtraman.2013.06.004.

Chapter 4

Impacts from Improvement of Ground Rail Accessibility to/from City Airport to Local Economies: Case Study of Tokyo, Japan

4.1 Introduction

The number of airline passengers has grown rapidly in the wake of international air transportation deregulation and liberalization, such as Open Skies and the emergence of low-cost airlines. The number of air passengers in the world in 2017 is about three times that in 1990, while the number of airline passengers carried in 2017 is expected to increase from 4.1 billion to about 10.0 billion by 2040, and the number of departures is expected to increase to about 90 million by 2040 (ICAO 2018).

To manage the increasing and changing demand, airport operators and governments in many countries/regions have sought to make multi-billion dollar investments in airport capacity development along with ground transportation improvement programs. These investments are expected to positively impact regional and/or local economic activity. For example, many empirical studies have highlighted the positive impact of international hub airports on regional and/or local economies in the case of the United States (US) and the European Union (EU) (Bel and Fageda 2008; Button et al. 1999; Button and Lall 1999; Kasarda and Lidsay 2011). Other studies have shown a strong correlation or interactive relationship between air passenger flows, quality of services/facilities, and economic development (Brueckner 2003; Baker, Merkert, and Kamruzzaman 2015; Green 2007; Debbage and Delk 2001; Sheard 2014; Hakim and Merkert 2016; Neal 2012; Florida, Mellander, and Holgersson 2015; Tittle, McCarthy, and Xiao 2013; Percoco 2010; Bilotkach 2015). These studies have generally considered airports as important infrastructure for accelerating face-to-face meetings, knowledge spillover, and innovation within cities, which can lead to local economic development. Meanwhile, urban planners have also recently expressed concerns that the economic potential of their cities could be enhanced by strategically improving accessibility to/from airports. National or provincial capital cities with extensive metropolitan areas such as Bangkok, Jakarta, Shanghai, Seoul, and Tokyo are likely to enhance the competitive advantage of their existing business centers by providing airport express rails. Such investments in airport rail links with faster passenger services could be an important tool to consolidate competitive advantages around in-city transit terminals, promote aviation-oriented urban regeneration within the central business district (CBD), and extensively shape the backbone of urbanization and local economic development in the long run (Murakami, Matsui, and Kato 2016).

However, few studies have looked in depth at the potential impact of improved first-/last-mile accessibility to/from airports on local economies, although ground transportation connecting the urban area to airports could also influence local economic activity. This study attempts to fill this gap by presenting empirical evidence from a case study in the Tokyo Metropolitan Area (TMA), which focuses on airport accessibility through urban rail transit. This study highlights rail transit as an airport access mode because rail transit is most popularly used for first-/last-mile trips to/from the airport in the TMA (Murakami and Kato 2020). Tokyo is a well-known megacity with a densely developed urban rail network in the region. The urban rail network has been developed as part of a long-term master plan that has been under development for years under the guidance of the central government (Kato 2014). Recent master plans have highly prioritized rail investments for improving accessibility to a city airport to handle rapidly increased air transportation demand and enhance international competitiveness (Kato et al. 2017; Morichi et al. 2001). In fact, eight new rail lines, including one airport access line, were put into operation in the TMA from 2000 to 2010. Therefore, Tokyo is a suitable case study for investigating the impact of improvement in rail access to the airport.

This chapter empirically analyzes the impact of improved rail accessibility to/from a city airport on the local economy in the TMA from 2000 to 2010. Population density, employment density, and land prices are used as indicators of the local economy. A quasi-experimental design using spatial difference-in-difference (DID) analysis, propensity score (PS) matching, and inverse probability weighting (IPW) is used to estimate the impacts. The spatial DID analysis enables us to estimate the economic impact of a policy treatment (in our case, improving urban rail accessibility to/from the airport), taking into account spatial autocorrelation. Combining spatial dependencies with a DID method has been used in recent spatial studies (Guignet and Martinez-Cruz 2018; Dubé et al. 2014; Heckert and Mennis 2012). PS matching is widely used to estimate an average treatment effect by comparing indicators of samples in a treatment group with those in a control group (Imbens and Rubins 2015; Shadish, Cook, and Cambell 2002). A PS is a conditional probability of assignment to the treatment group, given the covariates representing the characteristics of the samples that can be used to better match pairs of samples in the two groups (Rosenbaum and Rubin 1983). The IPW approach enables us to estimate the effects of specific treatments without the endogeneity caused by observable variables (Rosenbaum 1987). In the IPW approach, data from each sample are weighted according to an inverse of the PS. The above three methods are expected to verify our hypothesis that improving rail accessibility to/from the city's airport positively affected local indicators, in a rigorous manner.

This chapter proceeds as follows. The next section summarizes the recent development of airport rail services connecting the CBD with a city airport in the TMA. The methods of empirical analysis are presented, followed by the organization and description of data, estimation results, and discussion. Finally, our key issues and challenges for future research are summarized as concluding remarks.

4.2 Airport Rail Links in Tokyo Metropolitan Area

Metropolitan/urban rail connects many Asian cities to their airports, while long-distance rail connects European cities to their airports (Murakami, Matsui, and Kato 2016). Tokyo is also one of the typical major Asian cities where the airport rail link as part of urban rail, has connected the CBD with the airports, and its modal share of traffic is high.[2] TMA has two major airports, Haneda Airport and Narita Airport, officially known as "Tokyo International Airport" and

---

[2] Airport buses, private cars, and taxis are also available in addition to rail transit for airport access in TMA. The modal share of rail transit to/from Haneda Airport accounts for over 50%, followed by airport bus (about 20%), and private car (about 8%) (Murakami and Kato 2020).

"Narita International Airport," respectively. Haneda Airport is located about 15 km from the CBD. It used to be operated mainly for domestic service but is now used for both domestic and international services. With 85 million passengers in 2017, it is the busiest airport in Japan and the fourth-busiest airport in the world (ICAO 2018). This study focuses on the rail accessibility of Haneda Airport, a city airport of Tokyo, to or from the airport. Currently, there are two airport rail links that connect the CBD to Haneda Airport.

It should be noted that the airport rail links were considered part of an urban rail network in the TMA. It is well known that the TMA has a large and dense urban rail network. The urban rail network in the TMA was invested and developed based on long-term master plans for rail development proposed by the Council for Transport Policy under the guidance of the Ministry of Transport (Kato 2014). The urban rail master plans have been produced every nearly 15 years, and the most recent, the Masterplan 2030, was completed in April 2016 (Kato et al 2017). In the earlier master plans, relieving vehicle congestion was a major issue, as urban rail users in Tokyo suffered years of significant vehicle congestion due to insufficient capacity and rapid growth in urban rail demand. However, the latest urban rail master plan gives top priority to improving airport/high-speed rail (HSR) connectivity, as this is expected to help boost Tokyo's international competitiveness. This may reflect the government's recent economic growth strategy, which assumes that infrastructure investments in urban areas, particularly improving airport accessibility, will increase economic productivity and lead to higher economic growth. The 2000, 2015, and 2030 master plans proposed 29, 34, and 24 rail investment projects, respectively, including 3, 6, and 4 airport rail access projects.

4.3 Method

Spatial Difference-in-Differences

The DID analysis attempts to mimic an experimental research design using data from an observational study by studying the differential effect of a treatment on a "treatment group" compared with a "control group" in a natural experiment (Angrist and Pischke 2008). DID requires data measured from a treatment group and a control group at two or more time periods, at least once before "treatment" (Time 1) and at least once after "treatment" (Time 2). In our study, we assume that the treatment is an improvement of urban rail accessibility between an area and a city airport, and that the treatment group includes areas where urban rail airport accessibility has been improved, while the control group includes other areas. DID estimates the impact of a particular treatment by comparing changes in indicators between the treatment and control groups.

This study assumes a simple two-time framework DID that a treatment effect is calculated as the difference of changes in indicators between the two groups from Time 1 to Time 2, formulated as:

$$\tau_i = (y_{i2T} - y_{i1T}) - (y_{i2C} - y_{i1C}) \qquad (1)$$

where τ_i is the treatment effect in zone i, y_{i2T} is a local indicator under the condition that the treatment is implemented in zone i at Time 2; y_{i2T} is an indicator under the condition that the treatment is implemented in zone i at Time 1; y_{i2C} is an indicator under the condition that the treatment is not implemented in zone i at Time 2; and y_{i2C} is an indicator under the condition that the treatment is not implemented in zone i at Time 1. The average treatment effect can be estimated using a parametric approach that assumes a linear regression model in which the dependent variable is the indicator of the zone and the explanatory variables include 0/1 dummy variables representing treatment status and time status, and other covariates formulated as follows:

$$y_{it} = \beta_{TR}TR_i + \beta_{TM}TM_t + \beta_{DID}DID_{it} + V_{it}\theta + \varepsilon_{it} \qquad (2)$$

where y_{it} is the indicator in zone i at time t; TR_i is a dummy variable, which is 1 if zone i belongs to the treatment group and otherwise 0; TM_t is a dummy variable, which is 1 if the time is after the treatment (Time 2) and otherwise 0; DID_{it} is defined as a product of TR_i and TM_t[3]; V_{it} is a vector of other covariates in zone i at time t, and β_{TR}, β_{TM}, β_{DID}, and θ are unknown coefficients. An estimated coefficient $\hat{\beta}_{TR}$ represents selection bias; $\hat{\beta}_{TM}$ represents a time trend of the indicator; and $\hat{\beta}_{DID}$ represents the average treatment effect, which is our main concern.

In this study, we also introduce spatial autoregressive models to incorporate spatial-dependent responses and spatial error dependence. A spatial lag model (SLM), a spatial error model (SEM), and a general spatial autoregressive model with a correlated error term (SAC) are used. They are formulated as follows:

$$\text{SLM:} \quad \mathbf{y}_t = \beta_{TR}\mathbf{TR} + \beta_{TM}\mathbf{TM} + \beta_{DID}\mathbf{DID}_t + \rho \mathbf{W}\mathbf{y}_t + \mathbf{X}_t\boldsymbol{\theta} + \boldsymbol{\varepsilon}_t \qquad (3)$$

$$\text{SEM:} \quad \mathbf{y}_t = \beta_{TR}\mathbf{TR} + \beta_{TM}\mathbf{TM} + \beta_{DID}\mathbf{DID}_t + \mathbf{X}_t\boldsymbol{\theta} + \mathbf{u}_t, \mathbf{u}_t = \lambda \mathbf{W}\mathbf{u}_t + \boldsymbol{\varepsilon}_t \qquad (4)$$

$$\text{SAC:} \quad \mathbf{y}_t = \beta_{TR}\mathbf{TR} + \beta_{TM}\mathbf{TM} + \beta_{DID}\mathbf{DID}_t + \rho \mathbf{W}\mathbf{y}_t + \mathbf{X}_t\boldsymbol{\theta}\lambda \mathbf{W}\mathbf{y}_t + \mathbf{u}_t, \mathbf{u}_t = \lambda \mathbf{W}\mathbf{u}_t + \boldsymbol{\varepsilon}_t \qquad (5)$$

where ρ is a parameter for the spatial lag term, $\mathbf{W}$ is a spatial weight matrix, λ is a parameter for the spatial error term, $\mathbf{u}$ is an independent identically distributed error, and $\mathbf{X}_t$ is the matrix of independent variables not including constant.

Propensity Score Matching

PS matching estimates the treatment effect based on the difference between the treatment and control groups. Because the covariates are expected to be unbalanced between the two groups, they are balanced using a balancing score that yields a PS. The PS is defined as a probability of assigning a sample to the treatment group that varies between 0 and 1. The PS is usually estimated with a logit or probit model using the covariates, formulated as:

$$e_i = f\big(z_i = 1 | b(\mathbf{V}_i)\big) \qquad (6)$$

---

[3] In our study context, zones that have experienced the improvement of airport accessibility from 2000 to 2010 should have their TR value as 1, while other zones that have not experienced an improvement should have 0 as their TR. For 2000, TM should be 1, and for 2010, TM should be 0. For zones with accessibility improvement, DID should be 1 if the year is 2010 and 0 if the year is 2000; for other zones without accessibility improvement, DID should be 0 regardless of the year.

where e_i is a PS of zone i; z_i is a dummy variable representing an assigned group, which is 1 if zone i belongs to the treatment group and 0 otherwise; $b(\cdot)$ is a balancing score; and $\boldsymbol{V}_i$ is a vector of covariates.

PS matching finds pairs of samples from treatment and control groups with a similar score. In practice, several methods and criteria for matching have been proposed. In this study, the nearest matching method with a 1-to-1 matching restriction and the matching caliper method with two calipers of 0.01 and 0.005 are used. This study estimates an average treatment effect (ATE) and an average treatment effect on treated (ATT), which are shown as follows:

$$\text{ATE} = E(y_{i2T} - y_{i1T}) - E(y_{i2C} - y_{i1C}) \tag{7}$$

$$\text{ATT} = E(y_{i2T} - y_{i1T}|z_i = 1) - E(y_{i2C} - y_{i1C}|z_i = 1) \tag{8}$$

where $E(\cdot)$ denotes a function of taking an average. y_{i2T} is a local indicator under a condition that treatment is implemented in zone i at Time 2; y_{i1T} is an indicator under a condition that treatment is implemented in zone i at Time 1; y_{i2C} is an indicator under a condition that the treatment is not implemented in zone i at Time 2; and y_{i1C} is an indicator under a condition that the treatment is not implemented in zone i at Time 1. ATE represents the average treatment effect covering pairs of all samples in both treatment and control groups after the matching process, while ATT represents the average treatment effect covering pairs of samples in the treatment group through the matching process. Thus, ATT could show the treatment effect properly for samples in the treatment group by comparing a counterfactual case of an untreated condition.

Inverse Probability Weighting Approach

The IPW approach estimates unobservable $\hat{E}(y_{i2T}-y_{i1T})$ and $\hat{E}(y_{i2C}-y_{i1C})$ as follows:

$$\hat{E}(y_{i2T} - y_{i1T}) = \sum_{i=1}^{N} \frac{z_i(y_{i2T} - y_{i1T})}{e_i} \Big/ \sum_{i=1}^{N} \frac{z_i}{e_i} \tag{9}$$

$$\hat{E}(y_{i2C} - y_{i1C}) = \sum_{i=1}^{N} \frac{(1-z_i)(y_{i2C} - y_{i1C})}{1-e_i} \Big/ \sum_{j=1}^{N} \frac{1-z_j}{1-e_j} \tag{10}$$

where N represents the total number of zones, $E(\cdot)$ represents the weighted average, e_i represents the PS, y_{i2T} is a local indicator under a condition that treatment is implemented in zone i at Time 2, y_{i1T} is an indicator under a condition that treatment is implemented in zone i at Time 1, y_{i2C} is an indicator under a condition that the treatment is not implemented in zone i at Time 2, and y_{i1C} is an indicator under the condition that the treatment is not implemented in zone i at Time 1.

Then, ATE and ATT can be estimated using the IPW approach as follows:

$$\overline{ATE}^{IPW} = \hat{E}(y_{i2T} - y_{i1T}) - \hat{E}(y_{i2C} - y_{i1C}) \tag{11}$$

$$\overline{ATT}^{IPW} = \hat{E}(y_{i2T} - y_{i1T}|z_i = 1) - \hat{E}(y_{i2C} - y_{i1C}|z_i = 1) \tag{12}$$

The IPW approach has the advantage over PS matching in that (i) a subjective operation in selecting matched sample pairs using calipers can be avoided in PS matching; and (ii) the data can be fully utilized without discarding unmatched samples, which often occurs in PS matching.

4.4 Zone-Based Analysis

4.4.1 Data

We divide the TMA into 2,843 zones and collect the urban rail service data set as of 1 October 2000 and 1 October 2010. This zoning system was also applied to an analysis in the most recent urban rail master plan, Masterplan 2030, in which each zone has about one train station on average. Three socioeconomic and demographic data sets are collected as local indicators or dependent variables.

First, population data are estimated from the 2000 Census and the 2010 Census. Second, employment/population data are estimated from the 2001 Establishment and Enterprise Census of Japan and 2012 Economic Census for Business Activity, assuming that employment in 2001 and 2012 is the same as that in 2000 and 2010 based on data availability. Third, data on land prices are estimated from the annual surveys in 2000 and 2010 of official land prices under the Public Notice of Land Prices Act of Japan. This survey is conducted under the guidance of Japan's Ministry of Land, Infrastructure, Transport, and Tourism, which regularly investigates the land prices of approximately 26,000 points across the country on 1 January of each year. We estimate a representative land price in each zone by calculating an average land value when multiple land prices are available in a zone.

A data set of potential independent variables was also developed. First, the urban rail service is represented by total travel time from an origin to a destination, including the first-mile trip, waiting time at the rail station, in-train trip, transfer at the rail station, and the last-mile trip. In this study, airport accessibility is defined as travel time by rail between the airport and other zones.[4] This is because the travel time by rail is typically reduced when new rail lines are introduced or rail services in existing rail lines are improved for upgrading the airport accessibility. Second, the mobility of a zone traveling to other zones is defined as:

$$Mobility_{it} = \frac{1}{N-1} \sum_{j \neq i} T_{ijt} \tag{13}$$

where T_{ijt} is the travel time by train from zone i to zone j at time t. Third, a dummy variable of the urgent urban renewal area (UURA) is defined as 1 if a zone belongs to the UURA. Otherwise, it is 0. The UURA is an area designated by government ordinance to promote urgent and intensive

---

[4] Travel time between airport and zones is calculated based on rail routes with the shortest-travel time between them. It consists of the in-vehicle rail travel time between the airport station and representative stations of zones, waiting time at transfer stations, and first-/last-mile travel time to/from the airport/representative stations. Note that the representative stations in zones are defined as the stations that are closest to the representative nodes (centroids) of the zones. The in-vehicle rail travel time is defined as the daily average travel time on weekdays. The data were taken from railway company time tables.

renewal or improvement of urban districts through an urban development project (Ministry of Land, Infrastructure, Transport and Tourism, Japan 2019). This policy began in 2002, and the 24 areas were designated as UURA in the TMA between 2002 and 2010. Finally, other data sets were developed using the geographic information system. These include the distance between a zone centroid and Tokyo Station, the main hub in Tokyo; the distance between the zone centroid and the nearest station and Japan Railways (JR) station; the total length of roads in a zone; the road density in a zone; and a dummy for the Tokyo 23-ward area, defined as 1 if a zone belongs to the 23-ward area. Otherwise, the value is 0. JR stands for East Japan Railway Company, one of the major private railroad companies in the TMA. The 23-ward area is the most densely populated area in the TMA.

Since the above data set contains some missing values, including 108 missing data for population density, 62 for employment density, and 844 for land price, multivariate imputation by chained equation (Van Buuren and Groothuis-Oudshoorn 2011) is used to complement the missing values in the data set based on data availability.

Table 4.1 summarizes the descriptive statistics of the data set, while Figure 4.1 shows the changes in accessibility to Haneda Airport between 2000 and 2010 in the TMA.[5] The figure shows that travel time to Haneda Airport has improved particularly in the north and southeast of the TMA. These improvements largely follow the area where a new rail line was introduced.

Table 4.1: Descriptive Statistics of Zone-Based Data Set

Variables	Unit	Mean	S.D.	Min.	25%	50%	75%	Max.
Area	km²	5.53	13.02	0.06	0.82	1.77	4.54	331.31
Population density in 2000	per km²	8,044	8,153	1	1,855	6,922	12,373	255,310
Population density in 2010	per km²	8,617	7,177	0	2,092	7,510	13,168	51,090
Employment density in 2001	per km²	6,257	18,385	2	476	1,505	3,716	224,367
Employment density in 2012	per km²	6,850	20,815	1	508	1532	3720	330,314
Land price in 2000	¥/m²	376,539	604,491	5,000	147,607	240,667	393,325	11,725,000
Land price in 2010	¥/m²	426,596	1,264,214	590	99,150	192,000	360,500	28,000,000
Distance to Tokyo station	km	29.130	18.360	0.183	14.560	26.989	40.232	98.334
Distance to nearest station in 2000	km	1.276	1.505	0.015	0.367	0.745	1.605	13.316
Distance to nearest station in 2010	km	1.187	1.395	0.015	0.347	0.714	1.488	13.316
Distance to nearest JR station in 2000	km	2.730	2.704	0.028	0.921	1.921	3.675	25.715
Distance to nearest JR station in 2010	km	2.727	2.704	0.028	0.918	1.915	3.675	25.715
Accessibility to HND in 2000	minute	115.1	38.5	31.7	88.2	110.4	134.1	299.1
Accessibility to HND in 2010	minute	110.9	36.7	30.4	85.3	106.4	129.8	294.2
Mobility in 2000	minute	122.5	30.4	78.5	103.2	115.9	133.4	293.4

continued on next page

---

[5] Figure 4.1 contains some zones where the accessibility of Haneda Airport has had negative improvement from 2000 to 2010. One of the reasons for this is that the first-/last-mile travel time between centroids and representative stations in those zones has increased because representative stations were changed from 2000 to 2010 due to the changes in the rail route with the shortest-travel time between the zones and the airport.

Table 4.1 continued

Variables	Unit	Mean	S.D.	Min.	25%	50%	75%	Max.
Mobility in 2010	minute	121.2	30.2	77.9	102.3	114.7	132.1	292.7
Road density in 2000	km/km^2	12.46	6.35	0.41	7.33	12.18	17.12	31.58
Road density in 2010	km/km^2	18.74	10.04	0.52	9.40	20.17	26.77	45.97
Tokyo 23-ward (1/0)	n.a.	0.263	0.440	0	0	0	1	1
UURA (1/0)	n.a.	0.052	0.222	0	0	0	0	1

HND = Haneda Airport, JR = Japan Railways, km = kilometer, km^2 = square kilometer, m^2 = square meter, n.a. = not applicable, S.D. = standard deviation, UURA = urgent urban renewal area.
Notes:
(i) Japan Railways used to be a state-owned enterprise until 1987.
(ii) Exchange rate used is $1.00 = ¥107.8 for 2000 and $1.00 = ¥87.8 for 2010.
Sources: Authors, estimated with data from 2000 Population Census and 2010 Population Census of Japan; 2001 Establishment and Enterprise Census of Japan and 2012 Economic Census for Business Activity of Japan; the official land price under the Public Notice of Land Prices Act of Japan; and the Digital National Land Information of Japan.

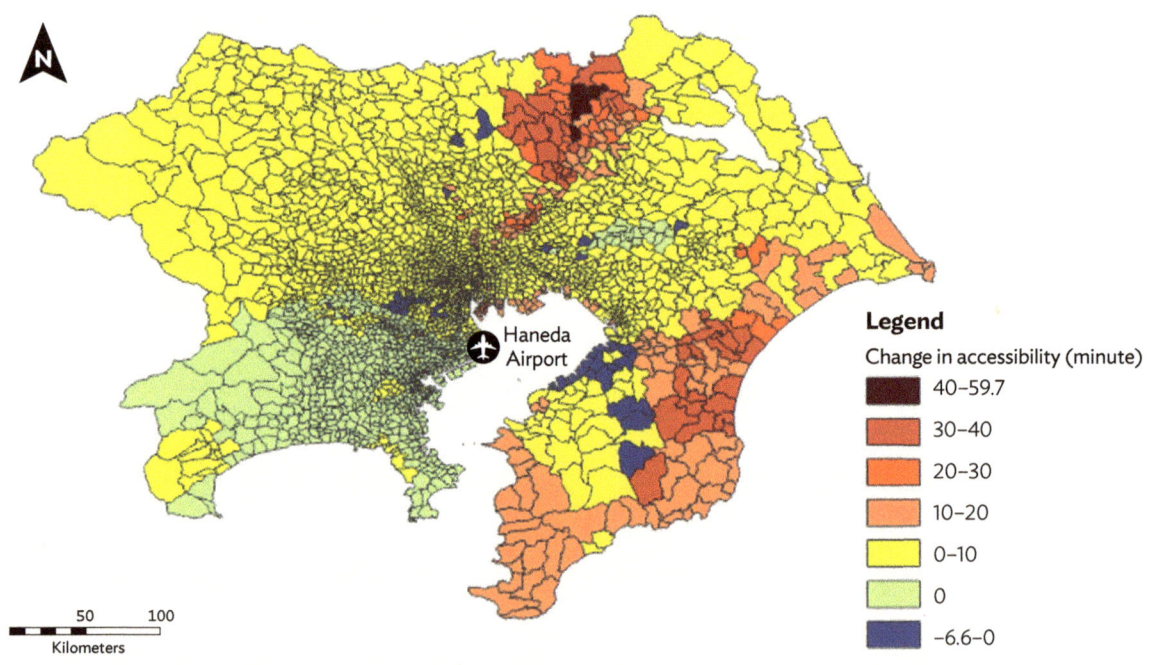

Figure 4.1: Changes in Accessibility to Haneda Airport in the Tokyo Metropolitan Area from 2000 to 2010

Note: This map was produced by Authors. The boundaries, colors, denominations, and any other information shown on this map do not imply, on the part of the Asian Development Bank, any judgment on the legal status of any territory, or any other endorsement or acceptance of such boundaries, colors, denominations, or information.
Source: Authors.

4.4.2 Results

This study defines the treatment group as a set of zones where Haneda Airport accessibility improved from 2000 to 2010, and the control groups as a set of other zones.

Estimation Results of Spatial Difference-In-Differences

To estimate the spatial models, we should define a spatial weight matrix to account for spatial autocorrelation. We assume an inverse of travel time between zones as elements of a spatial weight matrix after testing a number of options for the spatial weight matrix. Table 4.2 summarizes the estimation results of the DID analysis with ordinary least squares (OLS), SLM, SEM, and SAC, pertaining to population density, employment density, and land price, respectively. They show that the spatial lag and error terms ρ and λ are statistically significant in almost all models, implying that local indicators and other unobservable factors exhibit spatial autocorrelation. The log likelihood of SAC is larger than that of the others, while the Akaike Information Criterion (AIC) of SAC is smaller than that of the others. These performance indices may suggest that SAC is probably the best model to describe the local indicators.

The population density results show that the estimated coefficients of DID are significantly positive in all models. This means that more population has migrated to the area where accessibility to Haneda Airport had improved. This could be because new residential areas have been developed in the areas where the accessibility to the airport has been improved. They also show that TR, which is a dummy variable defined in equation (2) is considered significantly negative in all models. This means that the area where accessibility to Haneda Airport has been improved tends to have a lower population. In all models, UURA is estimated to be significantly negative. This is probably because UURA has promoted urban renewal and redevelopment mainly for businesses rather than residential areas.

Distance to the nearest JR station and mobility are also estimated to be significantly negative, while road density is significantly positive in all models. They are all reasonable. Tokyo 23-ward is significantly negative in all models. This could be because the Tokyo 23-ward area is close to the CBD and includes business and commercial areas rather than residential areas, unlike the suburbs where residential uses dominate.

Next, the results of employment density estimation show an insignificant average treatment effect, but a significant negative selection bias in all models. This means that the improvement in rail accessibility to Haneda Airport had no effect on the business cluster. The improvement was implemented in the areas with poorer access to Haneda Airport. They also show that UURA and Tokyo 23-ward have significant positive effects. These results are consistent with those of population density. Distance to nearest station, distance to nearest JR station, and mobility are significantly negative in all models, while road density is significantly positive in all models. They are also all reasonable. Finally, the estimation results for land price show insignificant DID in all models. TR is again estimated to be significantly negative in all models, implying that areas where accessibility to Haneda Airport has been improved tend to have lower land prices. In all models, UURA, road density, and Tokyo 23-ward have significant positive effects, while distance to nearest station, distance to nearest JR station, and mobility have significant negative effects in all models.

Table 4.2: Estimation Results of Spatial DID Models

	ln (Population Density)				ln (Employment Density)				ln (Land Price)			
	OLS	SLM	SEM	SAC	OLS	SLM	SEM	SAC	OLS	SLM	SEM	SAC
Intercept	8.57***	0.52	8.46***	0.56	13.37***	0.78***	12.73***	0.33	13.37***	0.78***	12.73***	0.33
	(0.11)	(0.33)	(0.31)	(2.67)	(0.06)	(0.08)	(0.55)	(7.73)	(0.06)	(0.08)	(0.55)	(7.73)
TR	−0.21***	−0.15***	−0.19***	−0.13**	−0.23***	−0.17***	−0.17***	−0.11***	−0.23***	−0.17***	−0.17***	−0.11***
	(0.04)	(0.04)	(0.05)	(0.05)	(0.03)	(0.02)	(0.03)	(0.03)	(0.03)	(0.02)	(0.03)	(0.03)
TM	−0.63***	−0.70***	−0.27	−0.41	−0.54***	−0.33***	−1.04	−0.61	−0.54***	−0.33***	−1.04	−0.61
	(0.05)	(0.06)	(0.40)	(1.21)	(0.03)	(0.03)	(0.76)	(7.23)	(0.03)	(0.03)	(0.76)	(7.23)
DID	0.17**	0.17**	0.15*	0.15*	0.03	0.04	0.03	0.03	0.03	0.04	0.03	0.03
	(0.06)	(0.06)	(0.07)	(0.07)	(0.03)	(0.03)	(0.04)	(0.04)	(0.03)	(0.03)	(0.04)	(0.04)
Area	−0.02***	−0.02***	−0.02***	−0.02***	0.003***	0.002*	0.003**	0.002*	0.003***	0.002*	0.003**	0.002*
	(0.00)	(0.00)	(0.00)	(0.00)	(0.00)	(0.00)	(0.00)	(0.00)	(0.00)	(0.00)	(0.00)	(0.00)
Distance to nearest station	−0.18***	−0.17***	−0.17***	−0.17***	−0.15***	−0.15***	−0.15***	−0.14***	−0.15***	−0.15***	−0.15***	−0.14***
	(0.01)	(0.01)	(0.01)	(0.01)	(0.01)	(0.01)	(0.01)	(0.01)	(0.01)	(0.01)	(0.01)	(0.01)
Distance to nearest JR station	0.01	0.01	0.01	0.01	−0.03***	−0.02***	−0.03***	−0.02***	−0.03***	−0.02***	−0.03***	−0.02***
	(0.01)	(0.01)	(0.01)	(0.01)	(0.00)	(0.00)	(0.00)	(0.00)	(0.00)	(0.00)	(0.00)	(0.00)
Mobility	−0.01***	−0.01***	−0.01***	−0.01***	−0.01***	−0.01***	−0.01***	−0.01***	−0.01***	−0.01***	−0.01***	−0.01***
	(0.00)	(0.00)	(0.00)	(0.00)	(0.00)	(0.00)	(0.00)	(0.00)	(0.00)	(0.00)	(0.00)	(0.00)
Road density	0.10***	0.10***	0.10***	0.10***	0.03***	0.03***	0.03***	0.03***	0.03***	0.03***	0.03***	0.03***
	(0.00)	(0.00)	(0.00)	(0.00)	(0.00)	(0.00)	(0.00)	(0.00)	(0.00)	(0.00)	(0.00)	(0.00)
Tokyo 23-ward (1/0)	−0.19***	−0.24***	−0.18***	−0.23***	0.71***	0.60***	0.68***	0.58***	0.71***	0.60***	0.68***	0.58***
	(0.04)	(0.04)	(0.04)	(0.05)	(0.02)	(0.02)	(0.02)	(0.03)	(0.02)	(0.02)	(0.02)	(0.03)
UURA (1/0)	−0.88***	−0.88***	−0.85***	−0.85***	1.34***	1.28***	1.30***	1.25***	1.34***	1.28***	1.30***	1.25***
	(0.09)	(0.09)	(0.09)	(0.09)	(0.05)	(0.05)	(0.05)	(0.05)	(0.05)	(0.05)	(0.05)	(0.05)
ρ	n.a.	0.93***	n.a.	0.91**	n.a.	0.99***	n.a.	0.99***	n.a.	0.99***	n.a.	0.99***
	n.a.	(0.04)	n.a.	(0.33)	n.a.	(0.00)	n.a.	(0.23)	n.a.	(0.00)	n.a.	(0.23)
λ	n.a.	n.a.	0.93***	0.92**	n.a.	n.a.	0.980***	0.97	n.a.	n.a.	0.98***	0.97
	n.a.	n.a.	(0.03)	(0.30)	n.a.	n.a.	(0.01)	(0.63)	n.a.	n.a.	(0.01)	(0.63)
N	5,680	5,680	5,680	5,680	5,680	5,680	5,680	5,680	5,680	5,680	5,680	5,680
LL	−8,077	−8,051	−8,053	−8,033	−4,940	−4,709	−4,854	−4,646	−4,940	−4,709	−4,854	−4,646
AIC	16,178	16,129	16,133	16,094	9,905	9,445	9,734	9,321	9,905	9,445	9,734	9,321

AIC = Akaike Information Criterion, DID = difference in differences, JR = Japan Railways, LL = log likelihood, N = number of observation, n.a. = not applicable, OLS = ordinary least squares, SAC = spatial autoregressive model with a correlated error term, SEM = spatial error model, SLM = spatial lag model, UURA = urgent urban renewal area.

Notes:
(i) Standard error in parentheses. ***p < 0.001, **p < 0.01, *p < 0.05.
(ii) DID = interactive term defined in equation (2); TM = dummy variable defined in equation (2); TR = dummy variable defined in equation (2).
Source: Authors' estimation.

Results of Propensity Score Matching

Table 4.3 shows the estimation results of the PS function with a logit model. All explanatory variables in the model represent respondents' social and economic attributes before the improvement of rail accessibility, since the variables must represent attributes of the samples before the assignment of the treatment or control. Note that some variables were included in the model despite their low statistical significance because they are expected to have a strong relationship with the dependent variable. Table 4.4 summarizes the estimation results of ATEs and ATTs with respect to population density, employment density, and land price with PS matching. This shows that both the ATEs and ATTs are statistically significant for employment density and land price when the caliper is 0.005. This suggests that a tighter matching is essentially required to properly test the treatment effect. Meanwhile, the estimated ATE and ATT of population density are insignificant.

Results of Inverted Probability Weighting Model

Table 4.5 shows the estimation results of ATEs and ATTs with respect to population density, employment density, and land price using the IPW method. This shows that the ATEs and ATTs are significantly positive for all indicators. They indicate that the improvement of Haneda Airport rail accessibility had significant positive effects on population density, employment density, and land price.

Table 4.3: Estimation Results of Propensity Score Function

Variable	Coefficient	Standard Error
Intercept	3.54***	0.97
Area	0.01	0.01
Population density in 2000	0.03	0.08
Employment density in 2000	0.13	0.14
Land price in 2000	0.08	0.05
Distance to Tokyo Station	0.03*	0.01
Distance to nearest station in 2000	0.11	0.08
Distance to nearest JR station in 2000	−0.12***	0.03
Accessibility to HND in 2000	0.12***	0.01
Accessibility to NRT in 2000	−0.04***	0.00
Mobility in 2000	−0.08***	0.01
Road density in 2000	0.02	0.02
Tokyo 23-ward dummy (1/0)	2.94***	0.26
UURA dummy (1/0)	0.82*	0.42
Number of observations	2,839	n.a.
McFadden's adjusted R^2	0.541	n.a.
Log likelihood	−753.3	n.a.
AIC	1,534.6	n.a.

AIC = Akaike Information Criterion, HND = Haneda Airport, JR = Japan Railways, n.a. = not applicable, NRT = Narita Airport, UURA = urgent urban renewal area.
Note: ***$p < 0.001$, **$p < 0.01$, *$p < 0.05$.
Source: Authors' estimation.

Table 4.4: Estimation Results of ATE and ATT with PS Matching

	Population Density			Employment Density			Land Price			Matched Number of Obs.
	ATE	t-stat.	p-value	ATE	t-stat.	p-value	ATE	t-stat.	p-value	
Model 1 (1-to-1 matching)	234.8	0.39	0.70	852.7	1.01	0.31	109,147	1.22	0.22	2,839
Model 2 (Caliper 0.01)	203.5	0.35	0.72	806.9	1.01	0.31	104,090	1.02	0.23	2,421
Model 3 (Caliper 0.005)	−243.8	−0.63	0.53	861.7**	2.20	0.03	215,674***	4.83	0.00	801
	ATT	t-stat.	p-value	ATT	t-stat.	p-value	ATT	t-stat.	p-value	Matched Number of Obs.
Model 1 (1-to-1 matching)	264.9	0.38	0.72	796.2	0.71	0.48	99,019	0.77	0.44	2,056
Model 2 (Caliper 0.01)	303.4	0.42	0.68	793.1	0.72	0.47	109,847	0.87	0.39	1,877
Model 3 (Caliper 0.005)	−39.2	−0.10	0.77	888.7*	1.66	0.10	238,647***	3.87	0.00	623

ATE = average treatment effect, ATT = average treatment effects on the treated, Obs = Observations, PS = propensity score.
Note: ***p < 0.001, **p < 0.01, *p < 0.05.
Source: Authors' estimation.

Table 4.5: Estimation Results of the Inverse Probability Weighting Model

	Population Density	Employment Density	Land Price
ATE	415.8**	694.7***	97,864***
	(148.8)	(195.8)	(20,031)
ATT	519.6***	770.8***	109,821***
	(130.5)	(197.8)	(223,501)

ATE = average treatment effect, ATT = average treatment effects on the treated.
Note: ***p < 0.001, **p < 0.01, *p < 0.05; parentheses denote standard error.
Source: Authors' estimation.

4.4.3 Robustness Analysis

To test the robustness of our estimation results, we estimate an additional model using OLS. Table 4.6 shows the estimation results of an OLS model with spatial diffusion effects. This model divides the zones into six subgroups according to the travel time saved to Haneda Airport. "TR 0-5" is defined as 1 if a zone experienced travel time savings to Haneda Airport of 0 to 5 minutes from 2000 to 2010, and 0 otherwise; "TR 5-30" is defined as 1 if a zone experienced travel time savings of 5 to 30 minutes, and 0 otherwise; "TR 0-30" is defined as 1 if a zone experienced travel time savings of 30 minutes or less, and 0 otherwise; and "TR 30<" is defined as 1 if a zone experienced travel time savings of more than 30 minutes, and 0 otherwise.

Table 4.6: Robustness Analysis – Estimation Results of OLS Model with Spatial Diffusion Effects

	Population Density		Employment Density		Land Price	
	Model PD-1	Model PD-2	Model ED-1	Model ED-2	Model LP-1	Model LP-2
Intercept	8.046***	8.053***	7.896***	7.897***	12.260***	12.245***
	(0.093)	(0.093)	(0.088)	(0.088)	(0.047)	(0.048)
TR 0-5	0.133*		0.280***		0.077**	
	(0.053)		(0.049)		(0.027)	
TR 5-30	−0.145*		0.354***		−0.005	
	(0.057)		(0.054)		(0.029)	
TR 0-30		0.026		0.308***		0.044
		(0.050)		(0.047)		(0.025)
TR 30<	−0.384*	−0.361*	0.094	0.088	−0.087	−0.077
	(0.163)	(0.163)	(0.153)	(0.153)	(0.082)	(0.083)
DID 0-5	0.099		−0.017		0.044	
	(0.064)		(0.060)		(0.032)	
DID 5-30	0.263***		−0.058		−0.029	
	(0.070)		(0.066)		(0.035)	
DID 0-30		0.167**		−0.034		0.016
		(0.059)		(0.055)		(0.030)
DID 30<	0.477*	0.473*	−0.097	−0.095	0.044	0.048
	(0.222)	(0.222)	(0.208)	(0.208)	(0.112)	(0.113)
TM	−0.696***	−0.699***	−0.417***	−0.418***	−0.376***	−0.378***
	(0.053)	(0.053)	(0.050)	(0.050)	(0.027)	(0.027)
Population density (*1,000)			0.014***	0.013***	0.003*	0.004**
			(0.002)	(0.002)	(0.001)	(0.001)
Employment density (*1,000)	−0.015***	−0.015***			0.014***	0.014***
	(0.001)	(0.001)			0.000	0.000
Land price (*100,000)	−0.011***	−0.011***	0.030***	0.030***		

continued on next page

Table 4.6 continued

	Population Density		Employment Density		Land Price	
	Model PD-1	Model PD-2	Model ED-1	Model ED-2	Model LP-1	Model LP-2
	(0.002)	(0.002)	(0.002)	(0.002)		
Distance to the nearest station	−0.205***	−0.215***	−0.218***	−0.215***	−0.125***	−0.129***
	(0.012)	(0.012)	(0.011)	(0.011)	(0.006)	(0.006)
Distance to the nearest JR station	−0.012*	−0.01	−0.050***	−0.050***	−0.019***	−0.018***
	(0.006)	(0.006)	(0.006)	(0.006)	(0.003)	(0.003)
Distance to Tokyo Station	−0.012***	−0.012***	−0.006***	−0.006***	−0.013***	−0.013***
	(0.002)	(0.002)	(0.002)	(0.002)	(0.001)	(0.001)
Accessibility to Haneda Airport	−0.006***	−0.006***	−0.016***	−0.016***	−0.006***	−0.006***
	(0.001)	(0.001)	(0.001)	(0.001)	0.000	0.000
Accessibility to Narita Airport	0.003***	0.003***	0.003***	0.003***	0.005***	0.005***
	0.000	0.000	0.000	0.000	0.000	0.000
Road density	0.105***	0.105***	0.059***	0.059***	0.019***	0.019***
	(0.002)	(0.002)	(0.002)	(0.002)	(0.001)	(0.001)
Tokyo 23-ward (1/0)	−0.254***	−0.263***	0.128**	0.132**	0.396***	0.386***
	(0.043)	(0.043)	(0.041)	(0.041)	(0.022)	(0.022)
UURA (1/0)	0.052	0.036	0.833***	0.839***	0.660***	0.635***
	(0.095)	(0.095)	(0.087)	(0.087)	(0.047)	(0.047)
N	5,686	5,686	5,686	5,686	5,686	5,686
AIC	15,913.226	15,953.803	15,197.466	15,197.194	8,173.485	8,227.535
LL	−7,937.613	−7,959.902	−7,579.733	−75,81.597	−4,067.743	−4,096.768

AIC = Akaike Information Criterion, DID = difference-in-differences, ED = effective density, JR = Japan Railways, LL = log likelihood, LP = land price, N = number of observations, PD = population density, UURA = urgent urban renewal area.
Notes:
(i) ***p < 0.001, **p < 0.01, *p < 0.05. Parentheses denotes robust standard error.
(ii) In the same way, "DID 0-5" is defined as the product of TR 0-5 and TM; "DID 5-30" is the product of TR 5-30 and TM; "DID 0-30" is the product of TR 0-30 and TM; and "DID 30<" is the product of TR 30< and TM.
(iii) TR is dummy variable defined in equation (2), and TM is variable defined in equation (2).
Source: Authors' estimation.

The results show that DID 5-30, DID 30< in Model PD-1 and DID 0-30 and DID 30< are estimated to be significantly positive for population density, while other DID-related variables are not significantly estimated. They also show that the estimated coefficient of DID 30< is greater than that of DID 5-30 and DID 0-30 in terms of population density, while the estimated coefficient of DID 30< is also greater than that of DID 0-30 in terms of land price, although they are not statistically significant. They suggest that greater travel time savings to Haneda Airport lead to more positive effects on population density and land price.

Impacts from Improvement of Ground Rail Accessibility to/from City Airport to Local Economies

4.5 Point-Based Analysis

4.5.1 Data

Next, we also use point-based land price data instead of aggregated zone-based land price data, as shown in the earlier analysis. The source of the land price data is the same as in the zone-based analysis, namely the 2000 and 2010 surveys of the official land price under Japan's Public Notice of Land Prices Act. One of the advantages of the point-based land price data is that we can incorporate the individual characteristics of land property, such as land area, building coverage ratio (BCR), floor area ratio (FAR), and built environment factors of each property such as land use patterns and accessibility to the nearest railway station. The geographic distribution of observed land points is shown in Figure 4.2.

Figure 4.2: Land Points Observed in Point-Based Analysis in Tokyo Metropolitan Area

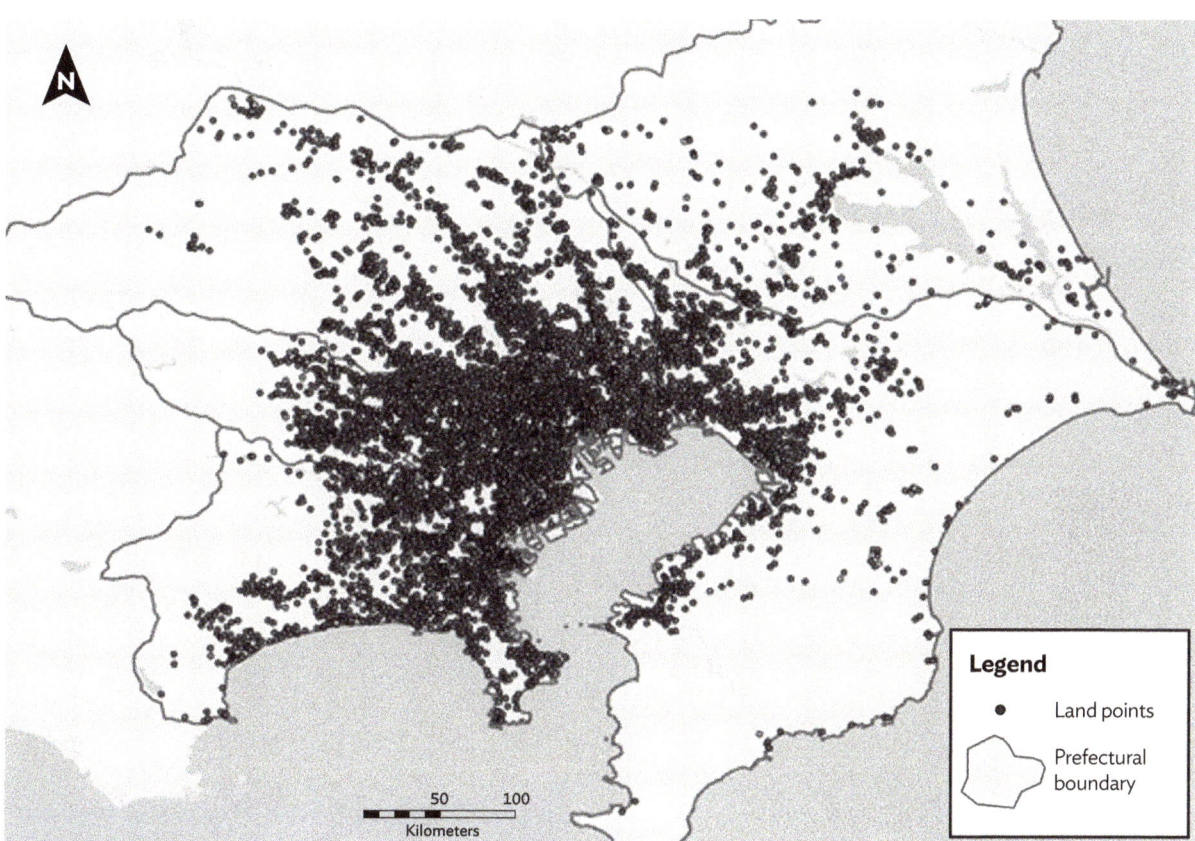

Note: This map was produced by Authors. The boundaries, colors, denominations, and any other information shown on this map do not imply, on the part of the Asian Development Bank, any judgment on the legal status of any territory, or any other endorsement or acceptance of such boundaries, colors, denominations, or information.
Source: Authors' estimation, with data from the official land price under the Public Notice of Land Prices Act, Japan.

Table 4.7 summarizes the descriptive statistics for the analysis with the point-based land price. Mobility is defined as the average travel time between zones from a given zone to all other zones by rail. Note that some of the descriptive statistics in Table 4.1 should be different from those in Table 4.7 because the data in Table 4.1 are zone-based, while in Table 4.7 they are point-based.

Table 4.7: Descriptive Statistics in Point-Based Analysis

Variable	Unit	Mean	S.D.	Min.	25%	Median	75%	Max.
Land price 2010	¥/m²	302,473	818,908	590	98,575	171,000	289,250	24,300,000
Land price 2000	¥/m²	338,715	607,231	2,300	154,000	227,000	337,000	13,100,000
Land area 2010	m²	494	5,198	47.0	136	174	235	347,824
Land area 2000	m²	483	5,115	47.0	136	174	235	347,824
Distance to nearest station 2010	km	1.49	1.81	0.00	0.55	1.00	1.70	24.4
Distance to nearest station 2000	km	1.53	1.80	0.00	0.55	1.00	1.80	17.0
Build coverage ratio 2010	%	58.4	12.1	0.0	50.0	60.0	60.0	80.0
Build coverage ratio 2000	%	31.4	26.8	0.0	0.0	40.0	60.0	70.0
Floor area ratio 2010	%	197	129	0	100	200	200	1,300
Floor area ratio 2000	%	205	134	0	100	200	200	1,000
Mobility 2010	min	122	25.4	77.9	106	118	133	293
Mobility 2000	min	123	25.5	78.8	107	119	134	293
Population density 2010	per km²	8,912	6,216	5	3,956	8,246	12,569	51,090
Population density 2000	per km²	8,340	5,898	4	3,609	7,480	11,911	49,671
Employment density 2010	per km²	4,787	14,194	5	730	1,571	3,299	237,596
Employment density 2000	per km²	4,693	14,125	3	729	1,547	3,343	224,367
Road density 2010	per km²	19.5	8.95	1.13	11.8	20.7	26.4	46.0
Road density 2000	per km²	12.8	5.47	1.01	8.81	12.4	16.5	31.6

km = kilometer, km² = square kilometer, m² = square meter, S.D. = standard deviation.
Sources: Authors, estimated with data from 2000 Population Census and 2010 Population Census of Japan; 2001 Establishment and Enterprise Census of Japan and 2012 Economic Census for Business Activity of Japan; the official land price under the Public Notice of Land Prices Act of Japan, and the Digital National Land Information of Japan.

4.5.2 Results

Table 4.8 shows the estimation results of the OLS models for point-based land prices, incorporating property attributes and built environmental factors. Model P-1 is a model with current land use patterns, while Model P-2 is a model with city planning zones under the City Planning Act and related laws in Japan. The results show that the estimated coefficient of DID is positive but not statistically significant.

Table 4.8: Estimation Results of OLS Models for Point-Based Land Prices

Variable	Model P-1 (Land use)	Model P-2 (City planning zone)
Intercept	13.953***(0.037)	12.838***(0.059)
TR	−0.296***(0.011)	−0.219***(0.010)
TM	−0.479***(0.015)	−0.433***(0.014)
DID	0.029 (0.015)	0.026 (0.014)
Distance to nearest station	−0.082***(0.002)	−0.061***(0.002)
Mobility	−0.013***(0.000)	−0.013***(0.000)
PD (*1,000)	0.015***(0.001)	0.009***(0.001)
ED (*1,000)	0.012***(0.000)	0.009***(0.000)
Road density	0.020***(0.001)	0.016***(0.001)
Tokyo 23-ward (1/0)	0.301***(0.012)	0.184***(0.012)
Building coverage ratio	−0.001***(0.000)	−0.001***(0.000)
Floor area ratio	0.000***(0.000)	0.001***(0.000)
Land use: Residence	−0.221***(0.017)	
Land use: Shop	0.296***(0.013)	
Land use: Office	0.124***(0.016)	
Land use: bank	0.582***(0.069)	
Land use: Hotel	−0.07(0.126)	
Land use: Factory	−0.462***(0.027)	
Land use: Warehouse	−0.383***(0.031)	
Land use: Farmland	−1.290***(0.133)	
Land use: Forest	−2.966***(0.062)	
Land use: Clinic	0.259***(0.056)	
Land use: Vacant	−0.066(0.097)	
Land use: Workshop	−0.271***(0.050)	
Land use: Other	0.028(0.015)	
City planning area: Category 1 low-rise exclusive residential districts		0.753***(0.046)
City planning area: Category 2 low-rise exclusive residential districts		0.504***(0.058)
City planning area: Category 1 medium-to-high-rise exclusive residential districts		0.567***(0.045)
City planning area: Category 2 medium-to-high-rise exclusive residential districts		0.556***(0.047)
City planning area: Category 1 residential districts		0.462***(0.044)
City planning area: Category 2 residential districts		0.573***(0.050)
City planning area: Quasi-residential districts		0.600***(0.052)
City planning area: Neighborhood commercial districts		0.652***(0.045)
City planning area: Commercial districts		0.738***(0.046)
City planning area: Quasi-industrial districts		0.434***(0.046)
City planning area: Industrial districts		0.264***(0.056)

continued on next page

Table 4.8 continued

Variable	Model P-1 (Land use)	Model P-2 (City planning zone)
City planning area: Exclusive industrial districts		0.117*(0.056)
City planning area: Fire prevention districts		0.322***(0.021)
City planning area: Quasi-fire prevention districts		0.242***(0.010)
City planning area: Urbanization control areas		−0.407***(0.047)
City planning area: Urbanization promotion areas and city planning areas other than urbanization control areas		−0.025(0.026)
Regional forest planning area		−1.884***(0.061)
Category 2 national park area		0.21(0.251)
National park area		0.144(0.177)
N	13,032	13,032
AIC	12,747	9,842
LL	−6,348	−4,889

AIC = Akaike Information Criterion, DID = difference-in-differences, ED = effective density, LL = log likelihood, N = number of observations, OLS = ordinary least squares, PD = population density.
Notes:
(i) ***$p < 0.001$, **$p < 0.01$, *$p < 0.05$; parentheses denote robust standard error.
(ii) TM is the dummy variable defined in equation (2), and TR is the dummy variable defined in equation (2).
Source: Authors' estimation.

4.5.3 Robustness Analysis

Table 4.9 also shows the OLS models' estimation results for point-based land prices by city planning zone. Although the DID estimates are not significant for nearly all city planning zones, only the commercial districts have significantly positive estimates for DID. This suggests that improving accessibility to the city's airport may increase land prices in the commercial districts.

Table 4.9: Estimation Results of OLS Models for Point-Based Land Prices by City Planning Zone

Variable	Category 1 Low-Rise Exclusive Residential Districts	Category 2 Low-Rise Exclusive Residential Districts	Category 1 Medium-to-High-Rise Exclusive Residential Districts	Category 2 Medium-to-High-Rise Exclusive Residential Districts	Category 1 Residential Districts	Category 2 Residential Districts	Quasi-residential Districts	Neighborhood Commercial Districts	Commercial Districts	Quasi-industrial Districts	Industrial Districts	Exclusive Industrial Districts
Intercept	14.384***	13.996***	14.367***	14.139***	13.344***	12.410***	13.829***	13.914***	13.970***	13.673***	13.747***	11.035***
	(0.059)	(0.546)	(0.256)	(0.448)	(0.087)	(0.324)	(0.324)	(0.130)	(0.169)	(0.143)	(0.285)	(1.271)
TR	−0.182***	−0.363*	−0.346***	−0.225***	−0.366***	−0.320***	−0.379***	−0.260***	−0.224***	−0.308***	−0.371***	−0.440***
	(0.013)	(0.169)	(0.022)	(0.049)	(0.023)	(0.066)	(0.076)	(0.037)	(0.055)	(0.043)	(0.084)	(0.081)
TM	−0.462***	−0.604***	−0.375***	−0.478***	−2.774**	−0.984	−0.493***	−0.454***	−0.363***	−0.192	−0.544***	−0.796***
	(0.017)	(0.217)	(0.029)	(0.059)	(0.939)	(0.758)	(0.099)	(0.046)	(0.068)	(0.259)	(0.099)	(0.087)
DID	−0.016	0.053	0.012	0.057	0.015	0.042	−0.078	0.032	0.145*	0.112	−0.013	0.122
	(0.018)	(0.219)	(0.031)	(0.064)	(0.032)	(0.089)	(0.103)	(0.050)	(0.073)	(0.060)	(0.115)	(0.112)
Distance to nearest station	−0.068***	−0.093***	−0.052***	−0.005	−0.057***	−0.067***	−0.033*	−0.073***	−0.068**	−0.041***	−0.078***	−0.028
	(0.003)	(0.020)	(0.005)	(0.010)	(0.004)	(0.009)	(0.014)	(0.011)	(0.023)	(0.008)	(0.022)	(0.015)
Mobility	−0.015***	−0.010***	−0.012***	−0.013***	−0.012***	−0.010***	−0.011***	−0.014***	−0.018***	−0.014***	−0.014***	−0.014***
	(0.000)	(0.002)	(0.000)	(0.001)	(0.000)	(0.001)	(0.001)	(0.001)	(0.001)	(0.001)	(0.002)	(0.002)
PD	0.021***	0.021	0.013***	0.029***	0.016***	0.001	−0.003	−0.003	−0.009**	0.016***	0.015	0.059**
	(0.002)	(0.013)	(0.002)	(0.005)	(0.002)	(0.005)	(0.006)	(0.003)	(0.003)	(0.003)	(0.014)	(0.019)
ED	0.014***	0.057***	0.019***	0.012***	0.013***	0.009***	0.054	0.016***	0.003***	0.024***	0.106*	0.129**
	(0.002)	(0.010)	(0.002)	(0.003)	(0.002)	(0.002)	(0.028)	(0.002)	(0.001)	(0.003)	(0.042)	(0.044)
Road density	0.019***	0.026**	0.011***	0.020***	0.018***	0.021***	0.024***	0.016***	−0.004	0.008*	0.003	0.008
	(0.001)	(0.009)	(0.002)	(0.004)	(0.002)	(0.005)	(0.006)	(0.003)	(0.003)	(0.003)	(0.007)	(0.008)
Tokyo 23- ward (1/0)	0.381***	0.251	0.365***	0.257**	0.281***	0.104	0.475**	0.194***	0.202***	0.186***	0.431***	−0.283
	(0.017)	(0.149)	(0.024)	(0.085)	(0.028)	(0.141)	(0.162)	(0.037)	(0.046)	(0.040)	(0.109)	(0.257)
Building coverage ratio	−0.008***	−0.011	−0.015***	−0.023**	0.039*	0.01				−0.004		0.039
	(0.001)	(0.010)	(0.004)	(0.008)	(0.016)	(0.013)				(0.004)		(0.020)
Floor area ratio	−0.002***	−0.001	0.001***	0.003***	0.001**	0.005***	−0.001	0.002***	0.003***	0.001**		
	(0.000)	(0.001)	(0.000)	(0.001)	(0.000)	(0.001)	(0.001)	(0.000)	(0.000)	(0.000)		
N	4,701	91	1,922	491	2,077	220	149	810	1249	622	110	102
AIC	1,549.259	44.03	791.446	283.051	1,036.282	122.778	63.828	519.273	1,881.804	311.218	53.105	37.432
LL	−761.629	−9.015	−382.723	−128.526	−505.141	−48.389	−19.914	−247.637	−928.902	−142.609	−15.552	−6.716

AIC = Akaike Information Criterion, DID = difference-in-differences, ED = effective density, LL = log likelihood, N = number of observations, OLS = ordinary least squares, PD = population density.

Notes:
(i) ***p < 0.001, **p < 0.01, *p < 0.05; parentheses denote robust standard error.
(ii) TM is variables defined in equation (2), and TR is dummy variable defined in equation (2).

Source: Authors' estimation.

4.6. Discussion

This study examined the causal effects of improved accessibility to the city airport by rail on local indicators using four methods: DID, spatial DID, PS matching, and IPW, with two data sets of zone-based land prices and point-based land prices. Our findings can be summarized as follows:

- The DID and spatial DID analysis with zone-based and point-based data showed that improving the accessibility of the city's airport has a significant positive impact on population density.
- DID analysis with point-based land price data by the city planning zone showed that the impact of improved accessibility to the city airport on land prices was significantly positive only in commercial districts.
- The PS matching analysis with zone-based data showed that the ATTs of improved accessibility to the city airport were significantly positive in terms of employment density and land price.
- IPW analysis with zone-based data showed that both the ATEs and ATTs of improved accessibility to the city airports were significantly positive in terms of population density, employment density, and land price.

How should they be interpreted? We should note that each method has advantages and disadvantages. First, the DID method is only appropriate when the assumptions of a parallel trend and a common shock are met. The parallel trend assumption requires that the time trend of the indicators in control group zones is the same as that in a counterfactual case in the treatment group zones, and the common shock assumption requires that events other than treatment that may have an impact on the indicators should occur together in the two groups. In our analysis, we tried to avoid possible violation of these assumptions by incorporating various covariates. However, there could still be some hidden factors that could affect the indicators. Since many zones in the control group are located in the western part of the TMA, as shown in Figure 4.1, unique local characteristics could affect the indicators. The results of our point-based analysis, using DID by city planning zone, also suggest that the effects of improving access to Haneda Airport were only observed in the commercial areas. The spatial DID has the advantage of incorporating spatial autocorrelation explicitly, since spatial interaction is considered important in spatial impact analysis. Specifically, improving rail accessibility could increase local economic performance near rail stations at the expense of economic output in other neighboring areas farther from the rail stations. This could suggest that ignoring the spatial interaction could bias the estimated impacts.

Next, PS matching can balance covariates with PS. Thus, it is applicable even when covariates vary between zones. In addition, PS matching has an advantage over the semiparametric approach because the risk of misspecification is lower with a parametric approach such as DID. This method can work if the assumption of a strongly ignorable treatment assignment is met. This assumption requires that the joint distribution of changes in the indicators of the treatment group ($y_{i2T} - y_{i1T}$) and the control group ($y_{i2C} - y_{i1C}$) is independent of an assignment variable z_i. This may be equivalent to a condition of "missing completely at random" (Rubin 1976). However, the validity of this assumption is difficult to verify. Additionally, this method does not incorporate spatial autocorrelation.

Finally, IPW can also incorporate covariates using PS, which is similar to PS matching but less subjective than PS matching, as shown earlier. Another advantage of IPW may be that it is applicable even when the distribution of the PS in the treatment group does not overlap well with that in the control group. Using this method also enables us to calculate the estimators directly. Note, however, that IPW is also subject to the assumption of strongly ignorable treatment assignment and does not account for spatial autocorrelation.

We maintain that ATT is preferable for impact analysis in our context than ATE. The reason is because we primarily want to know whether the improvement of urban rail access to the airport had an impact on the local economy in the improved zones. Then, the ATTs estimated from the PS matching and IPW should be highlighted for our study. Note that the estimated DID is the same as ATE, since it contains all samples in both groups. Our ATT test results from the PS matching and IPW conclude that the improvement of Haneda Airport rail access has significantly increased employment density and land prices in the zones where access to the airport was improved.

The significant increase in employment density may indicate that business or commercial agglomeration near the rail stations was encouraged by the improvement in urban rail accessibility to the city's airport. Better rail access to/from the airport enables locals to travel by train in less time and with greater reliability than by car; visitors also reach their destinations more easily. This could have a direct, indirect, or catalytic impact on business agglomeration. The direct impact may be the relocation of offices in airport-related industries, such as airport operators, airlines, airport air traffic control, ground handlers, airport security, immigration and customs, aircraft maintenance, and other airport activities. The indirect impact may be that of downstream industries that supply and support airport activities, including wholesalers that supply food for in-flight catering, oil refining activities for jet fuel, companies that provide accounting and legal services to airlines, and travel agents that book flights. The catalytic effect may also occur in industries other than airport or airport-related industries, such as tourism, including hotels, restaurants, and recreational facilities, as well as local transportation and global industries whose employees frequently travel by air to other regions/countries or frequently meet with visitors from other regions/countries who use air transportation.

The significant increase in land prices may also indicate an increase in economic productivity in areas where access to the urban rail airport has been improved. One of the factors in improving economic productivity is a direct effect of improved accessibility. Shorter first-/last-mile travel time to/from the airport allows local businesspeople to be more productive in their offices and allows visitors to stay longer in the areas, which could lead to further production and/or consumption. Another factor, as mentioned earlier, could be business agglomeration. The business cluster is expected to promote innovative activities by facilitating matching in the labor market, which allows employers to find skilled workers at a lower cost, improve knowledge sharing among workers by increasing opportunities for face-to-face meetings, and activate a learning process for local workers in communicating with others. There is potential demand for offices in areas where improving rail access to the airport could lead to an increase in land prices.

4.7 Conclusion

This study sought to provide empirical evidence of the effects of improving airport accessibility through urban rail in the TMA. Three types of quasi-experimental methods were used: spatial DID, PS matching, IPW with 2000 and 2010 panel data to statistically test the impacts. The estimation results show that employment density and land prices are significantly affected by the improvement of airport accessibility. These empirical findings could be helpful in understanding the impact of investments in airport ground access improvements and in examining the justification for billion-dollar investments in airport rail links, which have been widely debated in many cities.

This study provided useful insights into the economic impact of accessibility improvements on local economies in the TMA. However, several issues should be further examined. First, the data arrangement for the empirical analysis should be further explored. For example, this study assumed that the land price of the zone is represented by a simple average of the data at representative points in the zone, but this may introduce bias in the estimation because the land price should vary between areas in the same zone. A different method should be used to capture the land price of the representative zone, such as using different zoning systems where each zone has only one representative point of land price. In addition, other definitions of treatment and control groups might be helpful to better understand the impact of accessibility improvements. In this study, the treatment group was assumed to include the zones with improved accessibility and the control group was assumed to include the others. However, the treatment group could also include, for example, the zones with improved accessibility beyond a specific threshold, such as a travel time savings of 10 minutes or more. This is because local effects could only be materialized when the shock is greater than a certain level. In addition, further research with other data sets is needed to consolidate the findings of this study. For example, a similar empirical analysis should be conducted for other time periods in the TMA or in other cities.

References

Angrist, J. D. and J.-S. Pischke. 2008. *Mostly Harmless Econometrics: An Empiricist's Companion*. Princeton University Press.

Baker, D., R. Merkert, and M. Kamruzzaman. 2015. Regional Aviation and Economic Growth: Cointegration and Causality Analysis in Australia. *Journal of Transport Geography*. 43. pp. 140–150.

Bel, G. and X. Fageda. 2008. Getting There Fast: Globalization, Intercontinental Flights and Location of Headquarters. *Journal Economic Geography*. 8 (4). pp. 471–495.

Bilotkach, V. 2015. Are Airports Engines of Economic Development? A Dynamic Panel Data Approach. *Urban Studies*. 52 (9). pp. 1577–1593.

Brueckner, J. K. 2003. Airline Traffic and Urban Economic Development. *Urban Studies*. 40 (8). pp. 1455–1469.

Button, K. and S. Lall. 1999. The Economics of Being an Airport Hub City. *Research in Transportation Economics*. I. pp. 75–105.

Button, K., S. Lall, R. Stough, and M. Trice. 1999. High-Technology Employment and Hub Airports. *Journal of Air Transport Management.* 5 (1). pp. 53–59.

Debbage, K. G. and D. Delk. 2001. The Geography of Air Passenger Volume and Local Employment Patterns by US Metropolitan Core Area: 1973–1996. *Journal of Air Transport Management.* 7 (3). pp. 159–167.

Dubé, J., D. Legros, M. Thériault, and F. Des Rosiers. 2014. A Spatial Difference-in-Differences Estimator to Evaluate the Effect of Change in Public Mass Transit Systems on House Prices. *Transportation Research Part B: Methodological.* 64 (6). pp. 24–40.

Florida, R., C. Mellander, and T. Holgersson. 2015. Up in the Air: The Role of Airports for Regional Economic Development. *Annals of Regional Science.* 54 (1). pp. 197–214.

Green, R. K. 2007. Airports and Economic Development. *Real Estate Economics.* 35 (1). pp. 91–112.

Guignet, D. B. and A. L. Martinez-Cruz. 2018. The Impacts of Underground Petroleum Releases on a Homeowner's Decision to Sell: A Difference-in-Differences Approach. *Regional Science and Urban Economics.* 69. pp. 11–24.

Hakim, M. M. and R. Merkert. 2016. The Causal Relationship between Air Transport and Economic Growth: Empirical Evidence from South Asia. *Journal of Transport Geography.* 56. pp. 120–127.

Heckert, M. and J. Mennis. 2012. The Economic Impact of Greening Urban Vacant Land: A Spatial Difference-in-Differences Analysis. *Environmental Planning A.* 44 (12). pp. 3010–3027.

Imbens, G. W. and D. B. Rubins. 2015. *Causal Inference for Statistics, Social, and Biomedical Sciences: An Introduction.* Cambridge University Press.

International Civil Aviation Organization (ICAO). 2018. *The Annual Report of the Council 2017.* Montréal, Canada. https://www.icao.int/annual-report-2017/Pages/default.aspx (accessed 14 July 2019).

Kasarda, J. D. and G. Lindsay. 2011. *Aerotropolis: The Way We'll Live Next.* New York: Farrar, Straus and Giroux.

Kato, H. 2014. Urban Rail Development in Tokyo from 2000 to 2010. International Transport Forum Discussion Paper. Vol. 2014/05.

Kato, H., D. Fukuda, Y. Yamashita, S. Iwakura, and T. Yai. 2017. Latest Urban Rail Demand Forecast Model System in the Tokyo Metropolitan Area, Japan. *Transportation Research Record: Journal of Transportation Research Board.* 2668. pp. 60–77.

Ministry of Land, Infrastructure, Transport and Tourism, Japan. 2019. *Policies Related to Urban Renewal.* http://www.mlit.go.jp/toshi/crd_machi_tk_000008.html (accessed 14 July 2019).

Morichi, S., S. Iwakura, S. Morishige, M. Itoh, and S. Hayasaki. 2001. Tokyo Metropolitan Rail Network Long-Range Plan for the 21st Century. Presented at the 81st Annual Meeting of Transportation Research Board. Washington, DC.

Murakami, J. and H. Kato. 2020. The Intra-metropolitan Distribution of Airport Accessibility, Employment Density, and Labor Productivity: Spatial Strategy for Economic Development in Tokyo. *Applied Geography*. 125, 102309.

Murakami, J., Y. Matsui, and H. Kato. 2016. Airport Rail Links and Economic Productivity: Evidence from 82 Cities with the World's 100 Busiest Airports. *Transport Policy*. 52. pp. 89–99.

Neal, Z. 2012. Creative Employment and Jet Set Cities: Disentangling Causal Effects. *Urban Studies*. 49 (12). pp. 2693–2709.

Percoco, M. 2010. Airport Activity and Local Development: Evidence from Italy. *Urban Studies*. 47 (11). pp. 2427–2443.

Rosenbaum, P. R. 1987. Model-Based Direct Adjustment. *Journal of the American Statistical Association*. 82. pp. 387–394.

Rosenbaum, P. R. and D. B. Rubin. 1983. The Central Role of the Propensity Score in Observational Studies for Causal Effects. *Biometrika*. 70. pp. 41–55.

Rubin, D. B. (1976). Inference with Missing Data. *Biometrika*. 63. pp. 581–592.

Shadish, W. R., T. D. Cook, and D. T. Cambell. 2002. *Experimental and Quasi-Experimental Designs for Generalized Causal Inference*. 2nd Edition. Cengage Learning.

Sheard, N. 2014. Airports and Urban Sectoral Employment. *Journal of Urban Economics*. 80. pp. 133–152.

Tittle, D., P. McCarthy, and Y. Xiao. 2013. Airport Runway Capacity and Economic Development: A Panel Data Analysis of Metropolitan Statistical Areas. *Economic Development Quarterly*. 27 (3). pp. 230–239.

Van Buuren, S. and K. Groothuis-Oudshoorn, K. 2011. MICE: Multivariate Imputation by Chained Equations in R. *Journal of Statistical Software*. 45 (3). pp. 1–68.

Chapter 5

Economic Impacts of Airport Upgrading on the Regional Economy: Case Study of the People's Republic of China

5.1 Introduction

The airport is one of the most important elements of transportation infrastructure in many cities. The airport serves as a regional base for interregional and/or international transportation of leisure/business travelers and cargo. They function as gateways to international/domestic air transportation networks while also serving as cores of agglomeration in regions with local/regional businesses and employees directly and indirectly involved in supporting airport operations (Wu 2017; Brueckner 2003). It is widely believed that airport performance significantly affects the accessibility of regions in terms of interregional and/or international transportation and regional economic activities.

The transportation network of the People's Republic of China (PRC) has developed rapidly over the past decade. In 2017, 551.56 million passengers and 7.059 million tons of cargo were transported by air, and the annual growth rates are 12% for passenger ton kilometers and 8%–9% for cargo ton kilometers (CAAC 2018; IATA 2015). This has created the second-largest air transportation market in the world. The rapid growth in air traffic demand has caused serious traffic congestion at many airports in the PRC. This could hinder economic activities in the regions. Airport capacity expansion is considered a prerequisite for economic growth (Wu 2017) and has actually been implemented in many cities over the past decade. Increasing air traffic demand has required massive investment in new airports in many rural regions of the PRC, while the explosive growth in air traffic demand has also put pressure on existing airports in urban regions to increase their capacity, such as by expanding runways and renovating terminal buildings. Large cities such as Beijing, Shanghai, and Guangzhou, which are considered global hubs of air transport networks, are pioneering various strategies to upgrade their terminal facilities to improve operational efficiency in the PRC.

In general, the upgrading of a civil airport system can be categorized into three types. The first type is the upgrading of an existing airport, in which an existing airport is modernized through physical expansion, such as terminal extensions and flight area improvements, to increase air traffic capacity. The second type is airport relocation, in which the functions of the original airport are moved to another location where a new airport is created. The area of the original airport could be converted to another development. The third is a multi-airport system (MAS), in which a new civil airport is built, while the original airport remains in operation, resulting in two or more civil airports simultaneously serving air traffic in the region. Airport relocation, which used to be a rare event in PRC aviation, has recently become more popular. For example, in Qingdao, Dalian, and Xiamen, urban airports were closed when newly built airports away from the central business district (CBD) become operational. The introduction of MAS has also been explored in major cities such as Beijing and Chengdu, which are expected to complete construction of additional airports around 2020, after Shanghai completed the upgrading of MAS in 1999. One of the reasons that relocation of airports and/or MAS has recently become more prominent in the PRC is because investment in airport expansion in line with urban development is facing challenges in many cities. The development of new airports in urban areas has encountered difficulties in finding a suitable location, due to the increase in property prices in urban areas and the difficulty in finding consensus with local communities due to the expected negative impact of rapid expansion of urban boundaries. Airport upgrading aims to overcome the contradiction between improving air transportation capacity and rapid urbanization by relocating or building new secondary airports in peripheral areas, even if this requires additional efforts to improve ground access to remote airports.

Investment in airport upgrading is expected to have an impact on local and/or regional economic activity. Airport upgrading increases air traffic capacity and improves the airline network. Improved accessibility lowers trade costs and stimulates intra-industry trade and economic activity at the aggregate city level (Baker, Merkert, and Kamruzzaman 2015). Airport upgrading can also improve the socioeconomic function of a region. The phenomenon of airport cities—agglomerations of jobs anchored by the airport (Appold and Kasarda 2013) that have emerged at major airports in the PRC—is a unique response to growing population, employment, and economic activity. The location of advanced manufacturing services, including finance, insurance, and real estate, is particularly relevant because they are considered aviation-oriented.

Airport upgrading is seen as a transportation investment strategy to boost regional economies and resolve conflicts between urban development and the aviation industry. Many airport upgrading projects in the PRC have been completed in line with the rapid development of civil aviation and major changes in the aviation network and accessibility in the PRC. Although airport development policies in the PRC have been discussed with enthusiasm, there is still little evidence on whether airport upgrading really stimulates economic development.

This study examines the economic impact of investment in airport upgrading to increase air traffic capacity using an empirical data set in the PRC from 2000 to 2015. The impacts are estimated using an analytical framework of difference-in-differences (DID) models, which enable us to identify the causal effects of airport upgrading on the regional economy. The results of our empirical study are expected to contribute to debates on airport upgrading strategies not only in the PRC but also in other developing cities where airport capacity constraints are a major policy issue.

This chapter is organized as follows: first, models are formulated, including two-time frame DID and models with a continuous year frame DID. Next, the data set used for the empirical analysis is presented, followed by the results of the model estimates with a discussion of policy implications. Finally, the results and further questions are summarized.

5.2 Models

This study uses the DID method in a traditional two-time frame and a continuous-year frame to examine the impact of airport upgrading on the city's economic productivity as measured by gross domestic product (GDP) per capita. Since the observed years of airport upgrading vary from airport to airport, DID with the continuous-year frame may be more suitable and accurate to capture the short-term upgrading effect. Meanwhile, airport upgrading projects may also affect the regional economy over many years. Therefore, the two-time frame DID estimation could also capture the long-term economic impact of the airport's strategic positioning. There are several reasons to believe that airport upgrading or its strategy was not randomly assigned to cities. The decision to upgrade airports may depend on future strategic positioning and current traffic networking for long-distance commuting (Bonnefoy 2008). For cities designated as international or regional hub airports in the 2007 central government official document, an airport upgrading project is more likely.

For the DID analysis, cities in the PRC are divided into a treatment group and a control group. The treatment group includes the cities with airports where airport upgrading was implemented during the study period (from 2004 to 2015), while the control group includes other cities with airports. The DID analysis assumes a parallel trend hypothesis, i.e., the dependent variables of both treatment and control groups should have the same trend before and during the study period, except for an external shock given to the treatment group, i.e., airport upgrading in our study. This assumption guarantees a credible result of the causal impact of airport upgrading on the treatment groups.

First, the two-time frame model is specified as follows:

$$\ln y_{it} = \beta_{treat} Treat_i + \beta_{time} Time_t + \beta_{did} D_{it} + \boldsymbol{\theta} \boldsymbol{X}_{it} + \gamma_i + \varepsilon_{it} \qquad (1)$$

where y_{it} is regional GDP per capita of a city i at year t; $Treat_i$ is defined as 1 if the airport i belongs to the treatment group and 0 otherwise; $Time_t$ is defined as 1 if t is 2015 and 0 if t is 2004; D_{it} is defined as $Treat_i \cdot Time_t$; $\boldsymbol{X}_{it}$ is a vector of control variables; γ_i is a fixed effect with respect to the city; ε_{it} is the error component; and β_{treat}, β_{time}, β_{did}, and $\boldsymbol{\theta}$ are unknown coefficients. β_{treat} represents the treatment effect, which may imply a kind of selection bias; β_{time} represents the time effect, representing a change over time assuming a parallel trend; and β_{did} represents the DID effect, representing the effect of airport upgrading, which our study is concerned with. When β_{treat} is estimated to be significantly positive (negative), the cities with higher (lower) GDP per capita tend to be selected as the treatment group. When β_{did} is estimated as significantly positive, we can conclude that airport upgrading positively affects regional GDP per capita.

Next, the continuous-year frame DID is formulated as follows:

$$\ln y_{i\tau} = \sum_{\tau \in T} \tilde{\beta}_{treat,i} Treat_i \cdot YB_\tau + \tilde{\beta}_{did} E_{i\tau} + \tilde{\boldsymbol{\theta}} \boldsymbol{X}_{i\tau} + \tilde{\gamma}_i + \tilde{\delta}_\tau + \tilde{\varepsilon}_{i\tau} \qquad (2)$$

where YB_τ is 1 if year τ belongs to a series of years before the study period T (=2000, 2001, 2002, or 2003), and 0 otherwise; $E_{i\tau}$ is defined as $Treat_i \cdot YA_{i\tau}$ where $YA_{i\tau}$ is equal to 1 if a year τ is after the upgrading of the airport at city i, and 0 otherwise; $\tilde{\gamma}_i$ and ($\tilde{\delta}_\tau$) are the fixed effects in terms of city and time, respectively; $\tilde{\varepsilon}_{i\tau}$ is the error component; and $\tilde{\beta}_{treat}$, $\tilde{\beta}_{did}$, and $\tilde{\boldsymbol{\theta}}$ are unknown coefficients. When $\tilde{\beta}_{treat,i}$ is estimated to be statistically insignificant, it means that there is no difference in the dependent variables of the two groups before our study period (from 2004 to 2015). This is introduced because DID analysis typically faces the potential problem that a significant difference in the dependent variable between the treatment and control groups may be caused by a preexisting difference in the annual trend before policy implementation (Zheng et al. 2017; Sun et al. 2017). $\tilde{\beta}_{did}$ measures the DID effect, which represents the effect of airport upgrading in the short run, because E_{it} is assumed to change from 0 to 1 immediately after the airport upgrading. If the estimated DID effect is significantly positive, we can conclude that airport upgrading positively affects GDP per capita.

In addition to estimating the above two DID models with the full data set, we also perform model estimations with subgroups of our data set and robustness checks to corroborate our estimation results.

5.3 Data

An extensive panel data set from 2000 to 2016 in 88 prefecture-level cities in the PRC was originally developed to analyze the impact of airport upgrading projects on regional economic growth over the past decade. The cities are listed in the Appendix. The data set includes cities that operated one or more civilian airports, including for military and civilian purposes, before 2004 and that were not temporarily closed for some reasons, such as reorganization and upgrading, during the study period. Cities with airports newly opened between 2000 and 2003 were removed from our data set because the period from the introduction of the new airports to our evaluation years is too short to distinguish the effects of newly introduced airports from those of airport modernization. Note that the data set includes cities with airports whose grade index in-flight area is at grade 4C level or higher in 2016, as airports ranked below 4C could rarely be used by civil aircraft if there are few scheduled flights. See the definition of 4C in the Appendix.

The data set contains information on airport upgrading in each city, such as the year of airport upgrading, the type of airport upgrading, and the change in grade index of the flight area. In this study, airport upgrading was identified as a physical project that involves a construction phase of airport facilities to increase operational capacity. This means that the refurbishment of existing facilities is not regarded as airport upgrading. When airport expansion plans in each stage or official documents from the Civil Aviation Administration of China (CAAC) are available, especially for hub airports and main domestic airports, we specified the year of airport upgrading according to these plans. For smaller airports, we gathered airport upgrading information by fully utilizing internet resources, news reports, and/or other information provided by airport authorities. It should be noted that there is usually a 1–2 year period between the completion of the upgrade and the renewal of the license to permit new facilities (terminal, runway). Although it would be ideal to use the year in which the new facilities are officially commissioned, we assume the year of project completion as the upgrade year, mainly because data on official licensing are not available. If multiple upgrading projects were implemented during the study period, the earliest year of project completion is assumed to be the upgrade year.

Table 5.1 presents the descriptive statistics of the potential variables used in our empirical analysis. *Population density* represents the population per square kilometer in the main central urban areas. A prefecture-level city in the PRC often includes a major urban center (usually with the same name as the prefecture-level city) and a larger surrounding rural area with many smaller cities, towns, and villages. We used the population and area of the central urban area to measure population density. *Secondary industry* and *tertiary industry* represent the share of secondary industry and tertiary industry, respectively, in total GDP. *College students* represent the total number of full-time students enrolled in regular higher education institutions. Regular institutions of higher education include full-time universities, independently established colleges, colleges, institutions of higher professional education, institutions of higher vocational education, and others. *Local fixed asset investment* (LFAI) represents investment in fixed asset projects by all investors in a city. LFAI can be a good indicator of how much is being invested. *Foreign direct investment* (FDI) is defined as foreign direct investment as a share of total GDP. *Urban road density* is defined as the urban road area per person. Airport distance is defined as the distance of the road network between an airport and the city center. *City HSR availability* is defined as a dummy variable equal to 1 if HSR service is available in city i in 2016, and 0 otherwise. *Yearly HSR availability* is defined as an annual dummy variable equal to 1 if HSR service is available in city i in year t, and 0 otherwise. The city statistics data are from the China City Statistical Yearbooks from 2001 to 2017 accessed from the China National Knowledge Infrastructure and urban statistical bulletins on local government websites. Airport statistics data are from the Statistical Yearbook of Civil Airport published by CAAC. Railroad data are from the China Railway Statistical Yearbook.

Table 5.1 first shows that the average regional GDP per capita increased from CNY26,402 in 2004 to CNY80,895 in 2015, reflecting the rapid economic growth in the PRC. Note that CNY1 was equivalent to approximately $0.83 in 2004 and to $0.62 in 2015. Second, the average number of regional air passengers also increased from 2,285,000 in 2004 to 8,555,364 in 2015. The lowest number of air passengers in our study period is 705, while the highest is 94,393,000, which indicates the diversity of air traffic demand across regions. Third, the average population density slightly decreased from 1,062 in 2004 to 931.0 in 2015. This may be due to suburbanization in cities, including the physical extension of urban areas, which may have dispersed geographic distribution of the population. Fourth, the average share of secondary industry has decreased from 50.4% in 2004 to 44.3% in 2015, while the average share of tertiary industry has increased from 43.2% in 2004 to 51.4% in 2015. This is due to recent changes in the industrial structure of the PRC, which has shifted from a manufacturing-oriented economy to a service-oriented economy. Fifth, the average number of college students per 100 urban residents soared significantly from 208 in 2004 to 377 in 2015. The minimum was only 18 in 2015, indicating that educational opportunities still vary widely across regions. Sixth, the average LFAI increased significantly from CNY29,530 million in 2004 to CNY194,297 million in 2015. The standard deviation has also increased, which means that the inequality in regional investment may become greater during the study period. Seventh, the average FDI increased from 58,000 in 2004 to 190,510 in 2015. The growth rate of FDI from 2004 to 2015 was 228.5%, half that of local fixed investment (545.1%). This may indicate that the PRC economy has developed mainly through domestic investment rather than foreign investment. Eighth, the average urban road density has increased from 8.727 square meters (m^2) per person to 15.01, reflecting the aggressive investment in road infrastructure improvement during the study period. Ninth, the average distance to the airport before and after the upgrading is 16.67 km and 18.67 km, respectively. This indicates that airport upgrading, including airport relocation and/or the introduction of additional airports, was accompanied by the construction of new airports that are farther away from the downtown area. This is probably because urbanization in the central areas has made it difficult to find suitable land for airport construction near downtown areas. Tenth, the average HSR availability in the city is 0.705, which means that 70.5% of the studied airports have experienced the introduction of HSR during the study period. Finally, the average annual HSR

Table 5.1: Descriptive Statistics of the Data Set

Attribute/Variable (Unit)	Observation	Mean	Std. Dev.	Min.	Max.
Regional GDP per Capita (CNY)					
2000–2016	1,496	47,708	34,499	3,442	237,689
2004	88	26,402	15,686	3,442	86,523
2015	88	80,895	34,866	19,808	195,792
Air Transportation Passenger (persons)					
2000–2016	1,496	4,267,833	9,102,607	704	94,393,000
2004	88	2,285,000	4,877,000	7,191	34,883,190
2015	88	8,555,364	14,120,000	212,658	89,939,000
Population Density (person/km^2)					
2000–2016	1,496	1,097	963	50.48	11,449
2004	88	1,062	856.2	51.37	4,765
2015	88	931.0	668.1	56.19	3,406
Secondary Industry (%)					
2000–2016	1,496	48.0%	11.3%	14.4%	90.1%
2004	88	50.4%	11.8%	20.8%	86.4%
2015	88	44.3%	10.4%	17.1%	66.2%
Tertiary Industry (%)					
2000–2016	1,496	46.7%	11.0%	7.90%	79.6%
2004	88	43.2%	9.98%	12.0%	65.7%
2015	88	51.4%	11.2%	27.5%	79.6%
College Students (persons per 100 urban population)					
2000–2016	1,496	254.0	279.6	0	1,294
2004	88	208.1	210.1	8.123	842.1
2015	88	377.0	370.7	18.18	1,294
Local Fixed Asset Investment (CNY million)					
2000–2016	1,496	81,164	126,988	589.4	1,304,800
2004	88	29,530	38,021	1,315	247,480
2015	88	194,297	228,889	6,539	1,304,800
Foreign Direct Investment ($10,000)					
2000–2016	1,496	107,211	201,899	25	3,082,563
2004	88	58,000	88,485	45	379,917
2015	88	190,510	322,779	148	2,113,444
Urban Road Density (m^2 per person)					
2000–2016	1,496	10.97	6.612	0.380	64
2004	88	8.727	5.980	2	44
2015	88	15.01	7.280	1.780	54.24
Airport distance before upgrading (km)	88	16.67	11.95	1	75
Airport distance after upgrading (km)	88	18.67	12.01	2	75
City HSR availability (0/1)	88	0.705	0.456	0	1
Yearly HSR availability (0/1)	1,496	0.151	0.358	0	1

GDP = gross domestic product, HSR = high-speed rail, km = kilometer, m = meter, Std. Dev. = standard deviation.
Source: Authors' estimation, based on China City Statistical Yearbooks from 2001 to 2017 accessed by China National Knowledge Infrastructure; urban statistical bulletins of the local government websites; Statistical Yearbook of Civil Airport; and China Railway Statistical Yearbook.

availability is 0.151, indicating that the HSR network has been well developed in the PRC in many years during our study period. Note that the first HSR service between Beijing and Tianjin was introduced on 1 August 2008.

Figure 5.1 illustrates the relationship between regional GDP per capita and regional air passengers in 2004 and 2015, showing that air passengers tend to have a positive relationship with regional GDP per capita and that regional GDP per capita is higher in 2015 than in 2004, even with the same volume of air passengers. This could be due to the fact that better economic activities require higher demand for air transport services or vice versa.

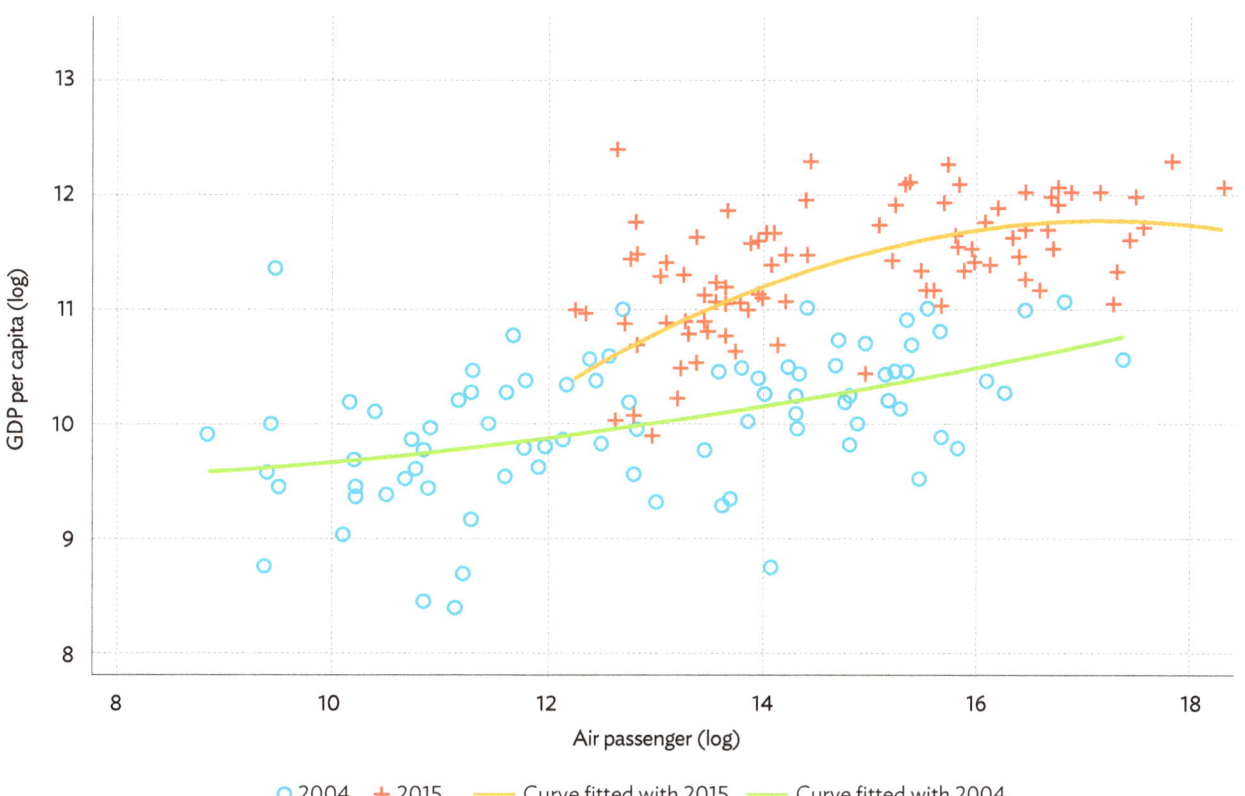

Figure 5.1: GDP per Capita Versus Air Passengers in 2004 and 2015

GDP = gross domestic product.
Source: Authors' estimation, based on the China City Statistical Yearbooks and Statistical Yearbook of Civil Airport.

5.4 Results

Estimation Results of DID Models

Table 5.2 summarizes the treatment and control groups in our data set, including HSR availability in each group. Note that all hub airports and the main domestic airports have experienced airport upgrading. First, this shows that two-thirds of cities in our data set experienced airport upgrading during the study period. This reflects the recent rush to expand airport capacity in response to rapid growth in air transportation demand at many airports in the PRC in recent decades. Second, this also shows that over 70% of the cities in our data set are connected to HSR transportation services. This could mean that cities with civilian airports have sufficient intercity travel demand to be connected to both air and HSR services. Third, it also shows that the proportion of cities with HSR services is higher in the treatment group than in the control group. This is probably because the cities with airport upgrading projects have seen such an increase in demand for intercity travel that HSR services are also required, along with an increase in airport capacity.

Table 5.2: Treatment and Control Groups in Data Set

City HSR Availability	Airport Upgrading Project		Total
	Yes (Treatment)	No (Control)	
1	41	19	60
0	16	12	28
Total	57	31	88

HSR = high-speed rail.
Source: Authors' estimation, based on the data collected from the Statistical Yearbook of Civil Airport and China Railway Statistical Yearbook.

Table 5.3 shows the estimation results of the models with two-time frame DID and continuous-year frame DID. In the two-time frame DID analysis, model T1 assumes no control variable but incorporates the city fixed effects, and model T2 adds control variables in addition to model T1. In the continuous DID analysis, models C1 and C2 assume only the city and year fixed effects, while models C3, C4, and C5 include the control variables. As for the models with two-time frame DID, the R^2s of models T1 and T2 are 0.49 and 0.80, respectively, which means that model T2 has significantly better model performance than model T1. This suggests that the covariates in the two-time frame DID are working. The estimation results of model T2 first show that the estimate of *Treat* is significantly negative, which means that the regions that experienced the airport upgrading had lower regional GDP per capita than the regions that did not experience it. This may indicate that the airport upgrading was implemented in the poorer regions to boost their economies in the PRC. Second, the results show that the value for *Time* is estimated to be significantly positive. This reflects the economic growth in the PRC. Third, the *College Students* variable is estimated to be significantly positive. This is reasonable because more students in higher education could help provide skilled labor, which should increase economic productivity. Fourth, both *secondary industry* and *tertiary industry* are estimated to have a significant positive relationship with regional GDP per capita. This is because both industries should lead to better economic performance than agriculture.

Fifth, *local fixed investment* and *urban road density* are also estimated to be significantly positive. They are also reasonable because both should contribute to regional capital, which is expected to increase economic productivity (Hu, Gan, and Gao 2012; Yu et al. 2012). Finally, the DID effect is estimated to be significantly positive. This means that airport upgrading significantly increases regional GDP per capita when controlling for covariates.

As for the continuous-year frame DID models, the R^2s of models C3, C4, and C5 are significantly better than those of models C1 and C2. Thus, models C3, C4, or C5 are preferable to the other models in terms of model fit. This also indicates that the covariates should be incorporated into the model for model performance. The estimation results of model C5 show that $Treat \cdot YB$ is estimated to be statistically insignificant in 2000, 2002, and 2003, but significant in 2001. An F-test is then conducted to examine the significance of introducing a set of interaction terms related to the treatment dummy and the year dummy. The *p*-value is 0.499, which means that a set of $Treat \cdot YB$ in model C5 is insignificant. Thus, we conclude that the trend of the treatment group is indifferent from that of the control group, which supports the parallel trend assumption. The estimation results of models C3, C4, and C5 show that *local fixed asset investment* and *urban road density* are estimated to be significantly positive, which is the same as the results in the two-time frame DID models. They are quite reasonable. The estimation results of models C3 and C4 show that *secondary industry* and *tertiary industry* are also estimated to be significantly positive. The results of model C4 also indicate that *air passengers* have significant positive association with GDP per capita. This is likely because one of the basic motivations of airport upgrading is to meet air traffic demand. This is also consistent with past empirical work on the causal effects of air traffic on regional economies in developed countries (Button and Lall 1999; Bel and Fageda 2008; Blumenthal, Wolman, and Hill 2009; Baker, Merkert, and Kamruzzaman 2015).

Past studies have also shown the importance of air travel in a more services-oriented economy (Brueckner 2003). As discussed earlier, the economic trend in the PRC is that the service industry is gradually replacing the manufacturing industry. In addition, the increasing size of airports may be linked to urban growth (Sheard 2014; Button and Lall 1999). A hub airport with large passenger traffic, also plays a role in promoting economic activities. Finally, the DID effect, represented by coefficient E, is again estimated to be significantly positive in models C3 and C5. Overall, the above estimation results suggest that airport upgrading significantly increased GDP per capita by 11.0% to 12.2% from the year before upgrading to the year after upgrading. The evidence from the two-time frame and the continuous-year analyses may imply that the positive impact of airport upgrading on the regional economy occurs shortly after the upgrading projects and may continue for many years after the upgrading projects.

Table 5.3: Estimation Results of DID Models

Variable	Two-Time Frame DID		Continuous-Year Frame DID				
Model	Model T1	Model T2	Model C1	Model C2	Model C3	Model C4	Model C5
Treat	0.312**	−0.177*					
	(0.15)	(0.09)					
Time	1.125***	0.365**					
	(0.24)	(0.17)					
Treat * YB$_{2000}$							−0.087
							(−0.04)
Treat * YB$_{2001}$							−0.073*
							(−0.04)
Treat * YB$_{2002}$							−0.058
							(−0.04)
Treat * YB$_{2003}$							−0.048
							(−0.03)
D	0.274	0.443**					
	(0.26)	(0.20)					
E			1.102**		0.122***		0.110**
			(0.05)		(0.02)		(0.04)
Air passengers				0.542***		0.028**	
				(−0.01)		(0.01)	
College students		0.155***		0.051		0.082	0.054
		(0.05)		(0.06)		(0.06)	(0.06)
Population density		−0.043		−0.007		−0.009	−0.014
		(0.07)		(0.023)		(0.023)	(0.030)
Secondary industry		4.617***		2.055***		1.998***	2.079
		(0.91)		(0.35)		(0.35)	(1.35)
Tertiary industry		3.699***		1.545***		1.505***	1.535
		(0.90)		(−0.37)		(0.37)	(1.34)
Local fixed asset investment		0.147***		0.162***		0.129**	0.162***
		(0.05)		(0.05)		(0.05)	(0.05)
Foreign direct investment		−0.026		−0.012		−0.009	−0.011
		(0.04)		(−0.01)		(−0.01)	(−0.01)
Urban road density		0.366***		0.202***		0.201***	0.200***
		(0.08)		(0.03)		(0.03)	(0.06)
F-test							0.499
Year fixed effect			Yes	Yes	Yes	Yes	Yes
City fixed effect	Yes	Yes	Yes	Yes	Yes	Yes	Yes
R-squared	0.49	0.80	0.31	0.70	0.91	0.90	0.91
Observations	176	176	1,496	1,496	1,496	1,496	1,496

Notes:
(i) *, **, and *** indicate statistical significance at 10%, 5%, and 1% levels, respectively; parentheses represent the standard errors.
(ii) D = variable defined in equation (1); DID = difference-in-differences; E = variable defined in equation (2); and YB = variable defined in equation (2).
Source: Authors' estimation.

Differences of Economic Impacts from Airport Upgrading by Airport Size

Although the analysis demonstrated a positive impact of airport upgrading on regional economic productivity, the DID effect was assumed to be the same for all airports once airport upgrading was implemented. However, the economic impact of airport upgrading can vary depending on the size of the airports. In the PRC, expansion and/or modernization projects at hub airports and major domestic airports are well supported by the public as they are believed to lead to significant positive economic impacts as part of the hub-and-spoke strategy of the air transport network, while projects at branch airports have often led to major political disputes as they have sometimes had poor economic impacts and resulted in chronic losses. In order to study the differentiated effects of modernization between two types of airports, the economic impact of airport upgrading on regional GDP per capita is further estimated using the data of two subgroups according to the classification of the grade index of the airport's flight area: one is a lower subgroup that includes small branch airports (rank 4C or 4D, as of 2016) that are mainly responsible for a limited number of domestic airlines; the other is a higher subgroup that includes airports (rank 4E or 4F, as of 2016) that are allowed to land and take off dual-channel aircraft without restriction, which greatly increases capacity and operational efficiency. See the details of the definitions for 4C, 4D, 4E, and 4F in the Appendix.

Table 5.4 shows the results of the estimation with the models for the continuous-year frame DID. Models L1 and L2 show the results estimated with the lower subgroup data with and without the covariates, respectively, while models H1 and H2 show the results estimated with the upper subgroup data with and without the covariates, respectively. The results in the lower subgroup show that the estimated DID effect is significantly positive. The increase in regional GDP per capita due to branch airport upgrading is estimated to be about 16%, which is about 4% higher than the coefficient estimated with model C3 and 5% higher than that with model C5, as shown in Table 5.3. Meanwhile, the results in the higher subgroup show that the DID effect is insignificant. Finally, the estimation results show that a set of $Treat \cdot YB$ is estimated insignificantly in the lower subgroup. This suggests that regional GDP per capita in the treatment group is indifferent to that in the control group, supporting the assumption of a parallel trend. In the higher subgroup, however, they are estimated to be significantly negative, which means that regional GDP per capita is significantly negative, implying that regional GDP per capita is significantly lower in the treatment group than in the control group in 2000–2003. This may imply that airport upgrading was carried out at the cities with lower regional GDP per capita at higher-ranked airports. The results may also indicate that the estimated coefficients of $Treat \cdot YB$ vary within a fairly narrow range of −0.240 to −0.177. This might suggest that the gap between the treatment and control groups is quite stable during 2000–2003. From this, we could also conclude that the parallel trend assumption is only weakly supported even in the higher subgroup.

In summary, we conclude that the economic impact of airport upgrading is significantly positive for smaller branch airports, but insignificant for larger airports. This may be because the marginal impact of airport upgrading decreases as the size of the airport increases. This may be quite unexpected compared with previous debates in the PRC that hub airports are more likely to have significant impacts than rural airports.

Table 5.4: Continuous-Year Frame DID Models Estimated with Two Subgroups

	Lower Subgroup		Higher Subgroup	
	Model L1	Model L2	Model H1	Model H2
Treat * YB_{2000}	−0.168	−0.168	−0.240*	−0.240*
	(0.10)	(0.10)	(0.12)	(0.12)
Treat * YB_{2001}	−0.114	−0.072	−0.181**	−0.179**
	(0.08)	(0.07)	(0.07)	(0.08)
Treat * YB_{2002}	−0.084	−0.011	−0.192***	−0.177**
	(0.07)	(0.07)	(0.06)	(0.07)
Treat * YB_{2003}	−0.092	−0.021	−0.198***	−0.194***
	(0.05)	(0.05)	(0.05)	(0.07)
E	0.150**	0.161***	0.02	0.035
	(0.07)	(0.059)	(0.05)	(0.039)
Population Density		−0.017		−0.082
		(0.029)		(0.069)
Secondary Industry		1.676		7.941***
		(1.437)		(2.625)
Tertiary Industry		0.924		7.625***
		(1.417)		(2.475)
College Students		0.02		0.017
		(0.092)		(0.038)
Local Fixed Investment		0.065		0.100**
		(0.083)		(0.043)
Foreign Direct Investment		0.021		0.028
		0.014		0.021
Urban Road Density		0.234***		0.075
		(0.069)		(0.077)
F-test				
City Fixed Effect	Yes	Yes	Yes	Yes
Year Fixed Effect	Yes	Yes	Yes	Yes
R-squared	0.88	0.88	0.94	0.95
Number of Cities	50	50	38	38

DID = difference-in-differences.
Notes:
(i) *, **, and *** indicate statistical significance at the 10%, 5%, and 1% levels, respectively.
(ii) E = variable defined in equation (2), and YB = variable defined in equation (2).
Source: Authors' estimation.

Robustness Analysis

The timing effect of policy implementation could significantly affect estimation results with econometric modeling, as Moser and Voena (2012) point out. Counterfactual regression analysis is also conducted using data from 2000 to 2012 to test the robustness of the DID effect, by following Shao, Tian, and Yang (2017) and Moser and Voena (2012). For this robustness test, we artificially assume that the years of airport upgrading from 2004 to 2015 were 4 years earlier than the actual years. Since the new year of airport upgrading that we artificially set in our robustness test is wrong, it is expected that the estimation results with the wrong data set should be insignificant. Table 5.5 shows the results of the counterfactual tests with the pooled data set and the lower subgroup, both of which showed significant DID effects in the earlier analyses, as shown in Tables 5.3 and 5.4. This shows that the effect of airport upgrading is statistically insignificant in either model, confirming the economic effect of branch airport upgrading on regional economies.

Table 5.5: Results of Counterfactual Tests with Pooled Data Set and Lower Subgroup Data

	All Samples	Lower Subgroup
E	0.051	0.086
	(0.029)	(0.06)
College Students	0.021	0.015
	(0.066)	(0.10)
Population Density	−0.007	−0.011
	(0.040)	(0.03)
Secondary Industry	2.003	1.680
	(1.359)	(1.46)
Tertiary Industry	1.47	0.878
	(1.354)	(1.45)
Local Fixed Asset Investment	0.093*	0.061
	(0.053)	(0.09)
Foreign Direct Investment	0.021	0.014
	(0.066)	(0.097)
Urban Road Density	0.198***	0.243***
	(0.061)	(0.07)
Year Fixed Effect	Yes	Yes
City Fixed Effect	Yes	Yes
R-squared	0.70	0.75
Observation	1,496	1,496

Notes:
(i) *, **, and *** indicate statistical significance at the 10%, 5%, and 1% levels, respectively; parentheses represent the standard errors.
(ii) E = variable defined in equation (2).
Source: Authors' estimation.

5.5 Discussion

As shown earlier, our empirical study found that airport upgrading generally has a positive impact on regional economies. Through further analysis, we conclude that airport upgrading has significant positive effects on the regional economy for smaller airports, but not for larger airports. What factors then influence the positive economic impact of airport upgrading? To investigate this, we additionally estimate new models based on model C3, where the DID effect is structured by introducing interaction terms. Airport distance and HSR availability are included in the interaction term with the DID effect. It is hypothesized that the DID effect is stronger when the accessibility of the airport is better, while it is weaker when the HSR is available.

The estimation results are summarized in Table 5.6. First, the estimation results of model C3-a indicate that *E*Airport Distance* has a significant negative association with regional GDP per capita. That is, the DID effect becomes smaller when the airport is farther from the downtown area. This is quite plausible, as it is expected that airport upgrading at the urban fringe has more economic impact than in non-urban areas, mainly due to better agglomeration effects in urban areas. This could suggest that the economic impact of the airport system is unlikely to work without the support of the urban environment, as shown by Appold (2015). The results may also indirectly suggest the pivotal role of airport ground access, along with airport capacity expansion, in characterizing airport-led economic development (Murakami, Matsui, and Kato 2016) in cities with an airport located far from the city center.

Table 5.6: Estimation Results of Model C3 with Interaction Terms

	Model C3-a	Model C3-b	Model C3-c
E	0.174** (0.087)	0.233** (0.095)	0.120** (0.049)
E * Airport Distance	−0.006* (0.004)		
E * City HSR Availability		−0.155* (0.093)	
E * Yearly HSR Availability			−0.005 (0.051)
College Students	0.025 (0.062)	0.034 (0.060)	0.023 (0.064)
Population Density	0.001 (0.039)	0.002 (0.039)	0.001 (0.040)
Secondary Industry Ratio	1.852 (1.365)	1.784 (1.356)	1.906 (1.360)
Tertiary Industry Ratio	1.397 (1.358)	1.318 (1.350)	1.440 (1.352)
Local Fixed Investment	0.110** (0.049)	0.098** (0.048)	0.110** (0.049)
Foreign Direct Investment	−0.009 (0.012)	−0.008 (0.012)	−0.008 (0.012)
Urban Road Density	0.181*** (0.053)	0.176*** (0.051)	0.189*** (0.056)
Year Fixed Effect	Yes	Yes	Yes
City Fixed Effect	Yes	Yes	Yes
R-squared	0.46	0.46	0.46
Observations	1,496	1,496	1,496

Notes: *, **, and *** indicate statistical significance at the 10%, 5%, and 1% levels, respectively. The numbers in parentheses represent the standard errors. E = variable defined in equation (2).
Source: Authors' estimation.

Next, the estimation results of model C3-b show that *E*City HSR availability* is estimated to be significantly negative. This suggests that the effect of airport upgrading on the regional economy is more remarkable in cities where HSR has not yet been introduced than in cities where HSR has been introduced. This is because the cities where HSR has been introduced tend to be large cities with higher-ranked airports, which could have a less significant effect, as shown earlier.

Finally, the estimation results of model C3-c show the insignificance of *E*Yearly HSR availability*, suggesting that the effect is not significantly affected by HSR availability. This may be unexpected since we hypothesized that the economic impact of airport upgrading decreases when HSR, another competitive interregional transportation service, is available. The independence of the economic impact of airport upgrading from HSR availability is probably because the impact mechanism of airport upgrading is different from that of HSR. The impact of airport upgrading may affect air-transportation-related industries or high-productivity industries that cover the global market, such as finance and insurance businesses, while the impact of HSR may affect medium-productivity industries that cover the domestic market, such as real estate, manufacturing, and service businesses.

5.6 Conclusion

This study empirically examined the impact of airport upgrading on regional economies using the DID method. The data set includes 88 cities with operating airports in the PRC and covers the period from 2000 to 2015. The two-time frame DID models and continuous-year frame DID models are employed to investigate the DID effect. A counterfactual test based on the upgrade year reset supports our main findings. This study reaches three main conclusions. First, the estimation results of the baseline models containing all sample cities showed that regional GDP per capita could be increased by 11.0% to 12.2% by upgrading the airports. Second, further estimation of models with two subgroups of larger and smaller airports showed that DID effects are significantly estimated in regions with smaller airports, but insignificant in regions with larger airports. These results suggest that the investment of branch airports in poorly developed regions could contribute to economic development despite their chronic losses. Third, in the discussion section, we find further evidence that airport location contributes to the distributional effects of airport upgrading on the urban economy, suggesting the importance of integrating airport planning with urban planning and comprehensive transportation planning. The additional analysis also found that HSR may not affect the economic impacts of airport upgrading.

Although this study did not find significant impacts of upgrading larger airports, upgrading larger airports cannot be described as unattainable. The caveat of this research is that we ignore the microscopic productivity effects of airport upgrading. For example, the airport side will generate employment sectors and economic activities around the airport to improve industrial productivity when the airport becomes larger after upgrading. Larger airports are more prominent than small airports in these aspects. Similarly, the hub-and-spoke air system will also promote air-related industrial agglomeration toward the city with larger airports and improve productivity. Therefore, in addition to improving accessibility, cities with larger airports could also experience positive spillover effects from improvements in air industrial productivity after airport upgrading and from industrial agglomeration emanating from surrounding cities as the airport becomes larger and predominant. Such analyses go beyond our research and suggest that our findings are more likely due to macro-level improvements in economic productivity. Another issue may be understanding the dynamics of airport upgrading impacts. Although our study showed that economic impacts occur immediately after airport upgrading and are likely to last for many years, it did not examine the time lag of economic impacts. This could be analyzed empirically with further models using the data. We await future research to learn more about the impact of airport upgrading on productivity improvement in developing economies such as the PRC.

Appendix 5.1: Cities and Their Regions in the Data Set

Table A5-1: Cities and Their Regions in the Data Set

City	Region	City	Region	City	Region
Beijing	Eastern	Changchun	Northeastern	Lianyungang	Eastern
Guangzhou	Eastern	Hefei	Central	Huangshan	Central
Shenzhen	Eastern	Hohhot	Western	Mianyang	Western
Chengdu	Western	Lanzhou	Western	Mudanjiang	Northeastern
Kunming	Western	Yinchuan	Western	Jingdezhen	Central
Xi'an	Western	Lijiang	Western	Changde	Central
Hangzhou	Eastern	Wuxi	Eastern	Luoyang	Central
Chongqing	Western	Yantai	Eastern	Nantong	Eastern
Xiamen	Eastern	Quanzhou	Eastern	Yibin	Western
Wuhan	Central	Zhuhai	Eastern	Luzhou	Western
Changsha	Central	Xining	Western	Pu'er	Western
Nanjing	Eastern	Shijiazhuang	Eastern	Ganzhou	Central
Qingdao	Eastern	Shantou	Eastern	Jiamusi	Northeastern
Dalian	Northeastern	Zhangjiajie	Central	Chifeng	Western
Haikou	Eastern	Baotou	Eastern	Yancheng	Eastern
Shenyang	Northeastern	Weihai	Eastern	Xiangyang	Central
Zhengzhou	Central	Yichang	Central	Baoshan	Western
Urumqi	Western	Yulin	Western	Nanyang	Central
Harbin	Northeastern	Jinhua	Eastern	Quzhou	Eastern
Jinan	Eastern	Changzhou	Eastern	Qiqihar	Northeastern
Tianjin	Eastern	Hulunbuir	Western	Wuhai	Western
Guiyang	Western	Taizhou	Eastern	Lincang	Western
Fuzhou	Eastern	Xuzhou	Eastern	Weifang	Eastern
Guilin	Western	Beihai	Eastern	Tongliao	Western
Wenzhou	Eastern	Zhoushan	Eastern	Nanchong	Western
Taiyuan	Central	Zhanjiang	Eastern	Fuyang	Eastern
Nanning	Western	Changzhi	Western	Jiayuguan	Western
Ningbo	Eastern	Liuzhou	Western	Dongying	Eastern
Nanchang	Central	Linyi	Eastern	Anqing	Central

Source: Authors.

Appendix 5.2: Aerodrome Reference Code

One of the methods used to categorize airports is the maximum size of aircraft for which the airport is designed. This study follows the definitions of the Aerodrome Reference Code given by the International Civil Aviation Organization (ICAO).

Table A5-2: Definitions of Aerodrome Reference Code for 4A to 4F

Numeric Number	Code letter	Wingspan (meter)	Outer main gear wheel span (meter)	Typical aircraft
4	A	< 15	< 4.5	PIPER PA-31/CESSNA 404 Titan
	B	15–24	4.5–6	BOMBARDIER Regional Jet CRJ-200/
	C	24–36	6–9	BOEING 737-700/AIRBUS A-320/EMBRAER ERJ 190-100
	D	36–52	9–14	B767 Series/AIRBUS A-310
	E	52–65	9–14	B777 Series/B787 Series/A330 Family
	F	65–80	14–16	BOEING 747-8/AIRBUS A-380-800

Source: International Civil Aviation Organization.

References

Appold, S. J. 2015. Airport Cities and Metropolitan Labor Markets: An Extension and Response to Cidell. *Journal of Economic Geography.* 15 (6). pp. 1145–1168.

Appold, S. J. and J. D. Kasada. 2013. The Airport City Phenomenon: Evidence from Large US Airports. *Urban Studies.* 50 (6). pp. 1239–1259.

Baker, D., R. Merkert, and M. Kamruzzaman. 2015. Regional Aviation and Economic Growth: Cointegration and Causality Analysis in Australia. *Journal of Transport Geography.* 43. pp. 140–150.

Bel, G. and X. Fageda. 2008. Getting There Fast: Globalization, Intercontinental Flights and Location of Headquarters. *Journal of Economic Geography.* 8 (4). pp. 471–495.

Blumenthal, P., H. L. Wolman, and E. Hill. 2009. Understanding the Economic Performance of Metropolitan Areas in the United States. *Urban Studies.* 46 (3). pp. 605–627.

Bonnefoy, P. A. 2008. Scalability of the Air Transportation System and Development of Multi-Airport Systems: A Worldwide Perspective. Ph D Dissertation. Massachusetts Institute of Technology.

Brueckner, J. K. 2003. Airline Traffic and Urban Economic Development. *Urban Studies.* 40 (8). pp. 1455–1469.

Button, K. and S. Lall. 1999. The Economics of Being an Airport Hub City. *Research in Transportation Economics.* 5. pp. 75–105.

Civil Aviation Administration of China (CAAC). 2018. *Statistical Bulletin of Civil Aviation*.

Hu, K., X. Gan, and K. Gao. 2012. Co-Integration Model of Logistics Infrastructure Investment and Regional Economic Growth in Central China. 2012 International Conference on Medical Physics and Biomedical Engineering (Icmpbe2012). 33. pp. 1036–1041.

International Air Transport Association (IATA). 2015. *Annual Review 2016*.

Moser, P. and A. Voena. 2012. Compulsory Licensing: Evidence from the Trading with the Enemy Act. *American Economic Review*. 102 (1). pp. 396–427.

Murakami, J., Y. Matsui, and H. Kato. 2016. Airport Rail Links and Economic Productivity: Evidence from 82 Cities with the World's 100 Busiest Airports. *Transport Policy*. 52. pp. 89–99.

Shao, S., Z. H. Tian, and L. L. Yang. 2017. High Speed Rail and Urban Service Industry Agglomeration: Evidence from China's Yangtze River Delta Region. *Journal of Transport Geography*. 64. pp. 174–183.

Sheard, N. 2014. Airports and Urban Sectoral Employment. *Journal of Urban Economics*. 80. pp. 133–152.

Sun, B. W., H. T. Yu, Z. R. Peng, and Y. Gao. 2017. High-Speed Rail and Manufacturing Agglomeration: Evidence from Beijing-Guangzhou High-Speed Rail in China. *Transportation Research Record: Journal of the Transportation Research Board*. 2606. pp. 86–95.

Wu, S. G. W. 2017. Airports, Market Access and Local Economic Performance: Evidence from China. SERC Discussion Papers. Spatial Economics Research Centre, LSE.

Yu, N., M. De Jong, S. Storm, and J. Mi. 2012. Transport Infrastructure, Spatial Clusters and Regional Economic Growth in China. *Transport Reviews*. 32 (1). pp. 3–28.

Zheng, S. Q., W. Z. Sun, J. F. Wu, and M. E. Kahn. 2017. The Birth of Edge Cities in China: Measuring the Effects of Industrial Parks Policy. *Journal of Urban Economics*. 100. pp. 80–103.

Chapter 6

Survival Analysis of Airport Upgrade Intervals: Evidence from the People's Republic of China

6.1 Introduction

In the People's Republic of China (PRC), about 4 billion domestic trips and over 100 million international trips were made in 2015 (Liu 2016). They continue to grow the fastest, accounting for 21.6% of the total increase in global air passenger traffic from 2015 to 2016 (ACI 2017). Meanwhile, the PRC has developed an extensive international air route network with 844 routes connecting 167 cities in 61 countries (CAAC 2018), and it is expected to expand further. Despite the prospects of continuing security concerns, economic uncertainties, and fierce traffic market competition from high-speed railways (HSR) in the PRC's domestic intercity transportation market, a little deviation from this upward trend in air traffic demand is anticipated. About 1 billion passengers are forecast to travel through airports in the PRC annually by 2022. In line with the strong growth in air traffic demand, there has been extensive investment in airport infrastructure, including the introduction of new airports and the expansion of existing airport facilities in the PRC. These airport investments have been made primarily to meet rapidly growing demand, but more recently to boost regional economic growth. This is because airports are expected to directly and indirectly create local jobs related to supporting airport operations, and this could lead to better economic performance in nearby regions, in addition to directly facilitating better quality interregional business/leisure travel and cargo transportation as the critical gateways of the global air traffic network (Brueckner 2003; Wu, Liang, and Wu 2016). In reality, the Civil Aviation Administration of China (CAAC) has emphasized airport upgrading projects, such as enhancing the capacity of existing airports, rather than increasing the number of airports in the country.

This chapter focuses on the Airport Upgrade Project (AUP). The AUP primarily refers to the construction of new facilities, such as terminal buildings and runways, at existing airports to provide additional space for future traffic demand. In the late 1990s, many airport authorities began using AUPs to expand capacity. In the 2000s, anticipated growth in air transportation demand required further new investment in stand-alone terminals to accommodate customs, entry and exit procedures, and runways to accommodate large-scale aircraft operations for long-haul flights. This trend continues in the PRC. The 11th Five-Year Plan (2006–2010) for National Civil Aviation proposed 78 AUPs, while the 12th Five-Year Plan (2011–2015) proposed 101 AUPs.

Many studies have examined a linkage between airport investments and their outcomes, such as impacts on regional economies and employment agglomeration. However, few studies have highlighted the potential factors that influence airport investments. AUPs could be motivated by factors such as urbanization structure changes in sociodemographic characteristics of cities, and growth in air traffic demand. It is a simple fact that an airport built more recently tends to be located far from the center of the metropolitan area it serves (Rodrigue 2017). This may reflect the physical expansion of urban areas, which has led to changes in the availability of space or the geographic distribution of population and influenced the process of airport investment. Although it is highly likely that airport planning and development are related to urban development, these factors have rarely been studied.

This study attempts to analyze a relationship between the socioeconomic characteristics of cities and the time intervals for airport upgrade, using historical data of airport development in the PRC. It focuses on the authorities' decision on airport upgrades in the face of local characteristics that change over time in terms of urban and airport development. The remainder of this chapter proceeds as follows. The next section provides a literature review on airport development. A statistical model is then developed to explain an airport upgrade interval assuming analogy to survival models, followed by the development of the data set used for model estimation. Then the empirical analysis is presented with a discussion of the results. Finally, conclusions and further perspectives are presented.

6.2 Literature Review

Many studies have examined the relationship between airport development and related factors. First, the impact of airports on regional economies has been well studied by many researchers such as Baker, Merkert, and Kamruzzaman (2015); Marazzo, Scherre, and Fernandes (2010); Bilotkach (2015); and Bel and Fageda (2008). The consensus of these studies is, not surprisingly, that airports have positive impacts on regional GDP, income growth in neighboring regions, increase in business establishments and headquarters, or promotion of a service-oriented economy in surrounding regions. However, there are few studies that empirically demonstrate the reverse effect, i.e., the impact of urban and/or regional factors on airport development, although urbanization and regional characteristics could influence airport-related development, including airport expansion. There are also many studies that focus the social impacts of airport externalities. Airports introduced in the 1980s or earlier were generally located on the periphery of cities. After the 2000s, they were surrounded by suburbs following the rapid expansion of the urbanized area. This has led to social problems as more people who have migrated from rural areas to the outskirts of cities have suffered negative externalities from airports such as aircraft noise and air pollution (Rodrigue 2017). Some studies have provided empirical evidence of the negative externalities of airports. For example, Feitelson, Hurd, and Mudge (1996) reported the effects of aircraft noise caused by airport expansion on people's willingness to pay for their residence. These studies extensively emphasized the social impact of airport externalities on residential and traffic planning around airports. However, the reverse effect has rarely been highlighted, even though airport externalities would encourage airport modernization, including relocation of airports and/or reallocation of air operations by introducing the multi-airport system to minimize the negative externalities of urban airports.

Meanwhile, some researchers have recently emphasized the integrated development of airports with neighboring areas, rather than only the development of airports. This reflects the recent practice of strategically planning some airport regions to promote linkages between the airport and its neighboring regions, including airport-related services and businesses (Smit, Koopman, and

Faber 2013). This creates a form of metropolitan development known as the "aerotropolis" (Rodrigue 2017). The concept of the airport city or aerotroplis has already been accepted in some developed countries, where busy city airports act as functional centers of large metropolitan areas, creating jobs for passengers and serving frequent travelers (Appold 2015; Brueckner 2003). For example, Appold and Kasarda (2013) have shown that employment in areas less than 2.5 miles from major US airports accounts for about 50% of employment in areas less than 2.5 miles from the central business district (CBD) of their respective cities. The PRC has also proposed a number of AUPs that follow the aerotropolis concept. For example, the authority has officially approved a development project for the Zhengzhou Airport Economic Zone along with the second-phase of expansion of the Xinzheng International Airport, formally establishing the first national economic zone (Kasarda and Lindsay 2011). This is expected to improve the match between airline business and airport-related industries through skilled labor and develop an industrial chain that attracts air travelers and other service sectors. It is debatable whether airport cities are anchored by airport size or city size (Cidell 2014). One of the remarkable findings is that the share of metropolitan employment in areas less than a mile away from top US airports is negatively related to the distance of airports from CBDs, but not to the size or the relative amount of air traffic to the metropolitan population (Appold 2015). These results may suggest that urban land use patterns, such as employment suburbanization, influence the scale and/or size of airport cities and provide the basis for further information on the trend toward airport-urban integration.

In addition, airport ground access has also been highlighted as a means for the first-/last-mile trips to/from airports, as more and more airports have recently been built in areas that are far from CBDs. However, airport ground access is increasingly seen as one of the major regional/social problems in many countries due to its negative impacts in terms of traffic congestion and environmental degradation (Humphreys et al. 2005). As private vehicle use continues to dominate airport access/egress trips in many developed countries (Humphreys and Ison 2005), public transportation for airport access is expected to reduce the environmental impact of airport access/egress trips while meeting growing consumer demand in terms of environmental sustainability (Budd, Ison, and Budd 2016). Loo (2008) has also empirically shown that airport ground access is one of the most important airport level-of-service (LOS) attributes for passengers' choice of airport. However, airport ground access has not been well studied in the context of airport development decision-making, although airport relocation should be determined to provide a balance between acceptable externalities and accessibility to the urban core (Rodrigue 2017).

In summary, many airport-related studies have analyzed the economic impacts of airport development, the negative externalities of airport operations, the expected impacts of the airport city, and the impacts of introducing ground access to the airport. However, few studies have shed light on the supply side of airport investment: what factors affect airport investment? This study attempts to fill this gap with a case study of airport development in the PRC.

6.3 Model

This study analyzes airport upgrades in the PRC using historical data and survival analysis. Survival analysis is usually applied in the field of epidemiology, but recently it has been extended to other research areas, such as the analysis of the life span of bridge structures. This study assumes an analogy with epidemiology, in which a human subject corresponds to an airport. In contrast, the death of a human being corresponds to the airport upgrade as an affected event.

The survival model can be divided into two parts: survival curve fitting and risk factors of modeling. The first part involves the use of a Kaplan–Meier (KM) estimator to estimate a survival curve, and the second part involves a quantitative analysis using a Cox model with time-varying covariates. In this study, a Cox regression model is used to assess the relationship between urban characteristics and airport upgrades. First, let $X_i = \{X_i 1. \cdots , X_{ip}\}$ be the values of the covariates of subject i, then a traditional Cox regression model has the form:

$$\lambda(t|X_i) = \lambda_0(t) \exp(\beta_1 X_{i1} + \cdots + \beta_p X_{ip}) = \lambda(t) \exp\left(\sum \beta_j X_j\right) = \lambda_0(t) \exp(\beta'X) \qquad (1)$$

Traditional survival models can be viewed as consisting of two parts: the underlying baseline hazard function, often denoted $\lambda_0(t)$, describing how the risk of an event per time unit changes over time at baseline levels of covariates, and the effect parameters $\exp(\beta'X)$, describing how the hazard varies in response to explanatory covariates. A partial likelihood function shown in equation (2) is maximized to estimate the unknown coefficient vector β:

$$L(\beta) = \prod_{i=1}^{n} \left[\frac{\exp\{\beta' Z_i(X_i)\}}{\sum_{\{j \in R(X_i)\}} \exp\{\beta' Z_j(X_i)\}}\right]^{\sigma_i} \qquad (2)$$

In our case, the events in question may occur multiple times for a single subject, and the covariates also vary over time. Most Cox models in medical research assume that an endpoint of death occurs only once during a disease-recovery process. In the case of airports, however, there is no event of death as in the case of a human being. Note that death should be a unique and once-in-a-lifetime event. However, in the case of infrastructure such as airports, multiple events usually occur during their lifetime, such as facilities upgrades. Therefore, the consideration of multiple events can play a significant role in the empirical analysis of infrastructure.

There are several approaches to dealing with multiple events in the analysis. A simple way to implement the analysis follows the counting process approach (Andersen and Gill 1982). The basic assumption is that all event types are equal or indistinguishable. In this way, the problem can be reduced to the analysis of time to first event, time to second event, and so on. Therefore, the risk set at time t for the event contains all subjects who are still under observation (i.e., whose ages are larger than t at the beginning of time t. Among the various model specifications, this study applies the Gap model (Shu and Schaubel 2016), in which the Cox model measures the time to each upgrade from the occurrence of a previous event. This model assumes that the clock is set to zero after each failure, which means that the Gap model can manage the time interval of the airport upgrade.

In this study, the event is assumed to refer to every airport upgrade since opening. In contrast, the risk (hazard) of an event per time represents the probability that an upgrade will occur at that time, as time since the last event is measured. The Cox model with time-dependent covariates, which examines the timing of the upgrade since the last upgrade in response to the explanatory characteristics, is necessary. The Cox model with time-dependent covariates is specified as below:

$$\lambda(t|X(t)) = \lambda_0(t)\exp(\beta'X(t)) = \lambda_0(t)\exp\left(\sum \beta_j X_j(t)\right) \quad (3)$$

The hazard at time t depends only on the covariates at the corresponding time t, i.e., $X(t)$. Note that the regression effect of $X(t)$ is constant β over time. The advantage of the Cox model with time-dependent covariate is that the model can compare the risk of an event between time-dependent covariates at each event time.

6.4 Data

To assess the relationship between the cross-city timing of the airport upgrade and distributional socioeconomic characteristics, the authors developed a data set of upgraded airport information, a year of airport upgrade, urban characteristics, and other airport-level and city-level characteristics.

Airport Upgrade

In the past, most cities in the PRC have upgraded their airports through a series of planning, approval, and construction phases that are directly guided by the government. Based on expected air traffic demand and other development needs of the city, the central government and provincial/city authorities permit physical upgrades to their airports and update licenses. Data are mainly collected through internet sources such as the official websites of airport authorities, mass media, and encyclopedias. The data set contains information on airport upgrade events, including the year of completion of the airport upgrade, airport upgrade strategy, and details on the airport upgrade.

Figure 6.1 shows the multiple AUPs in 79 cities covered by the data set. The X axis shows their ID (1-79), and the Y axis shows the years in which airport operations began and airport upgrades were completed. Each vertical line starting with the red point (opening year) represents the life span of an airport system with multiple AUPs. Note that the end of the line does not represent "death" or "censorship," but rather that no further airport upgrades were made until 2019. The data set originally included all civil airports in the PRC that were ranked 4D or higher status in 2019.

Figure 6.2 shows the geographic distribution of AUPs in the PRC in the 1980s, 1990s, 2000s, and 2010s, respectively. The circle represents the airport upgrade, and its size denotes the period between the last airport upgrade or the start of airport operations and the corresponding year. The colors of the circle represent the ICAO aerodrome reference code (ARC) of the airport immediately before the airport upgrade.

Airports that have been out of civil aviation service for years have been removed from the candidate airports in our data set. This results in the data set containing 122 AUPs, of which nine AUPs implemented airport relocation and two AUPs implemented multiple airport systems (MAS). With the exception of the first phase AUP at Chengdu in the 1960s, all AUPs were introduced in the 1980s or later.

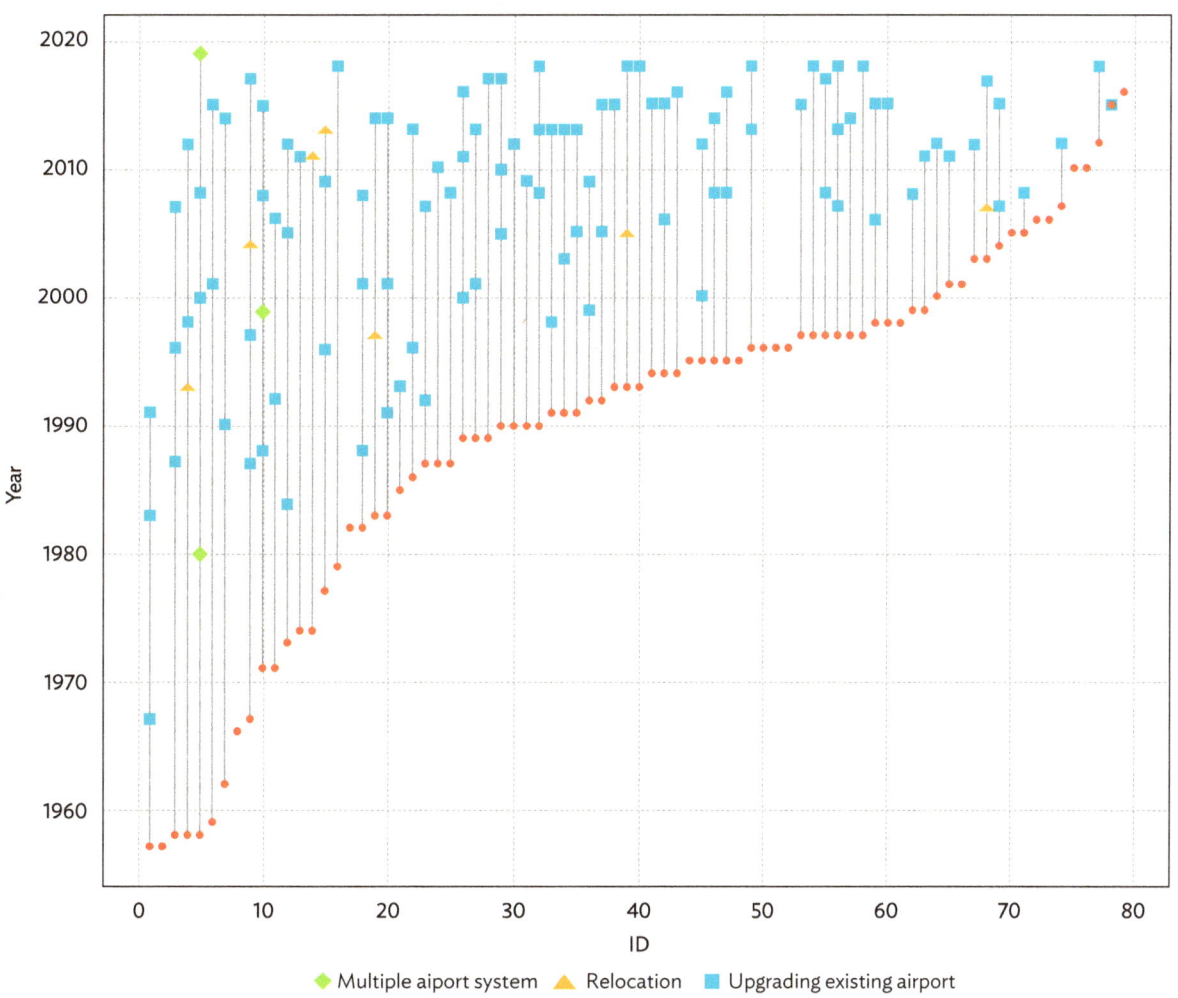

Figure 6.1: Multiple Airport Upgrade Projects in the Data Set

◆ Multiple aiport system ▲ Relocation ■ Upgrading existing airport

Source: Authors' estimation, based on the Statistical Yearbook of Civil Airport.

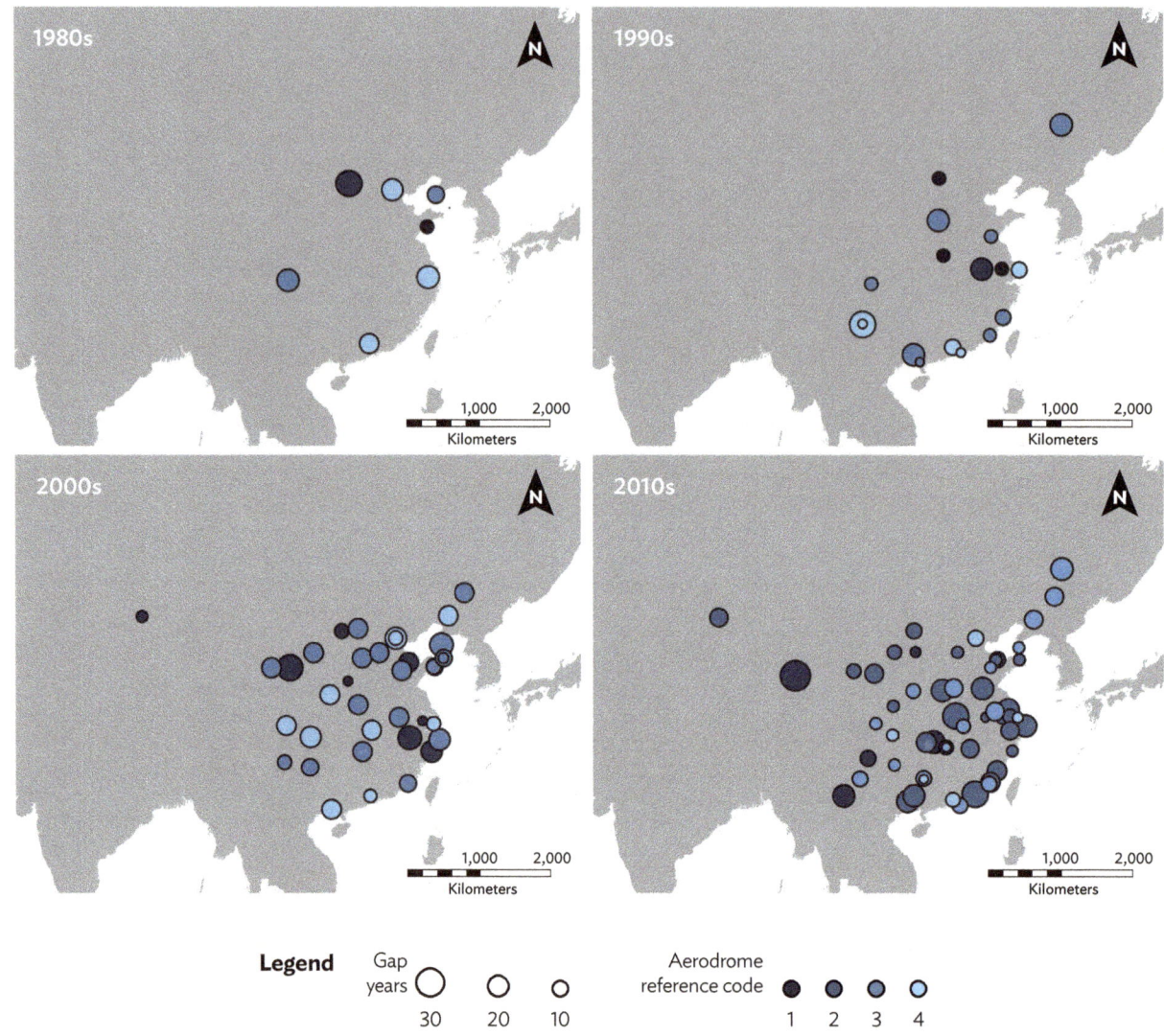

Figure 6.2: Airport Upgrade in Different Decades

Note: This map was produced by Authors. The boundaries, colors, denominations, and any other information shown on this map do not imply, on the part of the Asian Development Bank, any judgment on the legal status of any territory, or any other endorsement or acceptance of such boundaries, colors, denominations, or information.
Source: Authors' estimation, based on the Statistical Yearbook of Civil Airport.

Urban Characteristics

This study hypothesizes that the urban characteristics of a city where the airport has been upgraded affect the time interval of airport upgrade. The data on urban characteristics are obtained from the city statistics data from the China City Statistical Yearbooks accessed by China National Knowledge Infrastructure and from the urban statistical bulletins published on local government websites. When data were not available in the statistical yearbook, we searched other data sources, such as the official websites of local governments.

This study considers three types of variables related to urban characteristics. First, the urbanization rate represents a percentage of the urban population out of the total population residing in urban areas, which the central government defines. Our empirical analysis uses an "urbanization dummy" that takes the value of 1 if the urbanization rate is 50% or more, and 0 otherwise. Second, the tertiary industry ratio represents the ratio of tertiary industry added value to gross regional production (GRP) in a city. This represents the current economic situation at the time of the airport upgrade. An economic structure dominated by tertiary industry could be a risk factor encouraging airport upgrade projects from both a sustainable economic and aviation development perspective. Our empirical analysis uses a "tertiary industry dummy" that takes the value of 1 when the share of tertiary industry is 50% or more, and 0 otherwise. Third, urban population density represents the population density in urban areas. In our empirical analysis, we use the "urban population density dummy," which is set to 1 if the urban population density is 1,000 persons per square kilometer (km^2) or more, and 0 otherwise.

Airport/City Characteristics

We included factors related to airports and city characteristics in the empirical model. First, airports are classified according to their status by the Government of the PRC. As shown in Table 6.1, 23 major airports are designated as international hubs, regional hubs, or major domestic airports. Our model uses the variable "hub and main domestic airport dummy," which is defined to be 1 if an airport is one of the 23 major airports, and 0 otherwise.

Table 6.1: Airport Classification in the PRC

Special Airport City Category (Number)	Main Served City
International hub cities (3)	Beijing, Shanghai, Guangzhou
Regional hub cities (8)	Chongqing, Chengdu, Wuhan, Zhengzhou, Shenyang, Xi'an, Kunming, Urumqi
Main domestic airport cities (12)	Shenzhen, Nanjing, Hangzhou, Qingdao, Dalian, Nanchang, Nanning, Changsha, Xiamen, Harbin, Lanzhou, Hohhot

PRC = People's Republic of China.
Source: Authors.

Second, the city-tier system was introduced by the central government in the 1980s. The city-tier system facilitates the staged rollout of infrastructure and urban development throughout the country. The prospects of a city's commercial vitality and real estate development are based on its population size, economic size, and political rank. It has become a proxy for demographic and social segmentation. This study follows the most recent ranking by Phoenix News Agency. Our empirical study applies a "first- and second-tier city" dummy, defined to be 1 if a city belongs to the first- or second-tier city group, and 0 otherwise. Third, we also introduce a dummy variable for "tourism location," which has a value of 1 if a city is located in a tourism location or a county-level city, and 0 otherwise. A total of 11 cities are included in this group. Most airports built in county-level cities are located at high altitude and require a longer runway due to lower air density. Most county-level cities have seen only a small increase in visitors to date. However, it is likely that more airports will be built in the county-level cities in the future, mainly to replace inadequate ground transportation to connect them to major markets and to manage the increasing demand of tourist traffic. For example, Dunhuang Airport (DNH) is located in an oasis city in the Gobi Desert that lies on the ancient Silk Road and has become a major tourist destination. Note that its air routes have long been limited to connecting flights to adjacent major airports (e.g., Dunhuang–Xi'an/Lanzhou; Lijiang–Kunming; Hotan–Urumqi). Fourth, the ICAO Aerodrome Reference Code (ARC) represents a categorization of aircraft types based on their ability to use a given aerodrome. Rank 4E or higher is a basic requirement for cities that can accommodate large aircraft for long-haul international operations. Our empirical study applies the "4E/4F airport dummy," which is defined to be 1 if a city has an airport ranked 4E or 4F in ARC before airport upgrade, and 0 otherwise. Fifth, "distance to the city center" is also considered one of the potential explanatory variables in our empirical model. The distance is measured by a straight-line distance between the airport and the city center in kilometers. In the case of MAS, we took the average of the distances to the city center of each airport.

The descriptive statistics of our data set are summarized in Table 6.2. The mean value of the hub or major domestic airport is 0.4, with only 22 hub airport cities out of 79 samples contributing to it, which means that the upgrade times are relatively higher than those of branch airports. The mean value of the dummy for the proportion of urban population is 0.359, and the mean value of the dummy for the proportion of tertiary industry is 0.652, which represents the high status of tertiary industry of overall subjects. The mean value of the dummy for urban population density is 0.470.

Table 6.2: Descriptive Statistics of Data Set

Variable	Mean	Standard Error	Min.	Max.
Urban characteristics				
Urbanization dummy	0.359	0.481	0	1
Tertiary industry dummy	0.652	0.478	0	1
Urban population density dummy	0.470	0.500	0	1
Airport/city characteristics				
Hub and main domestic airport dummy	0.399	0.491	0	1
First/second tier city dummy	0.601	0.491	0	1
Ln (Distance to the city central)	2.819	0.632	0.693	4.317
4E/4F airport dummy	0.414	0.494	0	1
Tourism location/county-level city dummy	0.0808	0.273	0	1

Ln = log.
Note: 4E/4F = Indexes defined in Appendix of Chapter 5.
Source: Authors' estimation, based on the China City Statistical Yearbooks and Statistical Yearbook of Civil Airport.

6.5 Results

Survival Analysis of Airport Upgrade

Figure 6.3 shows the relationship between the time to first upgrade of airports and the age of airports in 2019. The time to first airport upgrade is defined as the period from the start of airport operations to 2019. This figure clearly shows that younger airports tend to have a shorter time to first upgrade. This means that airports that have been built recently tend to be upgraded within a shorter period of time after they begin operations.

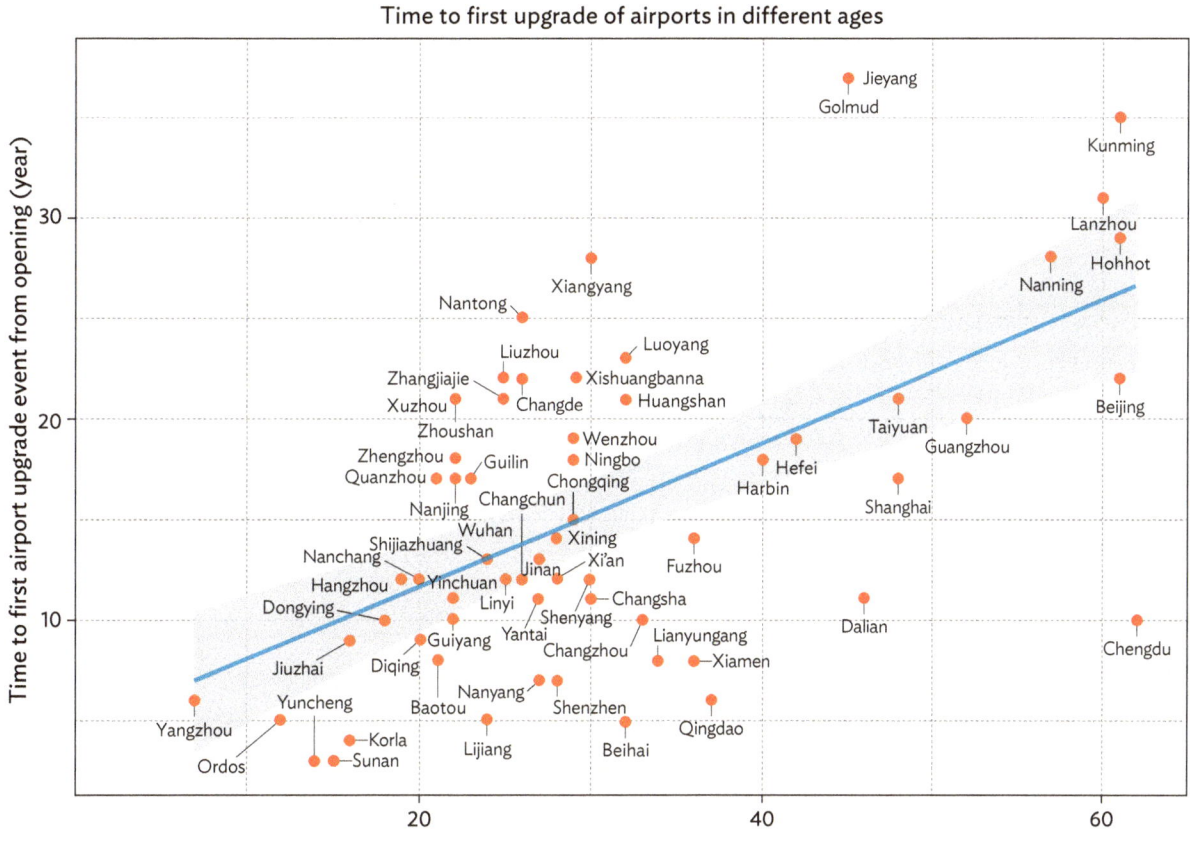

Figure 6.3: Time to First Upgrade of Airports versus Age of Airports as of 2019

Source: Authors' estimation, based on the Statistical Yearbook of Civil Airport.

The Kaplan–Meier method is widely used to estimate a survival function from censored survival data. Figure 6.4 shows a cumulative survival probability function and the Kaplan–Meier empirical hazard at each time point at which AUPs occurred. The hazard increases in the third year to about the 10th year and in the 15th year to about the 20th year. If we look at the risk rate (not that many cities were censored for more than 40 years), the hazard (upgrade probability) is higher between 10 and 13 years and then again between 22 and 25 years. Figure 6.5 also shows a cumulative survival probability and the Kaplan–Meier empirical hazard within 1 year of an upgrade since the last event. The hazard is higher between 5 and 15 years.

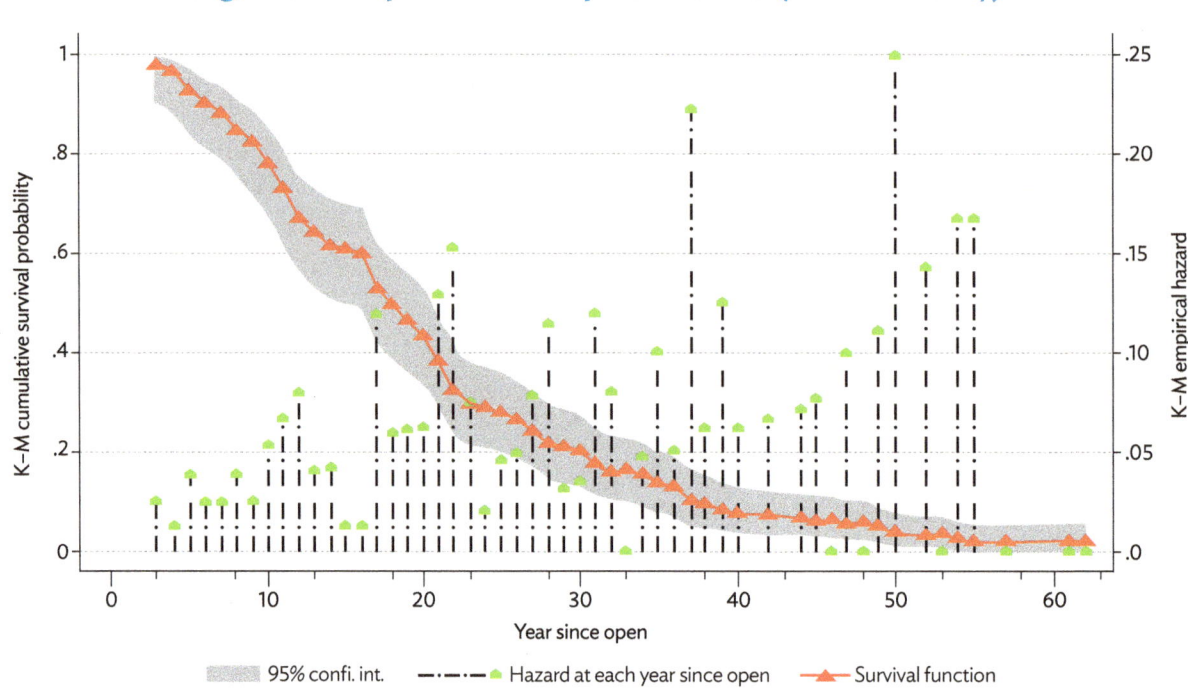

Figure 6.4: Kaplan–Meier Empirical Hazard (Time from Entry)

K–M = Kaplan–Meier.
Source: Authors' estimation.

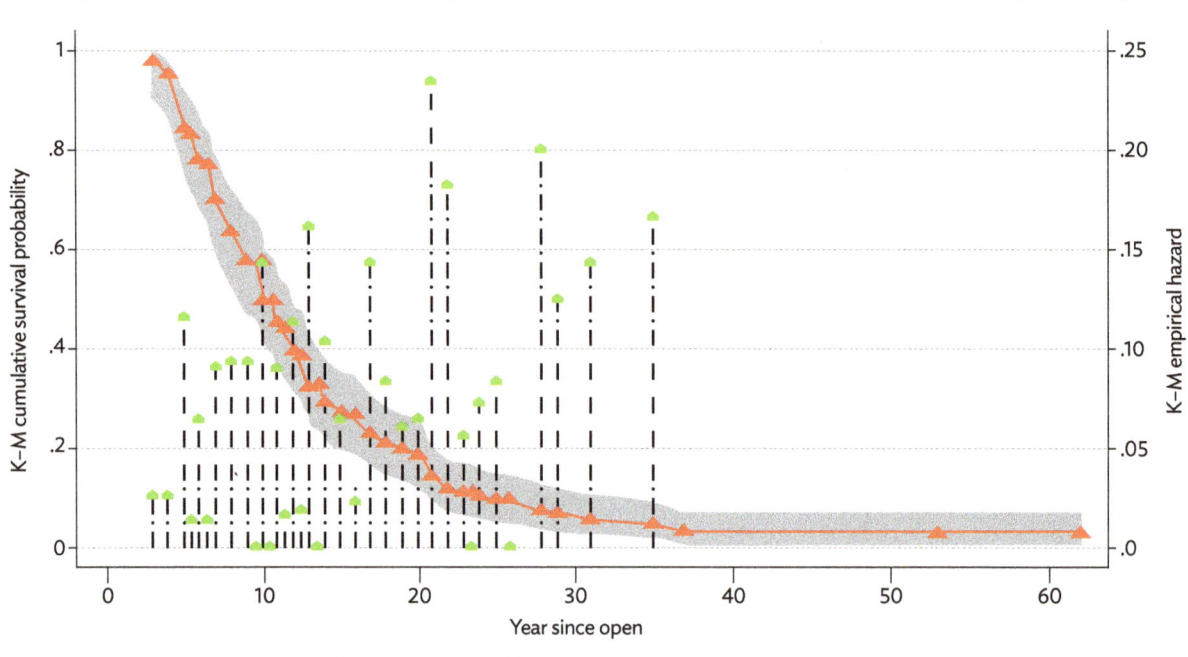

Figure 6.5: Kaplan–Meier Empirical Hazard (Time from Previous Event-Gap Model)

K–M = Kaplan–Meier.
Source: Authors' estimation.

Figure 6.6 shows the cumulative hazards for consecutive airport upgrade. It clearly shows that the "risk" of an upgrade project does not remain constant, while it depends on the previous upgrade. This means that the application of traditional Kaplan–Meier or Cox regression analysis may be inappropriate because risk factors are assumed to be fixed in the traditional approach. Thus, risks are typically measured at a baseline such as the geographic conditions of a city or at the end of the study period, such as the distance between the airport and the city center after the airport upgrade. This study then attempts to apply a model with a time-dependent indicator.

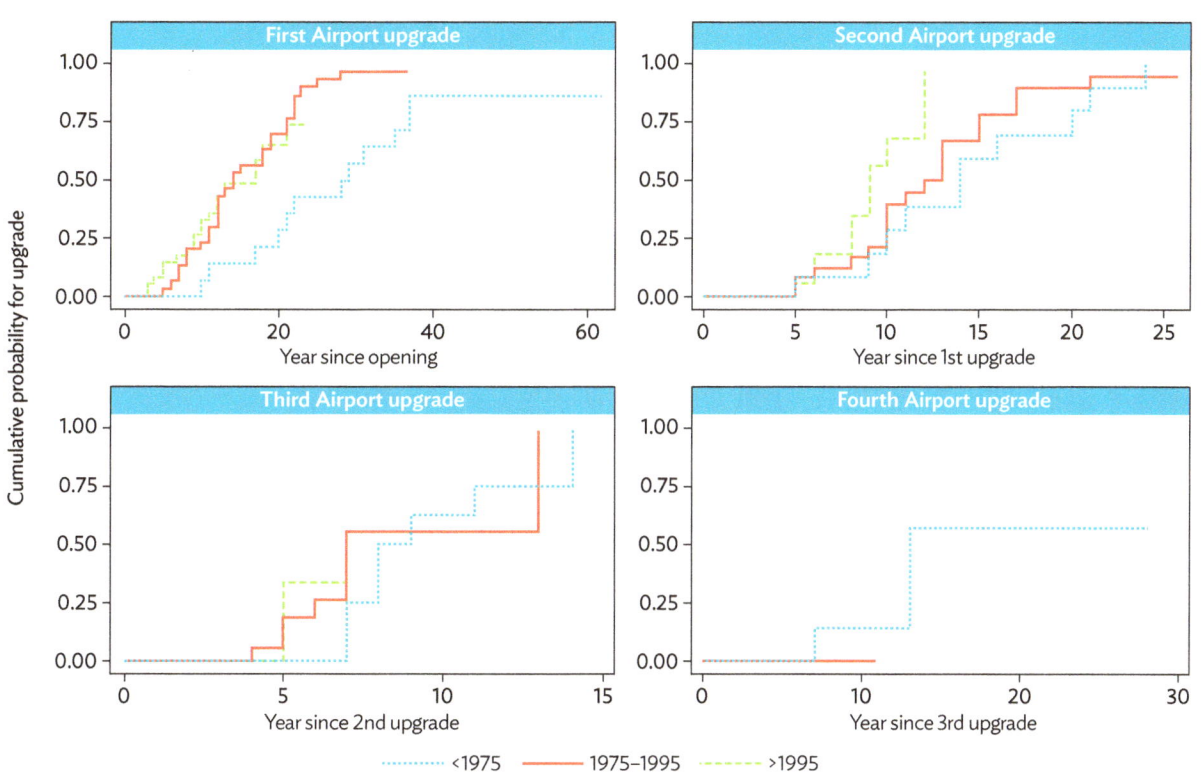

Figure 6.6: Cumulative Hazard for Consecutive Events

Source: Authors' estimation.

Estimation Results of Cox Regression

The effects of urban characteristics are measured based on the duration of the previous event. The fixed effect is included in our model, while each phased upgrade status is also considered. Table 6.3 summarizes the estimation results. Model 1 is the simplest model, where only the airport or city variables are introduced. Model 2 adds three dummy variables representing the AUP phases to model 1. The dummies for the second, third, and fourth or further upgrades are defined to take the value of 1 if the AUP was conducted in the second, third, or fourth or further phase after airport operations began, and 0 otherwise. These variables were introduced because the time interval for airport upgrades could vary depending on past experience with AUPs. In models 3 through 8, three urban characteristics were included in models 1 and 2. The three urban characteristics are examined independently because they are mutually highly correlated.

Table 6.3: Interval of Airport Upgrade and Urban Characteristics: The Gap Model

	Model 1	Model 2	Model 3	Model 4	Model 5	Model 6	Model 7	Model 8
Airport/City Characteristics								
Hub and main domestic airport dummy	0.39	0.24	0.40	0.27	0.42*	0.27	0.39	0.21
	(0.240)	(0.250)	(0.250)	(0.260)	(0.250)	(0.250)	(0.250)	(0.260)
First/second tier city dummy	0.59**	0.57**	0.58**	0.55**	0.61**	0.54**	0.58**	0.60**
	-0.25	-0.24	(0.250)	(0.240)	(0.270)	(0.240)	(0.270)	(0.270)
ln (Distance to City Central)	-0.02***	-0.02***	-0.02***	-0.02***	-0.02***	-0.02***	-0.02***	-0.02***
	(0.010)	(0.010)	(0.010)	(0.010)	(0.010)	(0.010)	(0.010)	(0.010)
4E/4F airport dummy	-0.33	-0.40	-0.58**	-0.57*	-0.52*	-0.45	-0.33	-0.4
	(0.270)	(0.300)	(0.280)	(0.300)	(0.290)	(0.310)	(0.270)	(0.310)
Tourism location or county-level city dummy	-1.62**	-1.43**	-1.74***	-1.55**	-1.48**	-1.24**	-1.62**	-1.46**
	(0.650)	(0.610)	(0.660)	(0.630)	(0.670)	(0.630)	(0.660)	(0.620)
Number of upgrades								
Second-phase upgrade		0.64**		0.60**		0.69***		0.65**
		(0.250)		(0.250)		(0.250)		(0.250)
Third-phase upgrade		0.93***		0.80**		0.97***		0.95**
		(0.360)		(0.380)		(0.360)		(0.370)
Fourth-phase or more upgrade		0.27		0.25		0.29		0.32
		(0.430)		(0.400)		(0.430)		(0.410)
Urban Characteristics								
Urbanization dummy			0.55***	0.43*				
			(0.210)	(0.230)				
Tertiary industry dummy					0.46**	0.30		
					(0.230)	(0.240)		
Urban population density dummy							0.01	-0.09
							(0.230)	(0.250)
City fixed effects	Yes	Yes	Yes	Yes	Yes	Yes	Yes	Yes
Sample size	79	79	79	79	79	79	79	79

Ln = log.
Notes: Standard errors are shown in parentheses; *, **, and *** represent 10%, 5%, and 1% statistical significance, respectively.
Source: Authors' estimation.

The estimation results first show that the distance between the airport and the city center is estimated to be significantly negative in all models. The results of all models indicate that a marginal increase in the distance between the airport and the city center results in a 2% decrease in AUP hazard. This means that the time interval for airport upgrade is longer when the airport is farther from the city center, holding other covariates constant. This could be reasonable because the space for airport upgrading, such as extending the existing runway, is more available in the urban fringe area than in the city center. More space allows the airport to implement AUPs more easily.

Second, the results also show that the estimated coefficient of the first- and/or second-tier city dummy is significantly positive, ranging from 0.55 to 0.61. This means that the time to upgrade airports tends to be shorter in larger cities. This could be because more business/personal communications to/from those cities have necessitated faster airport upgrades.

Third, the results of all the models show that the dummy for the tourism location or the county-level city is estimated to be significantly negative. This means that the airports in the tourist or rural cities may have a longer interval of AUPs. The airports in these cities tend to have invested only once at the beginning. The extreme case is Hotan, one of the oasis cities in the Gobi Desert. Hotan Airport (HTN) has had a 4D runway (3,200 meters long) for over 50 years, but only handled about 0.5 million passengers in 2014, which is significantly less than airports of the same class in the eastern and central regions of the PRC. The definition of 4D can be found in the Appendix of Chapter 5. However, since it has become a major tourist destination, it may require an AUP.

Fourth, the estimation results of model 2 show that the dummies for the second- and third-phase upgrade are estimated to be significantly positive. This implies that the time interval from the first-phase AUP to the second-phase AUP and the interval from the second-phase AUP to the third-phase AUP are shorter than the interval from the start of the operation to the first-phase AUP.

Fifth, the estimation results of models 3 to 5 show that the urbanization dummy has a significant positive relationship with the hazard, while the tertiary industry dummy also has a significant positive relationship. This means that an airport located in a more urbanized city or in a more tertiary-industry-oriented city could have a shorter interval for airport upgrade.

Sixth, the estimation results of models 7 and 8 show that the urban population density dummy is insignificantly associated with the hazard. This is first because population density is seldom considered in the past airport upgrade. Since most cities have vast territories, population and airport activities have their own location distribution. Second, past relocation projects have taken action to seek more development space. However, this is not the same as the high population density of these cities. They were built in the early stage of the PRC's urban development and were too close to the city. This reflects the conflict between urban and air development in urban land use and the location of urban airports, but may not be entirely due to population density. Thankfully, the covariate "distance between airport and city" provides a reasonable result and recommends to policy makers that the distance between the newly built airport and the city center should be estimated as much as possible in further urban expansion to avoid the cost of relocating the airport.

Finally, the estimation results also show that the dummy for the hub and the major domestic airport are unexpectedly all insignificant. This means that airport-related investment is not biased toward hubs and major domestic airports. This may suggest that policy makers may have intended to promote economic development by upgrading airports in less developed regions where interregional ground transportation service is poor and/or existing airport service is poorer than that in developed cities.

6.6 Discussion

The above analysis has shown that urban characteristics have a significant relationship with the time interval of airport upgrades. First, a more urbanized city has a shorter time interval for airport upgrades. This is probably because a city with a higher proportion of urban population should have a greater demand for air travel, which leads airport authorities to decide sooner whether to upgrade the airport.

Second, a city with higher production from tertiary industry has a shorter time interval for airport upgrade. Assuming that airport investment contributes to economic development, there could be bidirectional effects between airport upgrades and the city's industrial structure. On the one hand, the tertiary industry creates more interregional communication opportunities, so physical airport expansion becomes necessary to accommodate air travel demand. On the other hand, an airport upgrade can improve the capacity of the airport, which encourages airlines to fly to more cities and establish their operational hubs, so that foreign firms and/or firms from other regions have more opportunities to start a new business in the city, particularly in the service industry such as finance, insurance, and real estate.

6.7 Conclusion

This chapter examined the airport's continued investment in transportation capacity improvements in response to changes in airport and urban characteristics. Survival analysis is applied to the empirical data set of 122 airport upgrade projects in 79 cities in the PRC to understand the time intervals for airport upgrade. First, the Kaplan–Meier curve revealed that the probability of upgrading airports is higher from 5 to 15 years after the last event. Then, Cox regression models were estimated, which showed that the degree of urbanization and the share of tertiary industry production in total production have a significant negative relationship with the time interval of the airport upgrade, while the airport status and the distance between the airport and the city center have a positive relationship with the time interval. They suggest that urban characteristics may influence airport upgrade decision-making.

References

Airports Council International (ACI). 2017. ACI Annual Report 2016.

Anderson, P. K. and R. D. Gill. 1982. Cox's Regression Model for Counting Processes: A Large Sample Study. *The Annals of Statistics*. 10. pp. 1100–1120.

Appold, S. J. 2015. Airport Cities and Metropolitan Labor Markets: An Extension and Response to Cidell. *Journal of Economic Geography*. 15 (6). pp. 1145–1168.

Appold, S. J. and J. D. Kasarda. 2013. The Airport City Phenomenon: Evidence from Large US Airports. *Urban Studies*. 50 (6). pp. 1239–1259.

Baker, D., R. Merkert, and M. Kamruzzaman. 2015. Regional Aviation and Economic Growth: Cointegration and Causality Analysis in Australia. *Journal of Transport Geography*. 43. pp. 140–150.

Bel, G. and X. Fageda 2008. Getting There Fast: Globalization, Intercontinental Flights and Location of Headquarters. *Journal of Economic Geography*. 8. pp. 471–495.

Bilotkach, V. 2015. Are Airports Engines of Economic Development? A Dynamic Panel Data Approach. *Urban Studies*. 52. pp. 1577–1593.

Brueckner, J. K. 2003. Airline Traffic and Urban Economic Development. *Urban Studies*. 40. pp. 1455–1469.

Budd, L., S. Ison, and T. Budd. 2016. Improving the Environmental Performance of Airport Surface Access in the UK: The Role of Public Transport. *Research in Transportation Economics*. 59. pp. 185–195.

Cidell, J. 2014. The Role of Major Infrastructure in Subregional Economic Development: An Empirical Study of Airports and Cities. *Journal of Economic Geography*. 15. pp. 1125–1144.

Civil Aviation Administration of China (CAAC). 2018. *Statistical Bulletin of Civil Aviation*.

Feitelson, E. I., R. E. Hurd, and R. R. Mudge. 1996. The Impact of Airport Noise on Willingness to Pay for Residences. *Transportation Research Part D: Transport and Environment*. 1. pp. 1–14.

Humphreys, I. and S. Ison. 2005. Changing Airport Employee Travel Behaviour: The Role of Airport Surface Access Strategies. *Transport Policy*. 12. pp. 1–9.

Humphreys, I., S. Ison, G. Francis, and K. Aldridge. 2005. UK Airport Surface Access Targets. *Journal of Air Transport Management*. 11. pp. 117–124.

Kasarda, J. D. and G. Lindsay. 2011. *Aerotropolis: The Way We'll Live Next*. Penguin.

Liu, C. 2016. China to Build 66 New Airports Over the Next Five Years, https://www.thenanfang.com/china-to-boost-airport-infrastructure-by-billions/?msclkid=62bc888dce8911ecb4c2a939c7727722.

Loo, B. P. Y. 2008. Passengers' Airport Choice within Multi-Airport Regions (MARs): Some Insights from a Stated Preference Survey at Hong Kong International Airport. *Journal of Transport Geography*. 16. pp. 117–125.

Marazzo, M., R. Scherre, and E. Fernandes. 2010. Air Transport Demand and Economic Growth in Brazil: A Time Series Analysis. *Transportation Research Part E-Logistics and Transportation Review*. 46. pp. 261–269.

Rodrigue, J.-P. 2017. *The Geography of Transport Systems*. New York: Routledge.

Shu, X. and D. E. Schaubel. 2016. Semiparametric Methods to Contrast Gap Time Survival Functions: Application to Repeat Kidney Transplantation. *Biometrics*. 72. pp. 525–534.

Smit, M., M. Koopman, and J. Faber. 2013. *The Economics of Airport Expansion*. Delft: CE Delft.

Wu, W. Y. Liang, and D. Wu. 2016. Evaluating the Impact of China's Rail Network Expansions on Local Accessibility: A Market Potential Approach. *Sustainability*. 8. p. 512.

Chapter 7

Detailed Case Surveys: Airport System Development Practices in Ha Noi, Jakarta, and Manila

7.1 Introduction

This chapter attempts to supplement a series of findings shown in the previous chapters by providing more detailed case surveys on airport system development in Asia's developing cities, especially Ha Noi, Jakarta, and Manila. All three cities have national capital status in Viet Nam, Indonesia, and the Philippines, respectively, but these cities represent different stages and phases of development (Table 7.1). Of the three cities, Ha Noi still has the smallest size in terms of urbanized area, population, and gross domestic product (GDP), but had shown the fastest growth in urbanized area and population from 1990 to 2015. Manila and Jakarta have already reached the megacity scale, with a total population of over 10 million, with different urbanization patterns. Manila accommodates 17.6 million inhabitants within a moderately urbanized area of 2,030 square kilometers (km^2), which translates into a relatively high population density of 8,680 inhabitants per km^2. In contrast, Jakarta, with 18.6 million inhabitants, is spread over a largely urbanized area of 5,009 km^2, resulting in a relatively low population density of 3,717 inhabitants per km^2. Jakarta records higher figures for economic output, productivity, and growth than Ha Noi and Manila. Such heterogeneous conditions of urbanization, population, and economic development conditions are likely to require different practices in airport system development, as suggested in Chapter 3. Key information and local knowledge on (i) airport system development, (ii) ground transportation, and (iii) land use coordination for economic development were obtained from public reports, project materials, corporate websites, traffic databases, news articles (see references), and the three interview surveys conducted from July 2021 to September 2021 and summarized in the following sections for each of the case cities.[6]

---

[6] See Acknowledgments for the profile of four interviewees.

Table 7.1: Comparison of Ha Noi, Jakarta, and Manila in Urbanized Area, Population, and Economic Production

	Ha Noi	Jakarta	Manila
Urbanized area 2015 (km²)	1,095	5,009	2,030
Urbanized area Growth 1990–2015 (%)	+191.2	+43.2	+47.9
Population 2015 (million inhabitants)	3.7	18.6	17.6
Population growth 1990–2015 (%)	+221.1	+68.5	+88.3
Population growth 2015–2035 (%)	+92.6	+46.5	+49.6
Population density 2015 (inhabitants per km²)	3,340	3,717	8,689
GDP 2015 ($ billion)	28.0	427.3	197.8
GDP per capita 2015 ($)	7,655	22,952	11,214
GDP growth 1990–2015 (%)	+207.4	+295.2	+117.1

GDP = gross domestic product, km² = square kilometer.
Source: Authors, with data from European Commission (2018) and UN Department of Economic and Social Affairs (2018).

7.2 Ha Noi

As the national capital of Viet Nam, Ha Noi is connected to 32 international and 11 domestic destination cities by air transportation services, with an annual volume of 76,986 departure movements in 2018 (Figure 7.1). The most connected city is Ho Chi Minh City, with an annual volume of 39,091 departure movements. Ha Noi has a single-airport system to handle the relatively small to medium volume of international and domestic air traffic. Noi Bai International Airport (HAN) is the 34th-busiest passenger airport and the 18th-busiest cargo airport in Asia for 2018, with international traffic from the single airport accounting for 38.9% of total passenger traffic (25.9 million) and 72.7% of total cargo traffic (728,414 tons). In fact, Noi Bai International Airport is the largest airport in the country for cargo transportation, recording a 139.9% increase in passenger traffic from 2011 to 2018.

Figure 7.1: Air Traffic Flow to and from Ha Noi in 2018

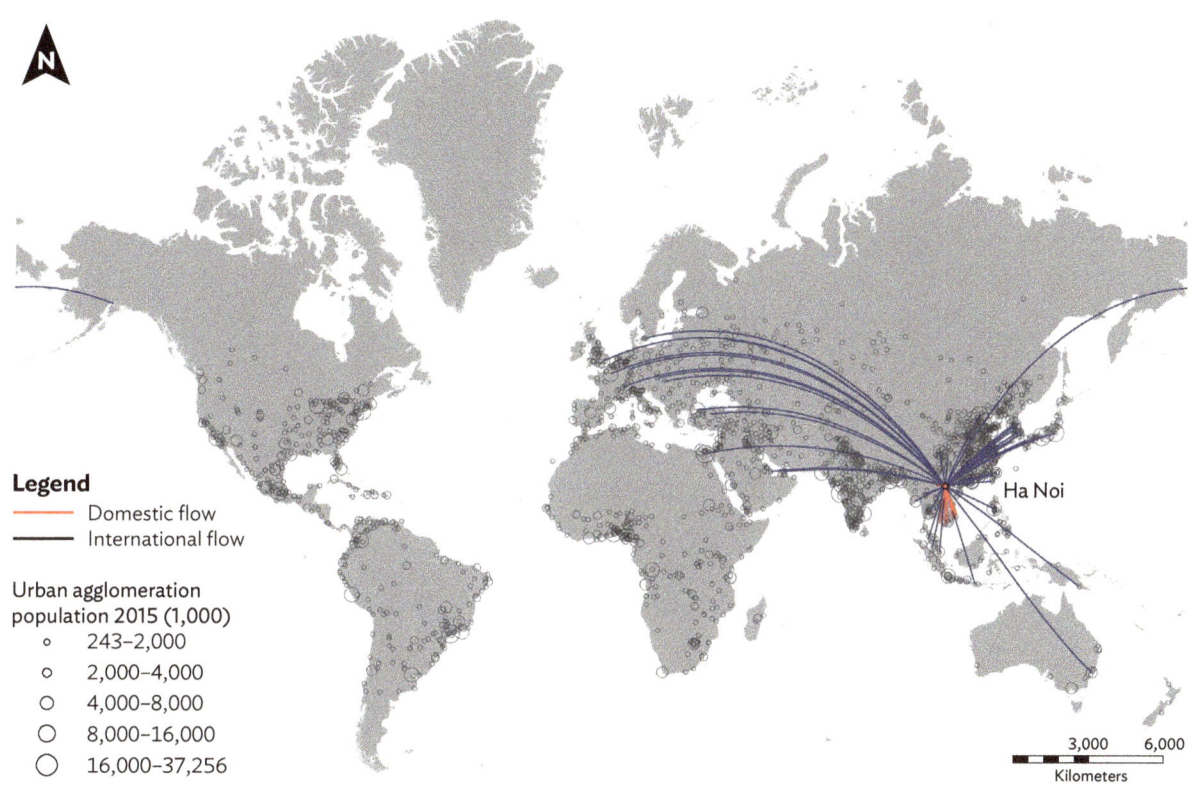

Note: This map was produced by Authors, with data from ICAO (2018), European Commission (2018), and UN Department of Economic and Social Affairs (2018). The boundaries, colors, denominations, and any other information shown on this map do not imply, on the part of the Asian Development Bank, any judgment on the legal status of any territory, or any other endorsement or acceptance of such boundaries, colors, denominations, or information.
Source: Authors, with data from ICAO (2018).

In response to rapidly growing air passenger traffic to and from Ha Noi, the capacity of Noi Bai International Airport, located about 35 km north of downtown Ha Noi, has been successively expanded over the decades. After the end of the Vietnam War and the reunification of the country in 1975, the military airfield was transformed into an international airport for commercial airline services in 1978. The first terminal (T1), with a total area of approximately 90,000 square meters (m²), became operational in 2001, followed by the addition of a second runway in 2006. Completion of these capacity expansion projects allowed Noi Bai International Airport to accommodate the Airbus A380 superjumbo in 2007 and to obtain SkyTeam hub status in 2010, although rapid growth in passenger numbers immediately overloaded T1.

In 2011, Viet Nam's Ministry of Transport and North Airport Corporation began construction of the second terminal (T2) adjacent to the existing T1 with a total investment of ¥76.1 billion, mainly funded by a Japan International Cooperation Agency (JICA) official development assistance (ODA) loan program (¥59.3 billion). In early 2015, T2 was put into operation with a total area of about 140,000 m² to handle 10 million–15 million international passengers annually. Crucially, since the inauguration of T2, T1's capacity has been dedicated to domestic passenger services. As a result of several airport capacity expansion projects, the entire Noi Bai International Airport system currently has a maximum capacity of 50 million passengers per year and still has developable land for another runway on a total area of about 565 hectares (ha).

It is important to note that the T2 construction project was accompanied by a number of large ground transportation projects (Vo Nguyen Giap Expressway and Nhật Tân Bridge) with a total investment of ¥27 billion and ¥80 billion, respectively, most of which were funded by the JICA ODA loan scheme (¥18.1 billion and ¥54.2 billion). The Vo Nguyen Giap Expressway, which opened in early 2015, connects Noi Bai International Airport at the northern end to the Nhật Tân Bridge at the southern end over a nearly straight stretch of about 12 km with a six-lane capacity. Opened in early 2015, the Nhật Tân Bridge serves not only as a symbol of the friendship between Viet Nam and Japan, but also as an alternative link to the existing Thang Long Bridge, which was built about 30 years ago across the 1 km-wide Red River. It is estimated that the completion of the Vo Nguyen Giap Expressway and Nhật Tân Bridge will reduce travel time between Ha Noi city center and Noi Bai International Airport by about 30 to 45 minutes. In theory, the broader economic development impacts of the airport capacity expansion (T2), combined with investments in ground transportation (Nguyen Giap Expressway and Nhật Tân Bridge), could flow to areas along the southern end of the new expressway corridor and around the southern end of the new bridge to improve accessibility and/or reliability, depending on land use coordination in the local context.

Since the 1990s, several large industrial areas have been developed around Noi Bai International Airport for Japanese high-tech manufacturing clusters. However, the land along the new expressway corridor is currently largely used for agriculture. The Ha Noi Planning Authority has envisioned a total area of over 2,000 ha between Noi Bai International Airport and the Red River for airport-related land use for economic development. According to the land use vision, the whole area can be divided into four conceptual districts: (i) "Gateway City" for agriculture, ecotourism, trading, and hi-tech park; (ii) "International City" for logistics, storage center, and cultural village; (iii) "Symbol City" for the amusement park and financial services; and (iv) "Eco-City" for tourism-related waters. In addition, a series of land use policies consider the improvement and/or resettlement of existing villages for social welfare and employment in the acquired agricultural area along the expressway. Specifically, the city agency is supposed to carry out land acquisition and adequate compensation by reimbursing the fees charged by real estate developers for land use rights or leasing of public lands. One of the biggest challenges in attracting competitive private developers and foreign firms is the provision of technical infrastructure (e.g., trunk roads, power, and water supply facilities, and sewerage and drainage systems), which requires additional development costs and investment in a large area.

The economic benefits of airport capacity expansion and two ground transportation projects can also be largely applied to a developable site at the southern end of the Nhật Tân Bridge. In fact, a total area of over 300 ha in Nam Thang Long has been developed as "Ciputra Hanoi International City" by Citra Westlake City Development Co., Ltd., a joint venture between Urban Development and Infrastructure Investment Cooperation (Viet Nam) and Ciputra Group (Indonesia), in accordance with the Hanoi City Master Plan. Ciputra Hanoi International City is expected to provide mostly residential condominium towers and low-rise housing units, as well as primary and secondary schools, gardens and golf courses, a clubhouse and retail space, a high-end hotel, and high-rise office buildings that meet international standards (Ciputra 2021; Tran 2015).

In addition, Ciputra Hanoi International City plans to provide a more direct link with downtown Ha Noi and Noi Bai International Airport through Ha Noi Metro Line 2 in four construction phases, funded by another Japanese ODA loan program. The airport rail link projects will apply concepts of transit-oriented development (TOD) and land value capture (LVC) to improve the locational advantages of the city center and the airport around Nam Thang Long Station (JICA 2020).

In December 2020, the Civil Aviation Authority of Vietnam (CAAV) publicly released its draft plan and vision for the national airport system for the next 3 decades, including the potential for developing and managing a multi-airport system in Ha Noi. The construction of a secondary airport has been proposed by Ha Noi to ease the traffic concentration at Noi Bai International Airport, which is estimated to carry 100 million passengers annually to and from Ha Noi by 2050. According to the 2016 Capital Region Master Plan, Ung Hoa district, about 54 km from the city center of Ha Noi, is one of four options for the construction of the new second airport, along with Ly Nhan district (Ha Nam province, 60–65 km), Thanh Mien and Binh Giang districts (Hai Duong province, 45–50 km), and Tien Lang district (Hai Phong city, 120 km). Indeed, the CAAV has not yet decided on the location of the secondary airport, and the Ministry of Transport has rejected a request to build the secondary airport in the capital by 2030 to conduct further feasibility studies based on the recovery and development of aviation after the COVID-19 pandemic.

7.3 Jakarta

As the national capital of Indonesia, Jakarta is connected by airline networks to 25 international and 16 domestic destination cities, with an annual volume of 278,362 departures in 2018 (Figure 7.2). The most frequently served city is Surabaya, with an annual volume of 49,412 departures. Jakarta has already established a multi-airport formation to handle the large volume of international and domestic air traffic. As the primary node, Soekarno–Hatta International Airport (SHIA) was the 8th-busiest passenger airport and the 17th-busiest cargo airport in Asia in 2018. International air traffic to and from Soekarno–Hatta International Airport accounts for only 23.5% of total passenger traffic (66 million) and 53.5% of total cargo volume (735,134 tons). Soekarno–Hatta International Airport recorded a 27.4% increase in passenger traffic and 26.3% increase in cargo volume from 2011 to 2018, much slower than Noi Bai International Airport in Ha Noi and Ninoy Aquino International Airport in Manila during the same period. Halim Perdanakusuma Airport (HLP), as a secondary node, had only 7.4 million domestic passengers (10.2%) and 34,423 tons of domestic and international air cargo volume (4.5%) in 2018.

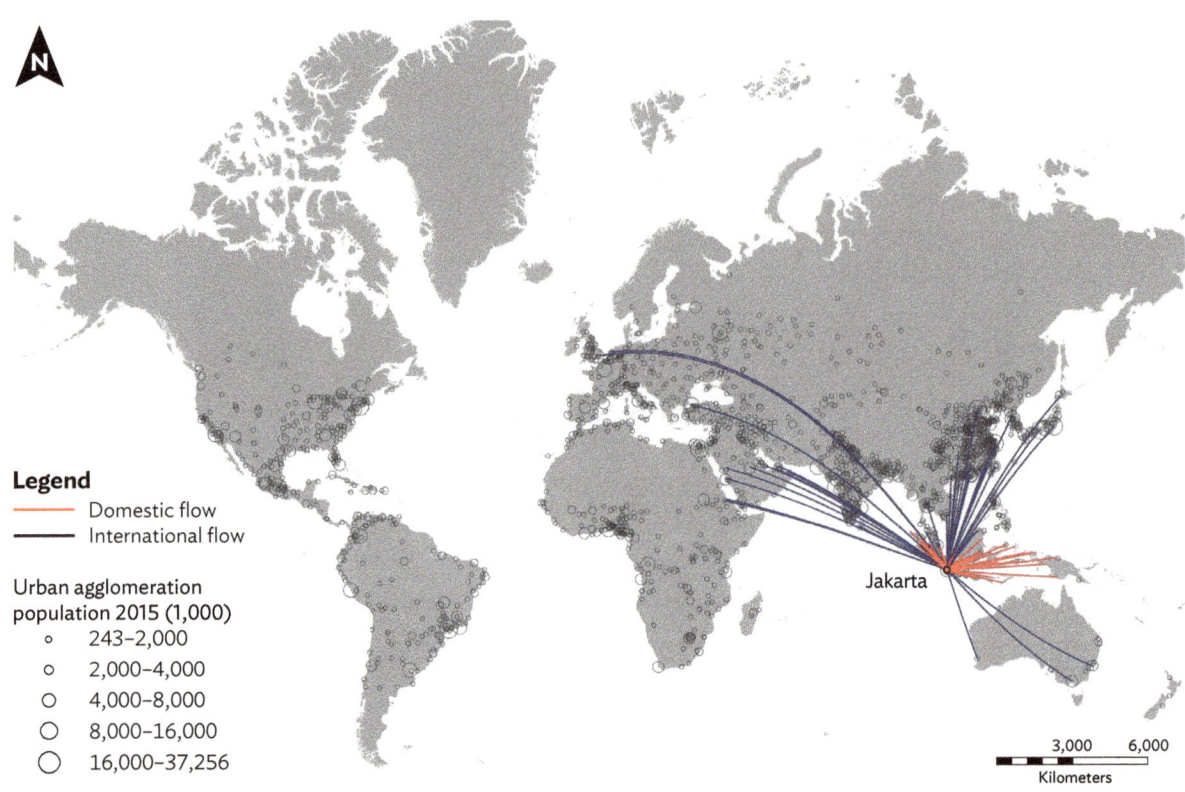

Figure 7.2: Air Traffic Flow to and from Jakarta in 2018

Note: This map was produced by Authors, with data from ICAO (2018), European Commission (2018), and UN Department of Economic and Social Affairs (2018). The boundaries, colors, denominations, and any other information shown on this map do not imply, on the part of the Asian Development Bank, any judgment on the legal status of any territory, or any other endorsement or acceptance of such boundaries, colors, denominations, or information.
Source: Authors, with data from ICAO (2018).

Jakarta has successively undertaken projects to build several airports, construct new airports, relocate airports, expand airport capacity, and construct other airports in recent decades. Kemayoran Airport (over Central and North Jakarta) and Halim Perdanakusuma Airport (known as Halim Perdana Kusumah Air Force Base, about 15 km from Central Jakarta) were Jakarta's two main airports until the opening of Soekarno–Hatta International Airport in 1985 (Figure 7.3). Kemayoran Airport was replaced by Soekarno–Hatta International Airport and gradually transformed into the Kemayoran CBD, which includes wide boulevards, green open spaces, high-rise office buildings, condominiums, hospitals, shopping streets, upscale hotels, entertainment centers, and government facilities. Since the closure of Kemayoran Airport in 1985, Halim Perdanakusuma Airport was used for general aviation and other limited charter flights for 29 years or until 2014.

On the other hand, Soekarno–Hatta International Airport was initially opened with Terminal 1 (T1) with a capacity of 8 million passengers per year for domestic flights in 1985, which was followed by the completion of Terminal 2 (T2) with a capacity of 18 million passengers for international flights in 1991. Since then, the primary airport has undertaken a series of projects to expand airport capacity

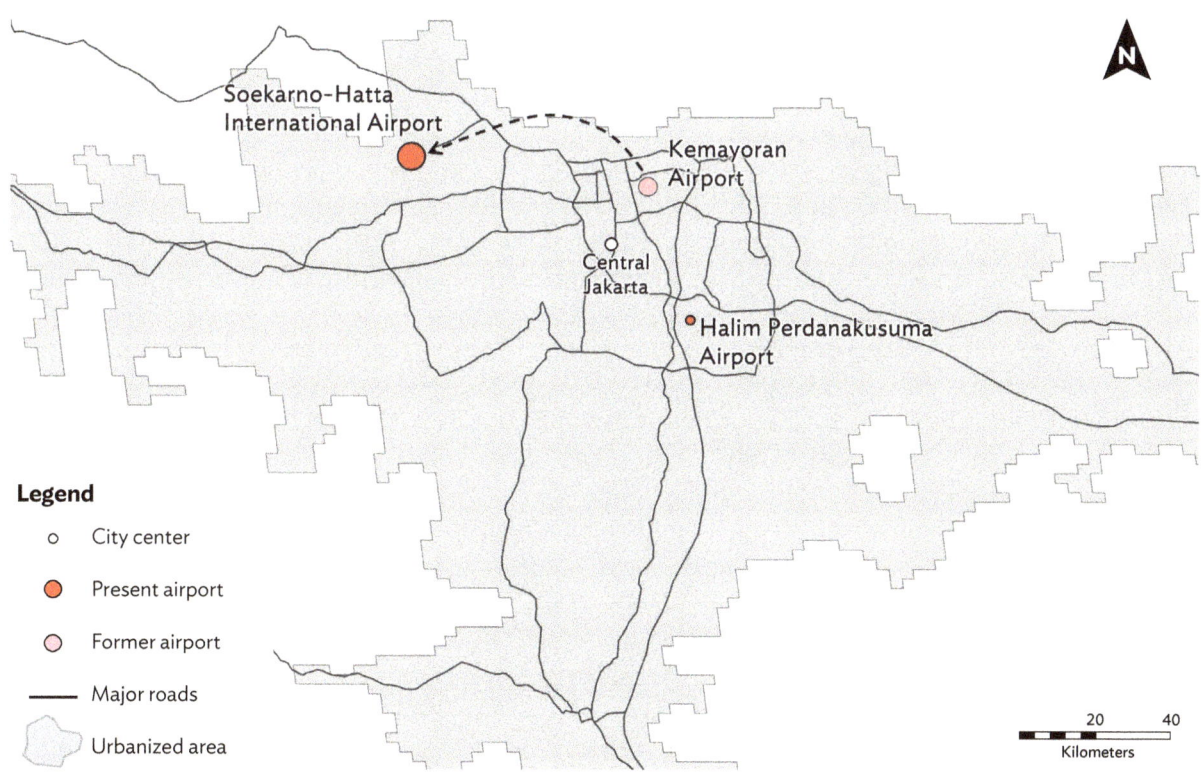

Figure 7.3: Location of Kemayoran Airport, Halim Perdanakusuma Airport, and Soekarno–Hatta International Airport in Jakarta

Note: This map was produced by Authors, with data from European Commission (2018). The boundaries, colors, denominations, and any other information shown on this map do not imply, on the part of the Asian Development Bank, any judgment on the legal status of any territory, or any other endorsement or acceptance of such boundaries, colors, denominations, or information.
Source: Authors.

on a total area of approximately 1,890 ha about 20 km northwest of Central Jakarta. The freight terminal development was completed along with Phase 1 of Terminal 3, which could provide a capacity of 22 million passengers per year for domestic flights in 2009 and international flights in 2011. Terminal 3 was further expanded and officially reopened as "Terminal 3 Ultimate" with a capacity of 25 million passengers, along with the development of a third runway and the integration of a commercial zone of 71,225 m^2 in 2016, according to the master plan for a world-class airport and aerotropolis designed by Angkasa Pura II, a state-owned enterprise for the management of Soekarno–Hatta International Airport and other airports in Indonesia. Soekarno–Hatta International Airport was originally designed by Paul Andreu based on the postmodern concept of "a cluster of small houses with red tile roofs set amid trees between large stretches of rice fields," which called for the integration of main terminals and several boarding pavilions. In fact, T1, T2, T3, and Soekarno–Hatta International Airport Station (a newly constructed airport rail link station) were connected in 2017 by the Airport Skytrain, which uses an Automated People Mover system with a total circulation length of about 3 km.

Angkasa Pura II plans to relocate the existing freight terminal to a new cargo complex on the west side of the airport district to accommodate increased air traffic to and from Soekarno–Hatta International Airport. Plans call for Terminal 4, with a capacity of about 45 million passengers per year, to be built on a total area of 130 ha on the north side of the airport district. However, the Tangerang Municipal Government rejected a number of proposals for further capacity expansion due to difficulties in acquiring land and relocating residential areas around Soekarno–Hatta International Airport. During the period, Angkasa Pura II reactivated Halim Perdanakusuma Airport as a secondary (commercial) airport to handle domestic (scheduled) flights with a capacity of about 2.2 million passengers per year in 2014, although the possibility of capacity expansion and land coordination for (re)development around Halim Perdanakusuma Airport is very limited or almost zero. On the other hand, the Indonesian government, together with Angkasa Pura II (and technical assistance and knowledge support from JICA), has assessed several sites for the development of the New Jakarta Airport and projected a total capacity of about 100 million passengers together with Soekarno–Hatta International Airport. Indeed, some greenfield sites within and outside the Jakarta Metropolitan Area can be identified for feasibility studies, but land acquisition, community resettlement, environmental impact, and/or metropolitan accessibility appear to be critical factors in selecting sites for new airport development.

The improvement of ground transportation infrastructure and services was of particular importance to Soekarno–Hatta International Airport because of severe traffic congestion and unreliable travel services on urban road systems to and from Central Jakarta. Nevertheless, the development of a rail link to the airport could only be realized in 2017 (Phase 1) and 2019 (Phase 2), largely due to the issue of land acquisition for new tracks and plan changes along the access corridor. The Soekarno–Hatta Airport Rail Link was eventually constructed with 24 km of existing commuter rail line from Manggarai to Batuceper and 12 km of the new track from Batuceper to Soekarno–Hatta International Airport (SHIA) station (Figure 7.4). Of the five airport rail link stations, SHIA and BNI City were newly built, whereas Batuceper, Duri, and Manggarai were upgraded to provide express services. The Soekarno–Hatta Airport Rail Link was initially opened between SHIA and BNI City in 2017 and extended to Manggarai in 2019. Kereta Api Indonesia, another state-owned enterprise for the sole operation of public railroads in Indonesia, formed a joint venture with Angkasa Pura II, to operate the Airport Rail Link service. The "direct" economic benefit of the Soekarno–Hatta Airport Rail Link (approximately $400 million capital investment) to travelers arriving at (or departing from) Soekarno–Hatta International Airport is still questionable due to the limited number of passengers and low fare revenue. According to the 2018 Airport Passenger OD Interview Survey (JICA 2019), the highest proportion of modal choices for airport passengers to access Soekarno–Hatta International Airport was taxi and online taxi (43.9%), followed by private car (29.8%) and large bus (17.3%), and the new airport rail link was rarely used by travelers. One of the most possible reasons for the Airport Rail Link's low ridership and modal share is its limited service coverage in Central Jakarta, where only three stations are directly connected by the express services to/from SHIA.

Figure 7.4: Soekarno–Hatta Airport Rail Link with Two New Stations and Three Renovated Stations

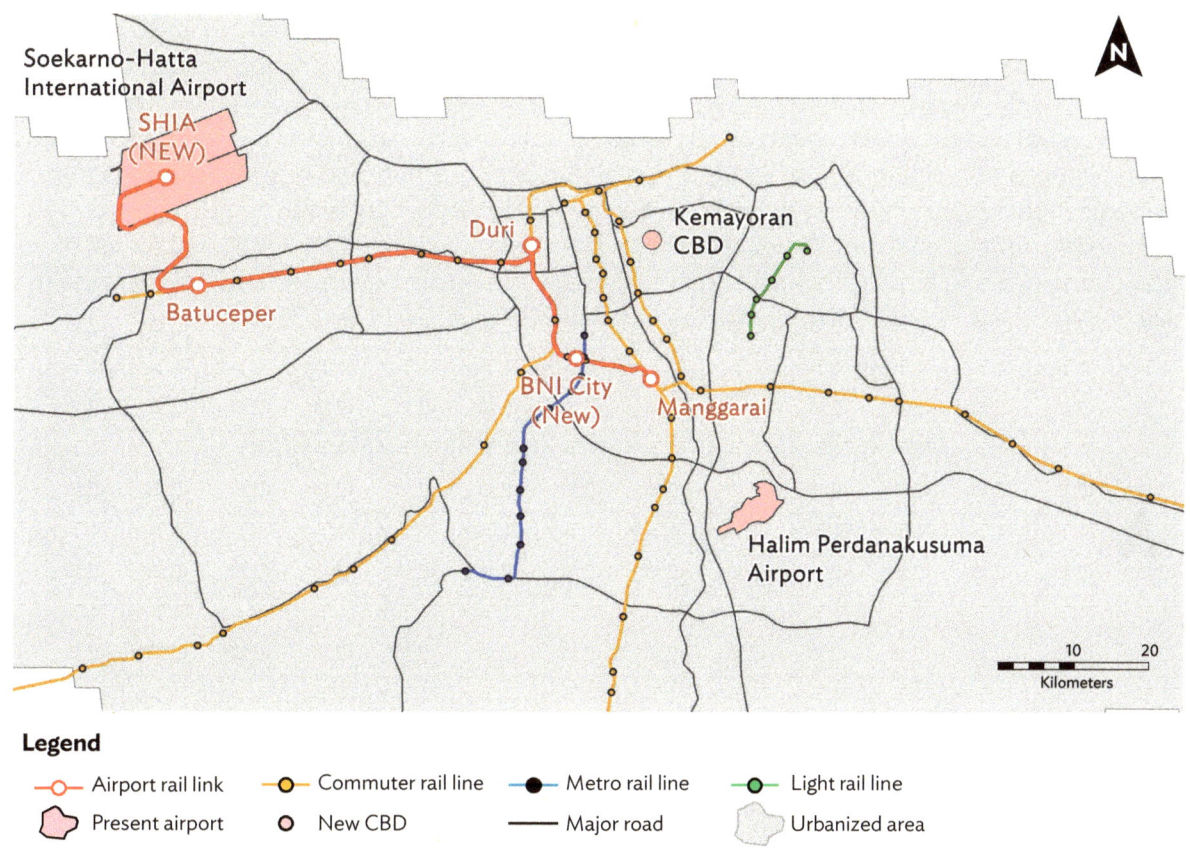

CBD = central business district.
Note: This map was produced by Authors, with data from European Commission (2018). The boundaries, colors, denominations, and any other information shown on this map do not imply, on the part of the Asian Development Bank, any judgment on the legal status of any territory, or any other endorsement or acceptance of such boundaries, colors, denominations, or information.
Source: Authors.

Instead, the "wider" economic benefits of the Soekarno–Hatta Airport Rail Link are likely to occur around some of the five stations to improve accessibility and agglomeration economies in Central Jakarta, depending on the connectivity of local feeder services and the availability of developable land. The most observable case is BNI City near Central Jakarta, accompanied by Dukuh Atas Transit-Oriented Development (TOD) around MRT Dukuh Atas BNI Station, Commuter Rail Sudirman Station, and Transjakarta Bus Rapid Transit.

Relatively large developable sites in the south of BNI City have been built for high-rise office buildings and hotels since the late 1990s. Many small land parcels in the north of BNV City should be consolidated into less developable sites for high-rise, mixed-use, and pedestrian-friendly redevelopment projects in accordance with the given TOD principles and land use incentives, such as bonuses for floor area ratio (FAR).

7.4 Manila

As the national capital of the Philippines, Manila is connected by airline networks to 23 international and 16 domestic destination cities, with an annual volume of 132,437 departures in 2018 (Figure 7.5). The most frequently served city for international flights is Singapore, with an annual volume of 11,188 departures, and for domestic flights is Puerto Princesa, with an annual volume of 10,130 departures. Despite the relatively large volume of international and domestic air traffic, Manila still relies on a single-airport system. Ninoy Aquino International Airport (MNL) is the 17th-busiest passenger airport and the 16th-busiest cargo airport in Asia for 2018, with its international traffic accounting for 51.0% of total passenger volume (45 million) and 61.2% of total cargo volume (738,698 tons). Ninoy Aquino International Airport recorded a 52.9% increase in passenger volume and an 80.0% increase in cargo volume from 2011 to 2018.

Figure 7.5: Air Traffic Flow to and from Manila in 2018

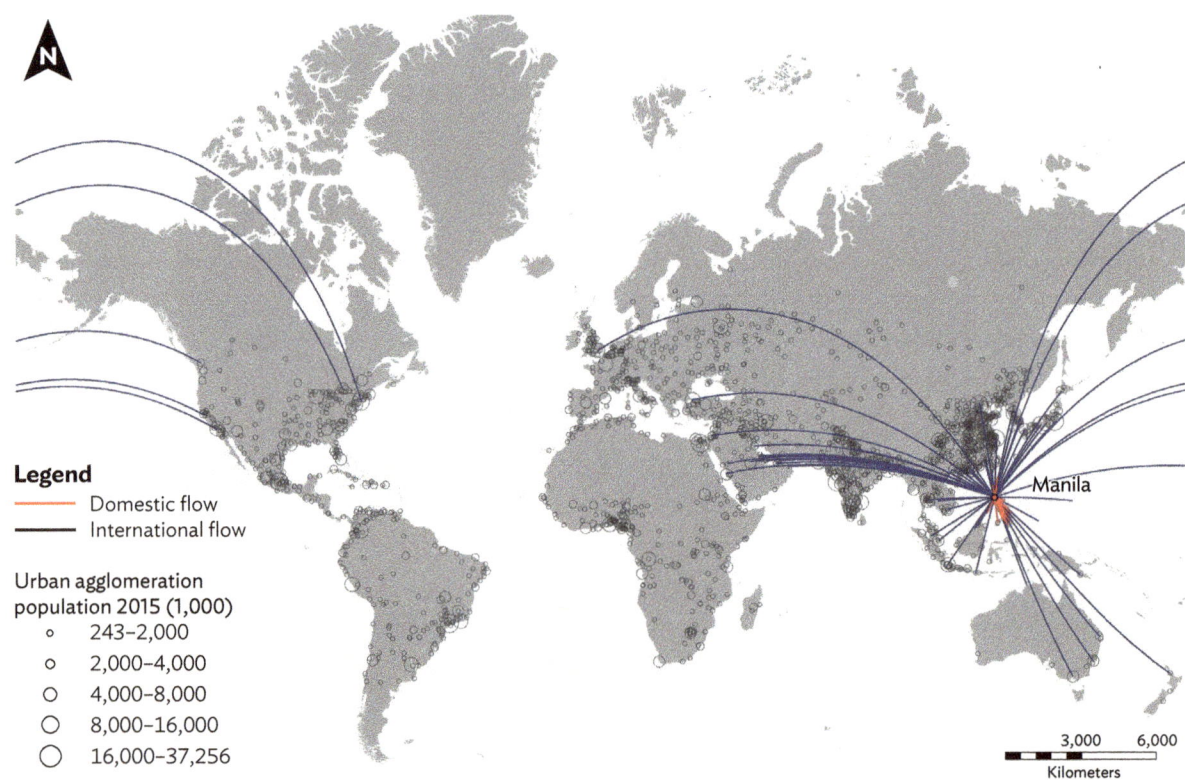

Note: This map was produced by Authors, with data from International Civil Aviation Organization (ICAO) (2018), European Commission (2018), and UN Department of Economic and Social Affairs (2018). The boundaries, colors, denominations, and any other information shown on this map do not imply, on the part of the Asian Development Bank, any judgment on the legal status of any territory, or any other endorsement or acceptance of such boundaries, colors, denominations, or information.
Source: Authors, with data from ICAO (2018).

Ninoy Aquino International Airport is located about 15 km south of downtown Manila. The inner-city airport, with a total area of about 400 ha, has sequentially undergone airport capacity expansion over several decades. The country's first airport was originally a US Air Force base and was moved to its current location in 1948. The international runway and taxiway were built in 1953 and the control tower and terminal building were completed in 1951, after which the airport was officially named Manila International Airport. In 1974, the airport was redesigned to improve its facilities. To this end, $29.6 million was provided through an Asian Development Bank (ADB) loan program. In 1981, construction of the new 67,000 m² Terminal 1 (T1) was completed, capable of handling 4.5 million passengers annually. In 1991, T1 reached its maximum capacity with an annual growth rate of about 11%. To celebrate the 100th anniversary of Philippine independence, construction of the "Centennial Terminal" or a Terminal 2 (T2) began in 1995 and was completed in 1999 with an area of 75,000 m² for 9 million passengers per year. About 75% of the project cost or ¥18.1 billion was funded through a Japanese ODA loan program. On the other hand, construction of a Terminal 3 (T3) began in 1997. However, the construction of T3 was suspended as the Philippine President, the government, and the Supreme Court declared the build–operate-transfer (BOT) contract void in 2003. In 2006, the Philippine International Air Terminals Co. Inc. accepted a $6 million settlement from the Philippine government and contracted the newly formed Takenaka Corporation to complete the suspended construction by 2008. In fact, T3 began partial operations in 2008 and became fully operational in 2014. The $640 million terminal project was largely funded by ADB and the Import–Export Bank of Japan through a $500 million loan program. The modern terminal building was designed by Skidmore, Owings and Merrill to handle a capacity of 13 million passengers per year with a floor area of 189,000 m² and a total parking area of 3,200 cars. Despite the successive completion of projects to expand airport capacity, severe traffic congestion continues to occur around Ninoy Aquino International Airport, both in the airspace and on the ground.

To ease increasing airport congestion and flight delays, the government decided to relocate some aviation services to Sangley Point, about 20 km west of Ninoy Aquino International Airport, in 2019. The Philippine Air Force has occupied Sangley Point for the Danilo Atienza Air Base. The revitalization of Sangley Point Airport as a hub for general aviation and turboprop cargo operations was completed in 2020 with a 2.4 km runway. Sangley Point's potential for further capacity expansion remains debatable due to its short runway, narrow road access, and land use constraints that would result in serious congestion at the northern end of the Cavite Peninsula. In fact, the Sangley Point International Airport (SPIA) Development Consortium, composed of local business tycoons, international consulting companies, and private real estate developers, has attempted to build a fully modernized, world-class, and green airport on newly reclaimed land in Manila Bay by launching an $11 billion project in a joint venture with the Cavite provincial government. Phase 1A of the plan calls for $2.3 billion investments to build the first runway and terminal building, as well as a new highway connector to handle 15 million passengers a year. Phase 1B would expand the airport's capacity to 25 million passengers per year with $2 billion in investment, and Phase 2 would require $6.6 billion in investment to build another runway and relevant facilities to accommodate 75 million passengers per year. However, not enough bids had been obtained for the development proposal by the end of 2021.

In 2016 and 2017, the Ninoy Aquino International Airport Expressway, consisting of a 7.75 km elevated expressway and a 2.22 km at-grade feeder road between the Skyway and the Bayfront district, was put into operation to not only reduce road traffic near the three airport terminals but also improve access to/from the Ninoy Aquino International Airport and Entertainment City. This ground transportation project, with a total cost of about $360 million, will benefit an estimated 80,000 travelers daily and reduce travel time between Entertainment City and the terminals from 25 minutes to 8 minutes and travel time between Skyway and the terminals from 1 hour to 20 minutes (Republic of the Philippines Department of Public Works and Highways 2021).

The airport expressway link brought time savings, especially for private cars, taxis, and ride-hailing services. Other modes of public transportation play a relatively minor role in transporting people to and from Ninoy Aquino International Airport. In fact, two rail stations have already been built near the airport (Baclaran LRT Station in 1984 and Nichols National Railways Station in 2010). However, both light rail transit and commuter rail lines do not connect directly to the airport terminals. Jeepney and other paratransit services are not viable options because they are not allowed to enter the airport district. In 2015, e-Jeepney was permitted on a trial basis for limited service within the airport district. The inadequacy of public transportation infrastructure and services around the Ninoy Aquino International Airport is largely due to the lack of inter-jurisdictional coordination of transportation between communities in the metropolitan area. Municipalities may reject new proposals for public transportation, including first- and last-mile link projects, for political reasons, such as a change of President, mayor, and/or public policy by-elections. In addition, such jurisdictional fragmentation in the provision of ground transportation infrastructure and services throughout the metropolitan area is likely to limit the potential economic benefits of developing a multi-airport system by worsening traffic congestion, increasing access and egress costs, and enhancing agglomeration diseconomies, accompanied by inadequate land use coordination among municipalities.

The urban areas around Ninoy Aquino International Airport are administered by three municipalities—Parañaque, Pasay, and Taguig. The municipalities can designate land use zoning codes to promote airport-linked economic development within their jurisdiction. Both Parañaque and Pasay classify many properties adjacent to the airport district as planned unit development zones, which allow flexibility in land use for diverse and complex real estate projects such as shopping malls, hotels, casinos, and other mixed-use property development.

In Parañaque, Entertainment City was developed in 2007 as a gaming and entertainment facility covering a total area of 44 ha along Manila Bay and owned by the Philippine Amusement and Gaming Corporation, a government-owned corporation that regulates the gaming industry. This Bayfront district has also been designated as an economic zone approved by the Philippine Economic Zone Authority since 2017. The development of integrated casino resorts directly linked to Ninoy Aquino International Airport is expected to increase demand for international leisure travel from Asia and the Pacific (Entertainment City Manila 2020). In Pasay, Newport City has been in operation since 2007 as a fully integrated residential and office complex with an entertainment complex covering a total area of 25 ha adjacent to T3 of Ninoy Aquino International Airport. The former Villamor Air Base was developed by Megaworld Corporation in partnership with the Philippines's Bases Conversion and Development Authority (BCDA) and transformed into Newport City, a world-class integrated complex for airport-linked commercial and residential services (Megaworld Newport Property Holdings 2016).

In Taguig, Bonifacio Global City (BGC) was also developed by BCDA in partnership with Ayala Land and Campos Group since the sale of military land totaling 240 ha in 1995. The BGC master plan features European-style communities with numerous amenities and residential services, including green spaces, high-end stores, and cultural facilities. Bonifacio High Street forms the commercial core of BGC with high-tech office towers and pedestrian-friendly shopping streets. Several domestic and foreign corporations have purchased land and committed to relocate their global, regional, and national headquarters to the BGC business district. The entire area is home to several educational institutions, including the University of the Philippines and De La Salle University, which offer graduate programs for professionals working in the business district. The Ninoy Aquino International Airport is accessible from some of BGC's seven gateways.

The Metro Manila Dream Plan 2030 (JICA 2014) shows the scope of multi-airport formation in Greater Manila Area with two additional gateway airports: (i) the upgrade of an existing airport in Clark, and (ii) the construction of a new international airport outside the metropolitan area. Clark International Airport is located about 100 km from downtown Manila and has long been debatable as to whether it should be considered a secondary or tertiary airport for Manila. Nonetheless, the construction of the North–South Commuter Railway with a total length of about 90 km from Tutuban Station in Manila to Clark Freeport and Special Economic Zone and Clark International Airport was planned to reduce road congestion, save transportation costs, and encourage a regionwide shift of economic activity from the congested capital city to the northern growth centers. On the other hand, the construction of the "new" Ninoy Aquino International Airport was proposed and implemented by San Miguel Corporation (SMC), one of the largest corporations in the Philippines. Since it is located on the coast of Bulacan (35 km north of downtown Manila), SMC's new airport construction project is often referred to as Bulacan International Airport. As the largest single investment in the country's history, the 2,500 ha development project includes not only four runways, airfield facilities, and terminal buildings for international and domestic flights with a maximum capacity of 200 million passengers per year, but also various components (e.g., airport and airline support facilities, access roads, parking facilities, utilities, residential units, industrial zones with a seaport, public services, and other ancillary facilities) as an "aerocity" at a total project cost of ₱735 billion ($14 billion) under a 50-year franchise agreement (SMC 2021). SMC is entitled to tax breaks, including income taxes, value-added taxes, percentage taxes, excise taxes, stamp duties, tariffs, and property taxes on land, buildings, and other real assets, during the construction period of up to 10 years. SMC is expected to subsequently pay profits equivalent to 12% of the internal rate of return to the government when the development project fully recovers investment costs (Lopez 2021).

7.5 Summary of Key Findings

This chapter presents eight key findings on airport system development practices in Ha Noi, Jakarta, and Manila as follows:

(1) The complexity of airport system development (e.g., construction of a single new airport, expansion of airport capacity, and formation of multiple airports) depends on the level of urbanization and the stage of economic development (Ha Noi, Jakarta, and Manila).

(2) International development agencies (e.g., ADB and JICA) can play an important role in enhancing the economic impact of airport capacity expansion along with ground transportation investments through loan programs and/or technical assistance in emerging economies (Ha Noi, Jakarta, and Manila).

(3) The location of a (former) military air base in a metropolitan area is one of the key determinants of multi-airport formation, as the choice of location for building new airports or relocating airports is somewhat related to the availability and accessibility of public land for airport capacity expansion (Jakarta and Manila).

(4) Asia's major corporations could take on the development and management of airport systems in an integrated way by internalizing the broader economic benefits of building new airports by developing land around new airport terminals and along ground transportation corridors if governments (or international development agencies) offer generous incentives to private partners, such as a range of tax breaks (Manila).

(5) Coordinating land use for airport-linked economic development often calls for acquiring land and relocating communities near airport-linked highway interchanges and/or rail stations. Military agencies may need to be involved in land use coordination for airport-linked development as public landowners in the vicinity of airports or former airbases (Ha Noi and Manila).

(6) Relocation of an airport may lead to significant and transformative development opportunities in inner-city locations, while limiting the possibility of secondary or tertiary airport use (Jakarta).

(7) The development of new secondary and/or tertiary airports is proposed to mitigate the concentration of traffic around existing primary and/or secondary airports in dense inner-city locations. However, the formation of multi-airports is likely to necessitate additional investments in ground transportation infrastructure and services, especially airport rail links for reliable passenger travel services, between city-center and city-fringe locations (Ha Noi, Jakarta, and Manila)

(8) Investment in an airport rail link requires coordination of development among jurisdictions and/or sectors to improve metropolitan-wide connectivity and last-mile accessibility, although the direct benefits of investing in an airport rail link for travelers (e.g., ridership, traffic mitigation, and reliability) are still debatable (Jakarta and Manila).

(9) The degree and pattern of broader economic benefits brought by airport system development may depend on land use zoning codes (e.g., flexible floor use and floor area ratio bonus for favorable land use) that are proactively adjusted by municipal governments around airports and/or along airport-linked ground transportation corridors (Jakarta and Manila).

Additionally, the detailed case studies implicitly show that the three capital cities in Asia continued to discuss and even promote airport system development projects during the COVID-19 pandemic. It can be anticipated that airport recovery scenarios will depend on changes in the composition of air traffic (e.g., domestic versus international) and the amount of proactive capital investment and supportive public policies for cities that want to be a regional hub in Asia.

References

Airports Council International (ACI). *Annual World Airport Traffic Dataset* (Years: 2011–2018). https://store.aci.aero/product-category/economics-statistics/annual-world-airport-traffic-reports-watr/.

Atlassian. 2021. Indonesia Jakarta Soekarno–Hatta International Airport. https://dlca.logcluster.org/display/public/DLCA/2.2.1+Indonesia+Jakarta+Soekarno-Hatta+International+Airport.

Ciputra. 2021. https://www.ciputra.com/en/portfolio/ciputra-hanoi-international-city/.

Entertainment City Manila. 2020. http://www.entertainmentcitymanila.ph/.

Hak Cipta 2020 Peta TPZ Kode A. https://jakartasatu.jakarta.go.id/portal/apps/webappviewer/index.html?id=fc51cd7c032b49e08261a1e5e3c89165.

International Civil Aviation Organization (ICAO). Traffic Flow Global Data (Shape File). https://store.icao.int/en/traffic-flow-global-data-shape-file.

Japan International Cooperation Agency (JICA). 2014. Roadmap for Transport Infrastructure Development for Metro Manila and Its Surrounding Areas. https://openjicareport.jica.go.jp/pdf/12149597.pdf.

Japan International Cooperation Agency (JICA). 2019. JABODETABEK Urban Transportation Policy Integration Project Phase 2 in the Republic of Indonesia. Annex 05: Working Paper on Transportation Surveys. https://libopac.jica.go.jp/images/report/12356390.pdf.

Japan International Cooperation Agency (JICA). 2020. Data Collection Survey for Hanoi Metro Line 2 Extension North. Final Report. https://openjicareport.jica.go.jp/pdf/1000042956.pdf.

Lopez, M. L. 2021. San Miguel Gets 50-Year Franchise for Airport City Project in Bulacan as Bill Lapses into Law. *CNN Philippines*. https://www.cnnphilippines.com/business/2021/1/4/SMC-franchise-Bulacan-Airport-City-lapses-into-law.html.

Megaworld Newport Property Holdings. 2016. Newport City. http://www.newportcity.com.ph/.

OAG. Traffic Analyzer 2021. https://www.oag.com/traffic-analyzer.

Republic of the Philippines, Department of Public Works and Highways. 2021. NAIA Expressway. https://www.dpwh.gov.ph/DPWH/PPP/projs/NAIA.

San Miguel Corporation. 2021. New Manila International Airport (NMIA). https://www.sanmiguel.com.ph/page/san-miguel-aerocity-inc.

Tran, H. A. 2015. Urban Space Production in Transition: The Cases of the New Urban Areas of Hanoi. *Urban Policy and Research*. 33 (1). pp. 79–97. https://doi.org/10.1080/08111146.2014.967393.

Chapter 8

Conclusions

8.1 Findings

This study first extensively reviewed the literature on airport system development. It then examined the development of airport systems in megacities around the world and in major Asian cities, and finally presented the results of empirical case studies in Asian cities on the impact of airport system development on regional economies.

In Chapter 2, the existing studies on airport system development were classified into five groups. The first group is macroeconomic studies that empirically examine the relationship between air traffic, airport capacity/connectivity, and economic growth. Although there are many studies on the relationship between air traffic or the airport system and regional economic indicators, little effort has been made to examine the causal relationship between airport system development and macroeconomic performance. The second group relates to airport-related development. In urban planning studies and practices, airports have tended to be overlooked over the last century despite their potential role in shaping urban form. But gradually, more researchers have highlighted the importance of major airports as development engines, as they attract a variety of speed-sensitive commercial activities and relevant value-added services. They proposed a number of concepts such as airport city and aerotropolis. The third group seeks to provide evidence for airport-centric development by analyzing the intra-metropolitan distribution of employment, with particular interest in transportation infrastructure and accessibility, including airports, as key determinants of economic growth under rapid suburbanization. Hedonic pricing studies demonstrating airport externalities are placed in the fourth group. Since the 1970s, numerous hedonic pricing studies have been conducted on the spatial impact of airport noise on residential communities, while a few case studies have examined the spatial impact of airport system development on surrounding properties. The last group relates to ground transportation and access to the airport by public transportation. A number of case studies from the United Kingdom (UK) and Australia discuss the role of ground access to airports by public transport from an environmental perspective. Although urban rail projects worldwide face issues of cost overruns and lack of demand in favor of global competitiveness and environmental sustainability, airport rail link projects may be justified for reasons of economic efficiency and competitiveness in the context of Asian hub cities with sufficient urban density.

Chapter 3 analyzed the development of airport systems in megacities in Asia and world regions through a comprehensive review of descriptive statistics. It was found that the construction of new airports was most popular in emerging megacities in Asia, while the expansion of airport terminals occurred sequentially in both established and growing megacities in North America, Europe, and

Asia. Airport relocation, on the other hand, has been limited to a few megacities in the People's Republic of China (PRC). It was also noted that multi-airport formation is relatively new, but is gradually occurring in established and growing megacities in Asia. New airports are typically built outside urban areas and connected by various airport rail systems, depending on the distance of access or egress to/from the city center. The construction of airport rail links has been intensive in recent decades and can be both proactive and reactive to the emergence and growth of megacities in Asia. Established megacities in North America, Europe, and East Asia have handled large air traffic flows with the development of multi-airport systems in global, regional, and national production networks, while emerging megacities in South Asia and Africa have not yet played a nodal role with the development of single-airport systems for limited air traffic flows. Population size (or megacity size) alone is not a determinant of airport system development, and megacities can be classified from single-airport system development to multi-airport system management in an evolutionary way. Nevertheless, the geospatial assignment patterns of air traffic flows within multi-airport megacities appear to follow different development paths. Megacities with the development of single- and multi-airport systems have shown different levels of economic production and growth in Asia and global regions.

In Chapters 4 through 6, case studies were conducted on the development of the airport system in Tokyo and in cities in the PRC. First, Chapter 4 attempted to provide empirical evidence on the impact of improving airport accessibility through urban rail transport in the Tokyo Metropolitan Area. Three types of quasi-experimental methods were applied: spatial difference-in-differences (DID), propensity score (PS) matching, and inverse probability weighting (IPW) with the panel data from 2000 to 2010 to statistically test the impacts. The estimation results showed that improving the accessibility of a city airport has a significant impact on employment density and land prices. Second, Chapter 5 empirically examined the impact of airport upgrading on regional economies using DID methods with a data set of 88 cities with operating airports in the PRC, covering the period from 2000 to 2015. To examine the DID effect, the models with two-time frame DID and continuous-year frame DID are used. A counterfactual test based on resetting the upgrade year supports our main findings. The estimation results of the baseline models, which include all sample cities, show that regional GDP per capita could be increased by 11.0% to 12.2% by upgrading airports. Further estimation of models with two subgroups of larger and smaller airports found that the DID effects are significantly estimated in the regions with smaller airports, but may not be significant in the regions with larger airports. In addition, airport location was found to contribute to the distributional impact of airport upgrading on the urban economy, suggesting the importance of integrating airport planning with urban planning and comprehensive transportation planning. The additional analysis also found that high-speed rail (HSR) may not have an impact on the economic effects of airport upgrading. Third, Chapter 6 examined the airport's continued investment in transportation capacity improvements in response to changes in airport and urban characteristics. Survival analysis was applied to the empirical data set of 122 airport upgrade projects in 79 cities in the PRC to understand the time interval of airport upgrades. The Kaplan–Meier curve showed that the probability of upgrading an airport is higher 5 to 15 years after the previous event. The estimated results of Cox regression models showed that the degree of urbanization and the share of tertiary industry production in total production are significantly negatively associated with the time interval of the airport upgrade, while airport status and the distance between the airport and the city center are positively associated with the time interval.

Chapter 7 attempted to supplement the findings of the previous chapters by providing more detailed case studies of airport system development practices in developing cities in Asia, particularly Ha Noi, Jakarta, and Manila. All three cities have national capital status in Viet Nam, the Philippines, and Indonesia, respectively, but these cities represent different stages and phases of development.

The findings include the following:

(1) The complexity of airport system development (e.g., construction of a single new airport, expansion of airport capacity, and formation of multi-airports) depends on the level of urbanization and stage of economic development (Ha Noi, Jakarta, and Manila).

(2) International development agencies (e.g., ADB and JICA) can play an important role in enhancing the economic impact of airport capacity expansion along with ground transportation investments through loan programs and/or technical assistance in emerging economies (Ha Noi, Manila, and Jakarta).

(3) The location of a (former) military air base in a metropolitan area is one of the critical determinants of multi-airport formation, as the choice of location for new airport construction or relocation is to some extent related to the availability and accessibility of public land for airport capacity expansion (Manila and Jakarta).

(4) Asia's major conglomerates could undertake the development and management of airport systems in an integrated manner by internalizing the broader economic benefits of building new airports through the development of land around new airport terminals and along ground transportation corridors, if governments (or international development agencies) offer generous incentives to private partners, such as a range of tax breaks (Manila).

(5) Coordination of land use for airport-linked economic development often calls for the acquisition of land and resettlement of communities near highway interchanges and/or rail stations associated with airports. Military agencies may need to be involved in land use coordination for airport-linked development as public landowners in the vicinity of airports or former air bases (Ha Noi and Manila).

(6) Relocating airports can lead to impactful and transformative redevelopment opportunities in inner-city locations, while limiting the possibility of secondary or tertiary airport uses (Jakarta).

(7) The development of new secondary and/or tertiary airports is proposed to mitigate the concentration of traffic around existing primary and/or secondary airports in dense inner-city locations. However, the formation of multi-airports is likely to necessitate additional investments in ground transportation infrastructure and services, especially airport rail links for reliable passenger travel services, between city-center and city-fringe locations (Ha Noi, Jakarta, and Manila).

(8) Investment in an airport rail link requires inter-jurisdictional and/or intersectoral development coordination to enhance metropolitan-wide connectivity and last-mile accessibility, although the direct benefits of investing in an airport rail link for travelers (e.g., ridership, traffic mitigation, and reliability) are still debatable (Manila and Jakarta).

(9) The degree and pattern of the broader economic benefits brought by airport system development depend on land use zoning codes (e.g., flexible floor use and floor area ratio bonus for favorable land use) proactively adopted by municipal governments surrounding airports and/or along airport-linked ground transportation corridors (Manila and Jakarta).

8.2 Discussion

This section highlights the answers to the three research questions posed in Chapter 1.

(1) What types of urban policies have been discussed and/or practiced with regard to airport system development in megacities?

Our study identified three types of urban policies for the successful implementation of airport system development. The first type is the locational strategy for airport system development (e.g., building a single new airport, expanding airport capacity, and forming multi-airports) in and around emerging, growing, or established megacities, taking into account three key conditions: the availability of developable land, accessibility to/from city centers, and scope of air traffic flow. National authorities are usually responsible for this type of policy making.

The second type is the strategic provision of ground transportation infrastructure and services, including airport rail links and expressways, in terms of airport infrastructure locational strategy and service provision within and around emerging, growing, or established megacities. This type of urban policy requires both inter-jurisdictional and intersectoral coordination among metropolitan-level stakeholders.

The third type is land use planning for aviation-oriented development, including designation of special economic zones, development policy guidelines, rezoning of land use, and development incentives around airports and along airport-linked ground transportation corridors in and around emerging, growing, or established megacities. This type of urban policy is typically initiated by municipal authorities in partnership with private developers, landowners (public and/or military), and other local stakeholders.

(2) How has airport system development influenced the spatial transformation of Asian cities?

Our study identified five stages of spatial transformation of emerging, growing, and established megacities with evolutionary development of the airport system. In the initial stage, the economic base of emerging cities is not yet strongly connected to larger production networks. A single-airport system, usually located near city centers in or around less urbanized areas, is likely to have limited influence on the spatial transformation of emerging cities in the early stages.

Second, cities that are part of larger production networks need to upgrade a single-airport system to handle increasing intercity passenger and cargo flows. Upgrading involves providing additional runways, taxiways, and new terminal buildings, usually at existing airports near city centers. An expanded single-airport system is likely to have some impact on the level and pattern of urbanization.

Third, growing cities need to further expand airport capacity to accommodate the continued economic development that accompanies rapid urbanization. However, as further expansion of airport capacity becomes difficult or even infeasible due to limited land in inner-city locations, growing cities tend to build a new airport in greenfield sites near or outside the city edge where developable land is available. In this development process, cities may choose to either close existing airports to create large-scale regeneration opportunities in inner-city locations or retain existing airports in inner-city locations to allow for the formation of multi-airports in metropolitan areas. Under either of these scenarios, development of the airport system is likely to bring additional decentralization effects to growing cities, while relocation of airports may bring densification effects to agglomeration economies near city centers.

Fourth, as newly constructed airports handle more passenger and cargo flows around or beyond city limits, growing cities tend to invest heavily in airport rail links and expressways to improve airport accessibility and travel time reliability to and from city centers. Such ground transportation projects are likely to lead to airport-related land development and a shift in competitive business locations in terms of accessibility, travel-time reliability, and agglomeration economies around airport-connected locations in urban areas.

Fifth, some capital-status and/or competitive megacities in advanced economies (e.g., London, Los Angeles, New York, and Tokyo) may adopt more complex multi-airport systems as part of their evolutionary integration into national, regional, and global production networks by deploying secondary, tertiary, and/or additional airports along with a variety of ground transportation technologies inside and outside urbanized areas on different development paths (e.g., from monocentric to polycentric urbanization).

(3) Could policy options for airport system development influence the economic performance of Asian cities?

Our empirical studies in Tokyo and cities in the PRC show that airport system development has had a positive impact on the local economies in the cities.

The Tokyo case study showed that improving the accessibility of the airport by rail has had significant positive impact on employment density. The significant increase in employment density may indicate that the location of businesses or commercial agglomeration near the train stations was encouraged by the improvement in urban rail accessibility to the city's airport. Better rail accessibility to/from the airport allows locals to travel by train in less time and with better reliability than by car, and also allows visitors to reach their destinations more easily. This could lead to direct, indirect, or catalytic impacts on business agglomeration.

The Tokyo case study also showed that improving airport rail access has had a significant positive impact on land prices. The significant increase in land prices may also indicate an increase in economic productivity in the areas where the airport urban rail accessibility has been improved. One of the factors in improving economic productivity is a direct effect of improved accessibility. Shorter first-/last-mile travel time to/from the airport allows local businesspeople to be more productive in their offices and allows visitors to stay longer in the areas, which could lead to further production and/or consumption. Another factor could be the agglomeration of businesses mentioned earlier. The cluster of businesses is expected to promote innovative activities by facilitating matching in the labor market, which allows employers to find qualified workers at a lower cost, improve knowledge sharing among workers by increasing opportunities for face-to-face meetings, and activate the learning process for local workers in communicating with others. The potential demand for offices in areas where rail access to the airport has been improved could lead to an increase in land prices.

A case study for cities in the PRC found that regional GDP per capita could be increased by 11.0% to 12.2% through airport upgrades. They concluded that airport upgrading has a significant positive impact on the regional economy for smaller airports, but may not for larger airports. Additional analysis indirectly revealed that airport access, along with airport capacity expansion, plays a critical role in airport-led economic development in cities with an airport located far from the city center. The results also suggest that the effect of airport upgrading on the regional economy is more remarkable in cities where high-speed rail (HSR) has not yet been introduced than in cities where HSR has been introduced. Additionally, the effect of airport upgrading is not significantly affected by the availability of HSR. The independence of the economic impact of airport upgrading from the availability of HSR is probably because the impact mechanism of airport upgrading is different from that of HSR. The effects of airport upgrading may affect the industries related to air transport or the highly productive industries that cover the global market.

8.3 Policy Implications

In summary, this study draws important conclusions from the above findings for the three levels of urban policy and development practices.

National-level authorities are expected to play a critical role in developing a locational strategy for more dynamic and complex airport systems to ensure the competitiveness and sustainability of emerging and growing megacities in larger production networks, with monetary and/or technical support from international development agencies.

Metropolitan-level entities are encouraged to collaborate horizontally in the strategic provision of ground transportation infrastructure and services, including airport rail links and expressways, to overcome the classic (but still existing) problem of jurisdictional and/or sectoral fragmentations and promote seamless travel experiences between cities and airports to improve accessibility, which in turn leads to airport-linked economic development.

Municipal- and/or district-level agencies can take strong initiatives to enhance and capture the net economic impacts (especially accessibility and agglomeration benefits) of dynamic and complex airport system development through proactive land use coordination and unique business promotion/stewardship in collaboration with private developers, landowners (public/military), and other local stakeholders.

The three levels of policy implications are interdependent, suggesting that the development and management of multilevel governance is essential for the competitiveness of emerging and growing cities (especially megacities), with the dynamic and complex development of airport systems on unique evolutionary paths to be successfully implemented in metropolitan, national, regional, and global production networks.

Finally, the economic success of emerging and growing Asian megacities with airport system development will depend largely on the path of recovery from the COVID-19 pandemic. While some analysts are pessimistic that global air traffic will never return to pre-COVID-19 forecasted levels, many countries are proactively making plans to reach a (new) normal state of business affairs by removing travel restrictions and reopening borders (IATA 2022a; ACI 2021). However, the actual recovery appears to be uneven across different regions of the world. Asia and the Pacific has so far shown the weakest performance of the major regions, reaching only 68% of 2019 travel levels by early 2022, in large part due to a slow recovery in international passenger markets (IATA 2022b). Nevertheless, the long-term recovery path of Asian megacities may be optimistic due to the mass of growing middle-class populations in the emerging markets (Andrianjaka 2017). Even in a pessimistic scenario, hub airports are expected to face capacity constraints after the recovery, so some types of infrastructure investments will need to be considered for sufficient airport capacity expansion (including ground transportation systems) to manage the resurging and growing passenger and cargo volumes in Asian megacities by 2040 (Gelhausen, Berster, and Wilken 2021). Essentially, such investment options are associated with the idea of green recovery to achieve some of the Sustainable Development Goals, such as "affordable and clean energy," "sustainable cities and communities," and "climate action" (IHLG 2019).

We foresee that green investments in airport system development could act as an important catalyst for emerging and growing megacities to implement a set of urban climate change mitigation strategies (e.g., spatial planning, urban form and infrastructure, electrification and net-zero emissions resources, green and blue urban infrastructure, and socio-behavioral changes) and to achieve a wide range of economic co-benefits (e.g., reducing congestion costs, improving labor productivity and city competitiveness, and reducing health-care costs related to pollution and diseases) (Lwasa et al. 2022). We also see the aforementioned multilevel governance as one of the critical enablers for mobilizing private capital investment in Asia's emerging and growing megacities with airport system development on sustainable trajectories.

References

Airports Council International (ACI). 2021. The Impact of COVID-19 on the Airport Business and the Path to Recovery. Advisory Bulletins. https://aci.aero/2021/03/25/the-impact-of-covid-19-on-the-airport-business-and-the-path-to-recovery/.

Andrianjaka, R. R. 2017. Middle-Class Composition and Growth in Middle-Income Countries. *ADBI Working Paper Series*. No. 753. https://www.adb.org/sites/default/files/publication/325056/adbi-wp753.pdf.

Gelhausen, M. C., P. Berster, and D. Wilken. 2021. Post-COVID-19 Scenarios of Global Airline Traffic until 2040 That Reflect Airport Capacity Constraints and Mitigation Strategies. *Aerospace*. 8 (10). pp. 300. https://doi.org/10.3390/aerospace8100300.

Industry High Level Group (IHLG). 2019. Aviation Benefits Report 2019. https://www.icao.int/sustainability/Documents/AVIATION-BENEFITS-2019-web.pdf.

International Air Transport Association (IATA). 2022a. Air Passenger Numbers to Recover in 2024. Press Release No: 10. https://www.iata.org/en/pressroom/2022-releases/2022-03-01-01/.

International Air Transport Association (IATA). 2022b. The Fight for Recovery in Asia-Pacific. Airlines. https://airlines.iata.org/analysis/the-fight-for-recovery-in-asia-pacific.

Lwasa, S., K. C. Seto, X. Bai, H. Blanco, K. R. Gurney, S. Kilkiş, O. Lucon, J. Murakami, J. Pan, A. Sharifi, Y. Yamagata. 2022: Urban Systems and Other Settlements. In IPCC. 2022. *Climate Change 2022: Mitigation of Climate Change. Contribution of Working Group III to the Sixth Assessment Report of the Intergovernmental Panel on Climate Change.* Cambridge, UK and New York, NY, US: Cambridge University Press. https://doi.org/10.1017/9781009157926.010.

www.ingramcontent.com/pod-product-compliance
Lightning Source LLC
Chambersburg PA
CBHW041243240426
43668CB00026B/2466